# CULTURE TO CULTURE

## MISSION TRIP DO'S AND DON'TS

# NAN LEAPTROTT

# CULTURE TO CULTURE

## Mission Trip Do's and Don'ts

Advancing the Ministries of the Gospel
AMG Publishers
God's Word to you is our highest calling.

*Culture to Culture: Mission Trip Do's and Don'ts*

Published by Living Ink Books
6815 Shallowford Road
Chattanooga, Tennessee 37421



ISBN 0-89957-156-5

First printing—July 2005

Cover designed by Daryle Beam, Market Street Design, Chattanooga, Tennessee
Interior design and typesetting by PerfectType, Nashville, Tennessee
Edited and Proofread by Melanie Rigney, Dan Penwell, Donna Clark Goodrich, and Warren Baker
Index compiled by Joe Zang, Lutherville, Maryland

---

Library of Congress Cataloging-in-Publication Data

Leaptrott, Nan.
Culture to culture : mission trip do's and don'ts / by Nan Leaptrott.
p. cm.
Summary: "A resource designed to assist those are who are led to Christian service in foreign countries and for those who travel abroad. It points out how misinformation about another culture can lead to a cultural divide as one faces different rules of protocol and etiquette"--Provided by publisher.
ISBN-13: 978-0-89957-156-0 (pbk. : alk. paper)
ISBN-10: 0-89957-156-5 (pbk. : alk. paper)
1. Missionaries--Training of. I. Title.

BV2091.L43 2005
266'.023--dc22

2005016753

Printed in Canada
11 10 09 08 07 06 05 –T– 8 7 6 5 4 3 2 1

I dedicate this book to the glory of God
who gave me a passion for people being valued
who led me to AMG Publishers
and Dan Penwell who guided me in the
writing of this manuscript.

*"The one who is in you is greater
than he who is of the world"*
(1 JOHN 4:4).

# Acknowledgments

There are so many people to thank for their help in making this book possible. If I listed them all, they would fill another complete book. You know who you are and I am grateful for your prayers and your help.

I must, however, make mention of a few people who went beyond friendship. Their contributions were immensely important and timely.

Dan Penwell heads my list of those to thank. Dan saw a potential for this book and took a chance on me, an unknown to him. He has become a treasured friend. Dan exemplifies Christian service in action. His attitude, his praise, and his support made me want to write the best possible book for him and AMG. He worked with me and prayed me through a very difficult personal time I experienced during the writing of this book. Thank you, Dan. You are the best.

Lonnell Johnson and his wife, Brenda, are longtime friends and business associates. Lonnell volunteered to help edit my book and to add his knowledge and expertise on African culture as a contribution. Lonnell recently returned from a sabbatical to Africa and is currently on leave of absence from Otterbein College, where he teaches African American literature and other courses. Brenda's friendship and belief in me is a treasure.

Dianne Greene, M.Ed, is my dear friend. She is a former high school English professor; a school guidance counselor; and an expert in language, grammar, and biblical knowledge. She not only prayed for me but also volunteered to edit my manuscript. She worked tirelessly on this project. Her love and compassion exceeds many. Dianne, you made this possible. Thank you.

Liz Garner and Penny Higgins who without their many acts of kindness and prayers this work would not have been completed. Dianne, Liz, and Penny are truly companions in Christ. Thank you, my dear friends.

Tom Allen, minister of education at my church and my friend, took one look at my outline and said, "Have you thought of developing your book this way?" Tom was right on target and his suggestions made this book flow. Sharing with me from his knowledge on Jewish traditions helped this section of my book immensely. Tom, thank you. Your powerful input and your constant dose of wit helped to get me through to the end.

My family is the heartbeat of my life. My longtime husband Richard supported me, loved me, and took care of many laborious details so I'd have the time to reach my goal of completing this book. My sons—Benjamin, Timothy, and Jeffry, and my daughters-in-love, Susan and Karol—encouraged me, prayed for me, and loved me unconditionally. Early on when I lost the use of an arm due to an accident, they cheered me to victory and would not let me give in or give up. I am so blessed to have such a caring family. Thank you my dear ones. And thanks also to David, Elizabeth, Russ, John, Zach, Anna, and James, the greatest grandchildren ever—your loving and funny ways gave me spirit. You know how much I love you.

# Contents

# Foreword

## Culture to Culture: Mission Trip Do's And Don'ts

When one crosses ocean and borders, the different rules of communication become enormously visible and often incomprehensible. Culture-based rules of interaction can seem baffling without an understanding of their origin or purpose. Quite simply, cultural guidelines reflect the ways in which people behave. This is a complex subject, which can be simplified by the understanding *that people behave in a manner consistent with their perception of reality.* That perception of reality is derived from the cultural setting into which one is born and conditioned.

*Culture to Culture* takes readers beyond their own cultural setting to give clear and precise information about global protocol. This essential tool will provide:

- An understanding of the underlying culture that dictates behavior
- A reference guide for points of protocol for world regions and for specific countries
- An understanding of the rules of global protocol, the sensitivities, and how to present a unified approach

- A plan to deduce the proper protocol when you encounter a new situation
- A method for developing an appropriate plan of action and interaction with those you meet, whether in Christian service, travel, or business
- A detailed guide for social interaction when dining in other countries and when hosting international guests on one's home turf

There are three ground rules for this book:

1. Not all nations are included directly in this book, yet all are represented by governing principles and cultural leanings.
2. The masculine pronoun is used in most cases. This simplifies the reading.
3. The approach used is an American one. People from other cultures who cross borders will take their culture with them, but the governing principles, protocol, and etiquette of the approached country will be the same.

The reader can depend on *Culture to Culture* for success in all their cross-cultural relationships. When Christian service is based on guidance of the Holy Spirit and coupled with a knowledge base, then this service is headed in the right direction.

# Preface

Each chapter in the regional country profiles (chapters 1–7) includes some or all of the following for the major countries in a specific region or continent.

- List of Countries Addressed
  - Introductory Remarks
  - Country or Region Overview
    - Mission Tip
    - Religious Factors
    - Governing Principles/Cultural Position
  - Country Profiles
    - Country
    - Cultural Position
    - Religious Factors
    - Communication Characteristics
      - Transaction
      - Interaction
    - Protocol & Etiquette
      - Forms of Address
      - Greetings
      - Handshakes

# Introduction:

## The Great Commission–
## Crossing the Cultural Divide

*Being* is an attitude. *Doing* is an activity. We are commissioned by God to *be* a reflection of Christ to the world. Then He invites us to *do.*

> Therefore go and make disciples of all the nations, baptizing them in the name of the Father, and of the Son, and of the Holy Spirit, teaching them to obey everything I commanded you: and surely I am with you always, even to the end of the age (Matt. 28:19, 20).
>
> The intensity of God's appeal is for:
>
> - the lost to be saved through Christ, His Son
> - Christ to be the main purpose of our lives
> - Christians to scatter and serve
>
> I must preach the good news of the kingdom of God to the other towns also, because that is why I was sent (Luke 4:43).

It takes the power of God working in us and the attitude of Christ to effectively cross cultural boundaries. Oftentimes, we believe that our positive spiritual intentions are all we need to become an effective missionary. Not true! A limited view of what it means to cross this cultural divide can impede our success as a missionary and hinder us as a messenger of Christ. The primary issues that can hinder us are:

1. An uninformed cultural view
2. An incomplete cross-cultural framework

## From Uninformed to an Informed Cultural View

In our own cultural setting we operate by rules of interaction that we don't consciously recognize. But when we deal with someone from outside our own culture, the rules of interaction become enormously visible and often incomprehensible. Why people behave the way they do is a complex subject that can be simplified by the understanding that *people behave in a manner consistent with their perception of reality.* That perception of reality is derived from the cultural setting into which one is born and conditioned.

In the world today travel, telecommunications, and economic interdependence have caused cultures to overlap and interact. Western culture, especially U.S. culture, has influenced almost every society. Television, movies, computer technology, and consumer goods carry U.S. culture around the world.

As countries become more westernized, and as immigrants build multicultural communities within the United States, we have come to believe others think, understand, act like us, and accept American ways because they are familiar with our culture. This is an illusion. Although those of the younger generations may wear denim and listen to our music, such customs do not change the fundamental beliefs that underlie their culture. Thus, we have a cultural divide. We can begin to understand this cultural dilemma by looking at Scripture and seeing how Jesus responded to cultural differences.

Jesus showed respect to all people and had no problems crossing cultural boundaries. How did he approach his mission cross-culturally? There are three distinct ways.

1. *Jesus was a knowledge-based person.* He learned about his own culture from his parents' teachings and his synagogue experiences, by being among his peers, and through historical and religious factors.

When Jesus was twelve, he was found in the temple listening and asking probing questions. As he began his ministry, he learned all he could about the different cultures and customs. Jesus didn't give up his Jewish culture. Even at the Crucifixion, Pilate referred to Jesus as King of the Jews. Christ did not change who he was. He was knowledgeable about different cultures and chose to meet people where they were. His encounter with the woman at the well is a good example. Jesus approached her with compassion and shared the truth. The Samaritan woman said to him, "You are Jew and I am a Samaritan woman. How can you ask me for a drink?" (John 4:9). Jesus answered her, "If you knew the gift of God and who it is that asks for a drink, you would have asked him and he would have given you living water" (John 4:10).

2. *Jesus approached people in love; his focus was to heal broken lives.* "Jesus left there and went along the Sea of Galilee. Then he went up a mountainside and sat down. Great crowds came to him, bringing the lame, the blind, the crippled, the mute, and many others, and laid them at his feet; and he healed them. The people were amazed when they saw the mute speaking, the crippled made well, the lame walking and the blind seeing. And they praised the God of Israel" (Matt. 15:29–31).

3. *Jesus crossed legalistic attitudes and behavioral patterns with humility.* He chose his words wisely. When he was accused of breaking the law or going against spiritual norms, Jesus replied, "I tell you the truth, the Son can do nothing by himself; he can do only what he sees his Father doing because whatever the Father does, the Son also does" (John 5:19).

Another example is when a woman caught in adultery was made to stand before Jesus and the crowd. The people were ready to stone her because that was the customary thing to do. Jesus knelt down and began to write in the sand, "If any one of you is without sin, let him be the first to throw a stone at her" (John 8:7). The crowd dispersed one by one, leaving Jesus alone with the woman. He stood, faced her, and asked: "'Woman, where are they? Has no one condemned you?' 'No one, sir,' she said. 'Then neither do I condemn you. Go now and leave your life of sin'" (John 8:7–10).

To be reflectors of Christ we must show respect to all people, humble ourselves, honor our global neighbor's differences, and put the focus on the other person. When we have an informed cultural view, we learn to adapt to other people's ways of action and how they interact. Nothing will be as we think. When we encounter something that may seem like a glitch, keep in mind that we are representing Christ.

Remember: be patient when you have to wait. Do not criticize or state how you do it back home. Be grateful for all courtesies shown you. Eat the food prepared for you. Worship in the manner in which your hosts do. It is imperative you become acquainted with the cultural differences.

Every culture has rules called protocols which will vary from culture to culture. It is important not only to know the rules but also to have an understanding of why the rules are in place.

---

## « MISTAKES TO AVOID »

1. Ethnocentrism: considering our own beliefs and behavior are superior or the only right ones.

2. Stereotyping: believing that all people in a group are alike and leaving no room for individual differences.

---

Protocol does not evolve randomly. There is both logic and purpose behind it. When the purpose of protocol is understood, its use becomes clearer and more dynamic. For example, if your mission work takes you to Japan, you will see that everything is done in a ritualistic manner. The Japanese hold their entire identity in formalities. If you belittle the many ceremonies, you have, in essence, belittled the person. Your casual attention to their ceremonial ways is perceived as a display of low self-esteem on your part. Etiquette is how protocol is put into action.

This book includes briefs that define protocol and etiquette for numerous countries. After we determine protocol and etiquette, we examine the culture.

Culture is based on personal experience, beliefs, and values. Culture is how and why things get done. Culture is also about expectations and the current stage of development of a civilization.

There are two aspects of culture: surface culture and reference culture. *Surface culture* is what you see at the onset. Culture can be compared to an iceberg. The surface of an iceberg is small in comparison to what's beneath the water. What you see first in a culture are things like music, dancing, dress, cooking and eating, fine arts, drama, and literature.

*Reference culture* is not recognized right away. It covers a myriad of issues, from body language, patterns of relationships, definition of sin, courtship practices, approaches to problem solving, ordering of time, social interaction rate, preference for competition or cooperation, notions about logic and validity, arrangement of physical space, and much, much more. Reference culture does not usually show up until there is a cultural divide in one's interaction. Make no mistake—it is this reference culture that most influences a society.

There are five ways in which culture influences: beliefs and values, etiquette and behavior, human relations, communication, and time.

1. Beliefs and Values: Historical and religious factors, assumptions and stereotypes, and view of women
2. Etiquette and Behavior: Forms of address, touch, space, gestures, gifts, and dining
3. Human Relations: Flexibility and adaptability
4. Communication: Non-verbal messages, verbal use, written and electronic styles

5. Time: How it is used, scheduled, important vs. unimportant, and maintaining tradition

---

## TRUTHS ABOUT STEREOTYPES

Stereotypes do exist. They are part of the information received from society. Most stereotypes contain a judgment about a certain group, i.e., good/bad, right/wrong, normal/abnormal, etc. Stereotyping someone or a society causes one to feel boxed in and doesn't allow any room for individuality. Stereotyping colors and distorts information. Internal thoughts and beliefs can sometimes be externalized without our being aware of what is happening. We stereotype another by the words we choose and the behavior we use.

---

### MOVING PAST STEREOTYPING

Everyone stereotypes others. This is due to our own cultural conditioning. Recognizing that we do stereotype is the first step in not making judgments about others. Consider every way in which you might consciously or unconsciously stereotype someone. When I moved to Pinehurst, North Carolina, I was one of a few southerners. I was surrounded by people whose habits were different from mine. One thing I noticed was that people didn't drop in to say "hello." I assumed they were not friendly. Nothing could have been further from the truth. They in turn thought southern friendliness was "just being nosy." This too was a wrong assumption. I helped to break our stereotypical molds by inviting my new acquaintances over for afternoon tea. We discussed openly our historical and religious origins, and what influence they had in shaping our perceptions. We discussed other factors that played a part in shaping our views: weather, transportation, speech patterns, etc. We grew to have great respect for each other's differences. However, even after many years, these friends still introduce me as their "token southern friend, who we never quite understand when she speaks." We have a good laugh and once again we have broken the ice for someone else to have better cultural understanding. Conversation by conversation, we dispelled stereotypical thinking.

---

**In cross-cultural service and travel, be less judgmental and more flexible and curious.**

---

It's also important to remove judgments and describe behaviors. When you look at behaviors without judging, you enhance your relationships. If someone has a different view of time, stop and consider: is this a judgment or an acquired behavior that is part of cultural conditioning? The same attitude goes for what you see in the media about certain groups of people. Stop and ask yourself if you are judging or seeing a particular behavior pattern. Of course, all behavior is not positive, and this needs to be addressed. But use caution about how you look at societies. When you look at how you might stereotype others, you need to develop a cross-cultural plan of action and interaction.

## Communication: Plan of Action and Interaction

A plan of action and interaction entails knowledge on what you need to accomplish and how you will go about accomplishing it. Without a plan, you leave everything to chance, and global mission service and travel are too important for that.

This part of your cross-cultural framework begins with recognizing the societal influences and the distinguishing differences each have. For simplification purposes, I present three fundamental cultural classifications:

- family/clan
- group
- individualistic societies

I put perimeters around cultural societies not to stereotype a society but to give some meaning to why people think, feel, act, and react in the manner they do. This is a broad stroke picture of culture at large. When I present individual country briefs, I will narrow the focus even more. For example, participating in Christian service and traveling in China will be much different than if you are in Japan, even though both are group societies.

## Three Types of Societies

*Family/Clan Societies:* The term family/clan may suggest a primitive social structure, but this is misleading. In fact, a large part of Western society is family/clan. What this means is that the primary focal point of the individual, the structure through which one derives one's identity, is the family unit. This unit can be more accurately defined as a clan, extended family, or tribe. It is a close-knit group whose members are associated through heredity and have a shared historical perspective. In family/clan cultures the family must survive at all costs, the family name (clan) must be protected, and the honor of the family must be defended.

1. Family/clan view of God: Family/clan societies view God differently than other cultures. They believe there is a distinct difference between man and God. God is man's infinite superior. The family/clan perception of reality is hierarchical, with the most powerful at the top, descending downward to lower levels. All these societies' group institutions—religious, professional, and personal—will be set up to reflect and maintain this view of reality. A family/clan view supports that the station in life in which one is born is the way it will always be, and there isn't anything one can do to improve his standing. The family/clan society feels completely dependent on God and will be distrustful of anyone who does not share its concept of God.

2. Family/clan cultures include: England, Latin America, Africa, Spain, Saudi Arabia, Argentina, Belarus, Bolivia, Brazil, and some parts of Canada, Chile, Colombia, Costa Rica, Egypt, Greece, Iraq, Ireland, southern Italy, Jordan, Mexico, Pakistan, Paraguay, Peru, Portugal, Syria, Turkey, and Venezuela.

***Group Societies:*** As in family/clan societies, group association is found in group societies. However, group societies engage in a much broader concept of the group. Group affiliation can be a town, a principality, a nation, or a race. The individual finds identity through affiliation with the large group. To maintain this group identity, it is important that the group foster homogeneity. All members are equal within the group. All participate and all share. The individual is not singled out. It is important to an individual's identity that he or she becomes just like everyone else. It becomes frightening for those who go beyond or reject the group and look for something different, something personal. Achievement by the whole is valued. Group culture supports the submersion of individual personality through the requirement of humility, promoting cooperation and sharing.

1. Group view of God: A group society senses its connection to the infinite as being continuous. A person's ultimate selfhood is oneness with the eternal. Group societies do not personalize the power by giving the force a name or even a pronoun. This perspective perpetuates a completely different form of reality, which is reflected in their daily life and social institutions. The individual and his personal achievements are not highly valued. It is the achievement of the whole that is valued. The social structure is arranged so people work together.

2. Group societies include: China, Hong Kong, parts of India and Indonesia, Japan, Malaysia, the Philippines, Singapore, South Korea, Taiwan, Thailand, and Vietnam.

***Individualistic Societies:*** In individualistic societies, each individual is free to construct his own personal identity. In fact, he must do so. The individualistic society contains a variety of institutions or groups that provide social structure. One can choose to find personal identity through family, religious affiliation, social group, business, or political organization, most likely choosing a combination of these. Individuals are responsible for themselves; the group will not care for them. It is through individual consent that any group is maintained as a unit. Conformity is neither demanded nor assumed. Reliance or dependence on any form of organization or institution is seen as a weakness or failure.

1. Individualistic view of God: Members of an individualistic society believe they can improve themselves and become closer to God. This changes the character of the power hierarchy. A member's spiritual identity is his relationship to God. A person's identity within a group is formed through sharing some kind of essential character with other members of the group. The individual in this kind of society believes he could not survive without some form of association.

2. Some individualistic societies include: Australia, the Flemish side of Belgium, Denmark, Estonia, Northern France, Germany (the most individualistic of all societies), Latvia, the Netherlands, New Zealand, Norway, Switzerland, and the United States.

After you have a frame around the classification of societies, you can view how these societies communicate.

## Global Communication Characteristics

In building relationships, it is important to know something about the people you will meet. Do they think like you? Do they have the same priorities? How are you likely to be received? Understanding a culture means understanding the way its people act, their view of life, and how they communicate with you. There are two aspects of global communication: *transaction communication* characteristics (their views and behavior) and *interaction communication* characteristics (the manner in which they communicate).

*Transaction communication* characteristics give you an idea of the person's power concept. Is he used to group power or personal power? Is power distributed laterally or hierarchically? The amount of power or lack of it in one's personal life will have a profound effect on how one interacts with you. Transaction communication characteristics include professional and personal environment, personal responsibility, expectation of others, main objectives, concept of accomplishment, problem solving, and decision making. When you have an understanding of someone's transaction communication characteristics, you'll arrive on his turf with knowledge and proficient acumen. You will experience fewer cultural misinterpretations and therefore, you will be more readily received.

*Interaction communication* characteristics give you pertinent information about:

- a person's perception of time and physical space
- how the player communicates most information, whether it is by language or gesture
- his ability to deal with uncertainty and change
- his degree of materialism and self-awareness

Included in the interaction characteristics are communication style, learning capabilities, feedback techniques, and time and change.

## Family/Clan Profile

*Transaction Communication Characteristics:* There are many layers of vertical hierarchy. It is assumed one is born into his station of life and there is little he can do to change that position. Leaders are inaccessible. In family/clan societies, it is extremely important to be obedient to the rules of society. The primary objection is to support the family. Remember, the family is more than the immediate family members. It is all the people. Family/clan societies expect mutual support and absolute loyalty. In family/clan societies, it is imperative to show respect to the group, to do one's job, and to contribute to the family unit. This is what keeps the members motivated. Getting what is asked for and feeling in control is very important. Be careful. Time and meeting content may be used for manipulation. Correspondence is controlled, limited, and personal. In family/clan societies, more emphasis is put on assessment of blame than on solving problems. Where the blame falls, there are severe consequences. Professional decisions are made at the top. Personal decisions are based on pride and emotion before the objective benefits are considered.

*Interaction Communication Characteristics:* With strangers, family/clan societies are formal and aloof. With those they know and trust, they are warm and welcoming. At first they will be cautious and formal and at times defensive and distrustful. They learn best when content is more visual than with detailed text. Generalization of data, coaching, and repetition are helpful. Family/clan societies avoid detail and do not want to be held accountable. Feedback is usually subjective, and not necessarily rational. Time is linear, and family/clan societies are process-oriented. Plans can grow; project definitions tend to be fluid. They do not use detailed plans. Plan to wait until time is right for them, and don't lose patience. Change is expected.

## Group Society Profile

*Transaction Communication Characteristics:* Power is shared, so there is a more horizontally layered hierarchy in group societies. People do not stand out. The physical plan is very open, but location of office or temple is important and symbolic. Ritual is important in commerce, public, and personal settings. Group societies contribute to their group and they expect outsiders to do the same. Conformity oils the society. To be accepted into a group society, the outsider must show humility, great respect, and a sense of mutual support to all he encounters.

A group society values status, strength, and craftiness from those with whom the members collaborate. In a group society, a person must succeed at the task he is given. He must get something from those with whom he is working so he can improve the position of his group. Saving face is everything to a group society. When a person in a group society achieves success within his group, then he perceives he has won. As an outsider, you must not single out a particular person within the group; rather, you must do everything to make your intentions for the good of the group. If you do, the person will feel like he has won greater respect within his group. Problems are evaded in group societies because if someone loses face, there is conflict. Therefore, all conflict is dealt with in privacy. When the problem is passed off or handled in privacy, ultimately no one admits to any problem. The outsider must find a solution and bring it to the group as a different method and never point a finger of blame.

All decisions in a group society are made by consensus. While it may appear to you that the group with which you are working and collaborating has the power to make decisions, there is always the unseen group that ultimately makes the decisions. They then pass their decisions down to the lower group. Usually, the unseen group is older and the lower ranked group thinks they are wiser. Age is highly respected in the group societies.

*Interaction Communication Characteristics:* Since one's individual actions do not stand out in a group society, he will at first be noncommittal to the outsider. When the relationship is built—and this takes some time—then he will be loyal forever. A person from a group society learns best when they are shown rather than showing them a complex, detailed plan. They also learn best in a group. Always address the group and never an individual. Feedback starts within the group. A consensus must be reached before they will allow you to take action. If the feedback has negative connotations, it will be avoided. A group society looks at and enjoys the process of completing a task. They are not goal oriented. Things will take as long as it takes and only when the time is right. This is difficult for an outsider to accept so patience is the order of the day. If there is to be change it will be construed as an error in your original thinking, and therefore resisted.

## Individualistic Society Profile

*Transaction Communication Characteristics:* An individualistic society has a multi-layered hierarchy. Anyone can come from humble beginnings and rise to the top in any area of life. Those who have achieved the most in their professional and personal life have more status. Status is extremely important to people in this type of society. They demand that they have private space.

Three main things drive a person in an individualistic society: personal achievement, personal growth, and independence. When collaborating with someone from an individualistic society, one must have integrity, perform well, and show great competence. Individualistic societies are goal driven. They expect others to have success by achieving and exceeding their goals. To fail at anything is a blow to the ego. Members of this type of society find it important to achieve in all aspects of life, not just at work. Just like decision-making, problems are approached from a rational view and they are addressed quickly. After the problem is solved, what went wrong is analyzed. People from individualistic societies are independent thinkers and use a rational approach in making their decisions. There is always someone at a higher level who will ultimately make the decision, but even then they expect rational reasoning from all others.

*Interaction Communication Characteristics:* Some individualistic societies including Germans, Finns, and Scandinavians are more formal in their communication. Westerners, the French, and Italians are less formal. All are more straightforward than people in family/clan and group societies. Individualistic people learn by detailed information and verbal text. They will independently verify the information they receive. If you ask for feedback from a person from an individualistic society, you will get it. It will be direct, impersonal, and objective. Time is linear. Punctuality is extremely important. An individualistic person likes detailed plans and observes schedules. Change is expected.

## Faith Points

There are many beliefs and religious practices you will encounter when conducting mission and service work. Your own faith and religious beliefs may be put to test. It is paramount to know what you believe and why you believe as you do. Second, have a reasonable knowledge about what others believe and how they worship. This book cannot address all religious practices but following are some general guidelines as to what to expect and how to show respect while standing firm in what you believe.

- Women and children are treated differently in many parts of the world.
- In some Arab countries women and men have different sections of the house with separate entrances—one entrance for the men and one entrance for the women.
- In some Arab regions women are not allowed to drive.
- In parts of India children are reared in brothels and most don't attend school.
- In Western Europe worship will be more formal and an overzealous evangelistic approach will not be appreciated.
- In New Zealand many churches have been turned into bars and restaurants, and there are great distances between locations of churches.
- Until recently the Bible was banned in China. Use caution when witnessing in this region of the world.

*Islam*

- The Koran is the Islam written code. It was first called *The Book of Fate.*
- The Koran promotes an attitude of surrendering to *Allah.* The commands and prohibitions are absolutes and cannot be questioned. The Koran supports an "eye for an eye." Whatever is done to you or one of yours can be meted back.
- In Muslin societies there are certain times for prayer—daybreak, noon, mid-afternoon, after sunset, and early evening.
- In mosques worshipers stand behind the prayer leader, all facing

the same direction. During the time of prayer worshipers are called upon to give alms. Before praying one must be *clean.*

- There is always a bowl and water as one enters the mosque.
- There is always a caller for prayer. If alone, worshipers kneel on a mat, face downward, and pray out loud. Do not pass the worshiper, make noise, talk, or stare. Stand a substantial distance away until the one praying has ended his prayer.
- Muslims have an obligatory observance to fast from food and drink during daylight hours in the ninth month of the lunar year. This is called Ramadan. Only the sick are exempt.

### *Hinduism*

- Hindus believe in reincarnation. The most prevalent view of Hindus is that one's soul inhabits many bodies until it finds rest.
- Hindus believe everyone is equal and what happens or doesn't happen to an individual is a result of *karma*—the effect of one's deeds that is reborn in another soul until the individual gets it right. They also believe that when an animal dies its soul goes straight to heaven.
- There are many sacraments among Hindus which are observed in the home beginning at birth until death.
- A Hindu woman is subordinate to her father first and then her husband. She cannot own anything but her jewelry. This does not mean that she does not have honor in society. Hindu men are urged to be kind to and treat women with respect.
- Do not confuse a *class* system with a *caste* system.

### *Buddhism*

- Buddhism is not a religion as it does not recognize a God.
- To the Buddhist, yoga and transcendental meditation are part of gaining inner peace and attaining oneness with self.
- A Buddhist does not believe that life is a preparation for eternity;

rather, it is a discipline. The here and now is what is most important. If one gives off good karma, good will return. If one gives off bad Karma, bad will happen.

- Buddhist doctrine is determined on merit and worship and is more a cult way of thinking.
- Women are not to shake hands with a Buddhist monk.

*Other Views*

- Confucius was a philosopher, not a founder of religion. Confucianists speak of sages and principles as the way of the ancients.
- Confucianism believes in destiny as determined by human action.
- In Thailand one does not step on a doorsill at a temple or in a home as Thais believe that the soul resides there.
- In South Korea the bottoms of the feet are considered least sacred but the top of the head in considered the most sacred.
- In Muslim countries the souls of the feet are considered unclean as is the left hand.
- In China people go to the ocean to pray for their dead.
- In some countries there is strong belief in witchcraft. Followers may drink and eat odd and even poisonous things in order to be healed or to cast out spells.
- In Israel, in certain religious areas, one does not drive or smoke on the Sabbath.

Observe these differences. Stand firm in your belief and at the same time show respect to others, then you will be able to carry the gospel message with clarity and purpose. In the process you may be able to convert those with very differing views.

*Summary*

Knowing the protocol in different societies is more than knowing how to shake hands. It is the knowledge of *how* to shake hands with the right person at the right time and in the right way to communicate respect, knowledge, and self-confidence. You have the choice of going through the motions or using your knowledge of protocol strategically. This could be compared to giving a presentation by simply listing facts as opposed to preparing a presentation that focuses on the needs of the receiver to solve his current problems or needs. Your overall plan should include the strategic use of protocol. Strategy is what gives us the opportunity to succeed or to fail. Strategy is necessary to any challenge if the participant wants to be able to influence others. Jesus' strategy was to reach out to the prostitute, the beggar, and the person in need to demonstrate God's love. He crossed over into many cultural settings and stood out as a person of humility and grace. We need to follow his example.

To develop a game plan for Christian service and travel, one should look to the end result:

1. What is your objective? Every participant must know what he or she is trying to accomplish.
2. Determine whether your mission objective requires a different approach than one to which you are accustomed.
3. Service is competitive only in the sense that one is vying for an opportunity to expand God's Word. The challenge lies in overcoming internal and external obstacles so you can obtain that goal.
4. Strive for a mutual quest for excellence through building the relationship with those you will encounter. Each side may present obstacles and challenges.
5. In the end, all can achieve success in expanding the Word of God. That won't happen as often if one approaches another society with myopic thinking. Leave your cultural blinders at home.
6. Be open and respectful of different approaches. Have no preconceived judgments and make sure your ideas are not set in stone. Be flexible and adaptable.
7. Leave your complaining at home. You are there to present a positive approach to the gospel. Living conditions probably will not be as comfortable as you have at home.

## Three Universal Rules

*1. Never try to become like people in another culture and never expect them to become like you.*

Each player must retain his own identity. The purpose of learning about another culture is to give you information to use in planning strategy. If someone tried to make you become like him and play only by his rules, you would naturally resist that person. Your identity would be threatened by his actions. You could not possibly trust him in any matter if you thought that his underlying objective was to make you become like him. Therefore, the objective of gaining trust will never be accomplished if you try to absorb another person's culture. No matter how hard you try, if you were raised an American, you will never become a Frenchman. You need to learn how to interact with another culture without losing your own identity.

*2. Never judge another culture as being good or bad relative to your own.*

As you go to other countries you will find rules of protocol and basic values that look completely different from your own. In fact, some cultures' mode of operation are so completely opposed to yours they may seem evil. There is no such thing as good or bad in cultural values. Values are relative to a society. You cannot truly respect another individual if you judge him to be less than you. Respect is the consideration you give someone whom you deem to have inherent value.

*3. Christian service is about people.*

We often focus on numbers, products, and results over interaction among people. This mind-set can creep into our endeavors even if our motive is well intentioned. Therefore, the importance of communication to the overall mission plan is obvious. Christian service is all about people. Don't leave home before you get that clearly in mind.

Jesus' entire ministry was about relating to people. He ate with them. He met in their homes. He always treated people with respect. This is the way of love. As a Christian goodwill ambassador, you must let what you do and say be your ultimate, personal best. You must rely on the power of the Lord Jesus Christ. When you do, you will enjoy your service and more importantly, your testimony will leave a positive impression on those you serve about Christ, the person you represent.

## Key Points

The world can be divided into three fundamental cultures: family/clan, group, and individualistic.

Be informed.
Have a plan.
Know your goals.
Ask how you can be a reflector for Christ.
Ask what you need to do.
Ask what you expect to give.
Ask what you hope you will receive.
Build bridges by being humble, kind, flexible, and sincere.
When you aren't sure, ask.

Prime directives for crossing the cultural divide effective are:

1. Never play the game by trying to become like your opponent and never expect your opponent to become like you.

2. Never judge another culture as being good or bad relative to your own.

3. Always remember that service and traveling as a goodwill ambassador is about people.

# 1. Western Europe

## (Including: Germany, Denmark, Norway, Sweden, England, France, the Netherlands, Italy, Spain, and Portugal)

### Religious Factors

The religious beliefs of the Celts and Teutons in northern Europe and the ancient Greeks and Romans in the south were not monotheistic but pantheistic. They all personified these spirits in some way; it was the interpretation of these spirits that differed. Greece, and later Rome, attached specific gods to specific functions of nature. Examples are:

Demeter, the Earth goddess
Poseidon, the god of the sea
Zeus, the god of the sky, who outranked them all

The Celts believed they were descended directly from gods. The Norsemen believed that their gods were restored to youth through magic, but otherwise died just like men.

The northern cultures reflected the belief in equality in their cultural institutions. They valued accomplishments in themselves as they valued them in gods, and believed that their gods could become angry with them and that consequences would ensue. They believed that nothing happened without a reason and that they could control what happened to them by modifying their behavior.

In contrast, southern Greeks and Romans believed the gods were more mischievous and fickle. Events occurred by the will of the gods and there was nothing a person could do. There was a sense that man controlled his own life. Man tried to get away with all that he could and hoped the gods were not looking.

Later, Roman Catholicism fit into this philosophy, with its provisions for confession and guaranteed absolution. The hierarchy and patristic tradition continued. Prior to Christianity, the Roman earthly father was also priest in his home. Thus, the concept of pope was easy for them to accept.

The Celts were the extreme opposites; they set up a society that reflected their egalitarian beliefs. They were ruled by an elite group of priests, called Druids, who were non-authoritarian judges and teachers. They settled disputes by consensus. The Celts were organized in clans; not in a dependent customary way but in an individualistic way:

- every man was required to marry outside his clan
- there was a system of fosterage in which another family raised a child until he reached adolescence
- clans were limited to four generations, at which point the property was divided and new clans were formed
- there was no automatic succession from father to son in clan leadership
- women had full equality with men and were allowed to own property

These factors ensured that no one could become too powerful. Each clan had complete autonomy. Regional decisions were made democratically.

In Ireland, the Celts believed that the gods resided in clans. These clans were constantly warring, struggling for power. They believed in a paradise ruled by deities. This was a strong predilection for a power hierarchy to exist, which naturally led to acceptance of the Catholic Church and its ecclesiastical hierarchy. The Protestant north remained in line with the beliefs of Great Britain.

The strong patristic hierarchy of the Romans overlies these societies. When the Romans left, the Roman Catholic Church spread to fill the void. Christianity, in the form of Roman Catholicism, pervaded Europe by the twelfth century. By the sixteenth century, the Reformation sent the power hierarchy of the church back to Rome.

## Governing Principles

Some countries lean to an individualistic approach, while others are more family/clan oriented. France had a strong Celtic society and the principles of "liberty, equality, and fraternity" which is still held today. As a result of a Celtic background in a Roman Catholic country, the French are strongly individualistic, but their focus is on their home life.

---

Although many Americans claim some common ancestry with Europeans and therefore assume that European customs may be more familiar, there are still enough differences to get the Americans in trouble.

---

Northern France leans more heavily to being individualistic in thought and behavior, and the south is more comfortable connected to their group (family/clan). Similarly, in Austria—a Germanic country with a Teutonic and Celtic heritage—there is a strong sense of power hierarchy. This is due to the fact that the Catholic Church held on to Austria with the help of the Hapsburg monarchy. This blend of cultures also extends into the more Catholic southern Germany.

## Country Profile: Germany

## (Culture Position: Strong Individualistic)

### Religious Factors

Germany is about 34 percent Catholics and 34 percent Protestants, primarily Lutheran. There are around three million Muslims in Germany. Over the past few decades, many Jews have immigrated to Germany from the former Soviet Union. The largest contingent of Jews is located in Munich.

### Communication Characteristics

*Transaction Communication Characteristics:* There is a strong level of hierarchy. Germans depend on personal achievement, are strongly independent, and exhibit a great amount of self-control.

---

**TRANSACTION ALERT**

Germans demand attention to order, careful planning of the simplest details, and exacting punctuality for all encounters. There is a time and place for everything.

---

The Germans place a great deal of emphasis on personal and professional achievement and on maintaining a sense of power. For a German to listen to you, one must show a great sense of integrity and must be competent and perform on a high level. Arrive prepared.

Problems are addressed quickly and rationally. If adequate planning has taken place, nothing should go wrong, according to the German mind-set. Everything one brings to the table will be verified by independent analysis.

*Interaction Communication Characteristics:* Germans communicate in a precise manner and a formal style. Be sure you err on the formal side of protocol. When a German gives feedback, he will do so in a direct, specific, objective, and impersonal manner. He will expect the same from you. At first, he will use a cautious (though not hostile) approach to an outsider. Germans think like engineers; they like a detailed approach.

I cannot stress punctuality enough. Do not arrive one minute before or one minute after the appointed time. Plans and schedules must be maintained and realistic. There must be good reasons for any change.

---

### ❮ INTERACTION ALERT ❯

Many Germans may speak English, but do not assume they will. Have all presentation materials, including brochures, translated and printed in German.

---

## Protocol & Etiquette

*Forms of Address:* Use the last name, preceded by title. The starkness of the last name sounds rude to American ears, but it is just the opposite in Germany. The easiness of friendship comes cheaply, and is insulting to the German. The correct manner is this:

Male: Herr Direktor Schmidt
Female: Frau Klinkenberg
Professional Female: Frau Doktor Becker

*Greetings:* Greet everyone in the room personally, unless it is a very large crowd. If it is a crowded room, rap on a table or lectern and greet everyone collectively.

The familiar form is *du* and *sie* for the formal.

*Handshakes:* The handshake is very firm and formal. Count silently and execute the handshake in this matter:

1. Connect.
2. Shake.
3. Disconnect.

Shake hands with everyone unless a large audience is being greeted. Do not reach across a person to shake someone else's hand. Shake the woman's hand first.

Do not shake hands across others who are in conversation. Do not shake hands across a threshold. Never shake hands with gloves on.

*Gestures:* Germans tend not to smile a lot in public. It is rude to yell and wave to get someone's attention in the distance. To get someone's attention, raise your hand, palm facing outward, with only the index finger extended. Men, when seated do not cross your legs with one foot resting on the other knee. Cross your legs knee over knee.

When in conversation, do not put your hands in your pocket. When walking down a street with a woman, the man walks curbside. When women walk together, the younger woman walks curbside. When two men and one woman are together, the woman walks between the men. On a path or hill, the man walks to the woman's left. Germans do not stand close together; do not intrude on their space. Do not sit until your host asks you to be seated and indicates where. Posture and bearing are important; sit up straight and do not slouch.

*Appropriate Attire:* Think conservative. Men wear dark suits with white, long sleeved shirts and a sedate tie. In less formal settings, a navy blazer and gray flannel pants are appropriate. A woman's attire can be a suit and blouse, with little jewelry. In a very casual setting one can wear jeans. Just make sure they show no signs of wear.

*View of Women:* Women are received graciously if they maintain an air of conservative appeal. While there are many professional women in Germany, a woman outside the German culture may be perceived by not having the clout to make decisions.

*Gift Giving:* It is inappropriate to give expensive gifts; however, a gift should be of good quality. Pens, pocket calculators, and books on American architecture are good choices. Unwrapped flowers are appropriate when going to someone's home for dinner. There should be an odd number but never thirteen. Do not bring red roses; they are reserved for courting. Do not bring calla lilies; they are used at funerals. Heather should not be included in the flowers; this is planted on graves.

*Dining:* If you are the host, allow your guest to be seated first. If you are a guest, ask your German host about the local special. Choose local cuisine, not American, when selecting a restaurant. If you are a guest in someone's home, do not begin to eat, don't even sip your beverage, until your host does. Both hands should always be on top of the table. Rest your wrists on the table, never the elbows, even if you are not using your hands.

---

### ❮ PROTOCOL & ETIQUETTE ALERT ❯

The most difficult obstacle course you may have is when you dine. Stay alert to the major differences you will face when you come to the table.

---

Germans eat continental style. The fork stays in your left hand, tines down, and the knife in your right hand. Never switch the fork to your right hand to put food in your mouth. Use the knife to push the food onto the back of the fork. The tines of the fork are turned to face the palm. Imitate your host if you are not sure what to do.

Never eat anything, even a sandwich, with your fingers. Never use your knife to cut potatoes, pancakes, or dumplings. It implies the food is not cooked properly. Finish everything on your plate, even in restaurants, or make a reasonable excuse.

Avoid discussing politics, World War II, and personal subjects. Never discuss money or possessions.

At a social setting, whenever a woman leaves the table or returns to the table, all men stand. However, men do not rise in a business setting. On taking leave, everyone helps each other with their coats. All shake hands upon leaving.

---

### PROTOCOL & ETIQUETTE ALERT

Germans value intellectual discussions and your image will be enhanced if you are able to discuss philosophy and German culture. Wait until after dinner to discuss your mission endeavors.

---

The guest makes the first move to go. If you visit someone and your host does not refill your glass, it is an indication that you should go. Do not ask for coffee with a meal. It is served after the meal.

### INTERESTING INFORMATION

*Compliments:* Compliments are highly suspect. Germans offer compliments only if something is truly outstanding. Be careful that any compliments do not sound insincere. Intelligence is valued highly. Subtle comments regarding your hosts' ideas during a meeting will have a positive effect. It is not customary for woman to thank a man when receiving a compliment.

To Germans, a good question indicates an intelligent observer. Use phrases like "That's a very good question" before you give the answer or

"That idea has a lot of merit; have you considered this idea?" before continuing with the solution you would like to see implemented. Listen intently to what they say and support their view, even when offering another opinion.

*Building the Relationship:* In Germany, the relationship building comes after the meeting not at the beginning.

*Entering a Door:* Men should allow people of higher status and seniority to enter the door first, but in social situations, proceed first.

## STRICTLY BUSINESS

In Germany their very formal communication style requires that you introduce yourself and your company first by letter. Your letter to ask for an appointment begins with "Gentlemen." The custom is to send an open letter so that those at the company may decide who the best contact would be.

The *protocol challenge* will be when a reply comes, inviting you to a meeting. The letter is signed with two signatures, both illegible, without typed names underneath. How will you respond? You notice a reference number under the letterhead. You send another letter to the company requesting the identification of this code number.

Germans use their signatures to maintain their privacy. Typing the names below their signatures would be too personal and revealing. The code indicates who sent the letter.

You reply to the invitation with your travel itinerary and the hotel you have chosen and you are faced with another *protocol challenge.* You arrive at the secretary's desk at precisely the prearranged time. You don't just take your coat off and drape it over a chair in the outer office. Rather, you shake hands with the secretary, introduce yourself, and then give the secretary your card so she can announce you.

The secretary escorts you to the correct office. The door will be closed. She knocks on the door and the person with whom you're meeting opens it, and asks you in. You enter the office. Herr Burger offers his hand. You shake firmly as he says "Burger." You respond with "Draper."

The starkness of the last name alone sounds rude to American ears, but it's just the opposite in Germany. You appear insincere and much too casual when you use your first name. Business should always be conducted with formality. Unless Herr Direktor understands American ways, your meeting will result in a difficult uphill battle. Notice the use of the title Herr Direktor. Germans love this. It elevates them, recognizes their accomplishments, and gives them their due respect. Use of the last name with Herr (or Frau for any woman over eighteen), or Herr with the professional title is correct. Note that women's professional titles are not so easy, because they are usually addressed by their husband's title. Dr. Schmidt's wife would be Frau Doktor Schmidt. It is best to stay with Frau Schmidt. You likely will not meet many women in high positions in Germany. Note that secretaries are addressed by the title Frau.

---

Remember that the handshake is a precise shake: connect, one firm shake, and disconnect. Do this with all people present.

---

You handled the introduction well, so you move forward toward your goal. Your host helps you with your coat, which has no missing buttons. Image is incredibly important. Things are not in order unless they look in order. Your host makes a mental note of your professional presence and is impressed. The conservative dark suit, the white shirt, subdued tie (stripes might have been too bold), and the polished shoes all indicate to him that you mean business. Without knowing it, you just cleared a major hurdle.

After you exchange formal greetings, and you've hung your coat up properly, you wait for your host to offer you a seat and ask you to sit down. Never sit down before your host suggests it. You allow your host to lead, to orchestrate the group on his own turf.

Make sure your presentation is highly professional, well organized, and detailed, with reference and support data. All information is impressively packaged. Information is provided in both English and German.

During the presentation, be prepared to answer questions in detail. Know where to find supporting documentation in your text. Look as old as possible. Germans trust seasoned executives, not whiz kids. Speak with a strong, confident, but unemotional voice. Your voice should never be hesitant. Be in control of your body at all times. Be at attention and keep hands still and out of pockets. Use language, not gestures, to express your ideas.

After you have finished your presentation and answer all questions, say that if there are no more questions, you will allow the others to review the information and you look forward to their response.

The Germans, being so meticulous in every detail, will want to pore over your proposal before coming to a decision. Do not push for an immediate answer. After a few days, you can send a letter asking if any additional information is needed.

Now it is time to take leave. Your host helps you on with your coat, which you allow (and reciprocate if he is leaving, too). You invite him and his wife to dinner that evening. You have already researched the city and found a special restaurant. Of course, this is only proper if your host is of comparable professional stature to you. You would include others at the meeting if they have similar status. Remember to shake hands with the secretary upon leaving. Shake once and then disconnect. Do this with all people present.

## Country Summary

- A strong level of hierarchy prevails in Germany.
- Go prepared.
- Order is everything.
- Germans communicate in a precise and detail manner.
- Punctuality is very important.
- Use a formal approach in everything.
- Dress conservatively.

- Dine continental style.
- Do not eat using your fingers.
- Keep both hands on top of table.
- Use compliments sparingly.
- Think engineer when communicating with a German.
- Business is conducted in a formal manner.

# Country Profile: Denmark

## (Cultural Position: Individualistic)

### Religious Factors

Christianity was introduced to Denmark in the twelfth century. The Reformation came in 1536. Today the primary religion is Protestant and the largest, strongest denomination is Lutheran. Lutheran pastors have played a significant part in Denmark's history. Danish philosopher Søren Kierkegaard worked to revitalize the Christian faith. Christen Kold in about 1850 pioneered the Danish "free school" system, based on N.F.S. Grundtvig's thinking that man, although created by God, is a free and responsible being.

### Communication Characteristics

*Transaction Communication Characteristics:* Hierarchy in Denmark is not as strong as in Germany. Comfort and convenience are extremely important. The Danes want contentment in whatever they embrace. They expect honesty and cooperation from foreigners. Cooperation is the key factor in problem solving.

---

## « TRANSACTION ALERT »

Solicit cooperation. It's important to be as flexible and cooperative as possible.

---

*Interaction Communication Characteristics:* The Danes are more relaxed than the Germans, but retain a formal side and do not use your first name. When giving feedback, Danes will be direct, specific, and objective. They learn best when presented with an organized and rational approach, so it is wise to use detailed text, data, and graphics. Punctuality and adherence to schedules are important and change is resisted.

Two mistakes not to make:

1. Do not compare your U.S. standard of living with others. You will turn them off if you brag about your material possessions, the vastness of our country, or your station in life.
2. Do not refer to Danes, Norwegians, or Swedes as Scandinavians. There is a strong national pride among the Nordic people, and past political rivalries—now replaced by commercial rivalry—cause them to insist on separate identities.

*Forms of Address:* Wait until it is suggested to call a person by his first name. Stand when you are introduced to someone. If he has a title, use it.

*Greetings:* If you ask, "How are you?" the Dane will think you really want to know and will tell you. Feel free to introduce yourself to a group.

*Handshakes:* Shake hands with both men and women. Shake the woman's hand first. The handshake is brief but firm. A handshake is as good as a contract. Shake hands upon meeting and leaving.

*Gestures:* Do not use the American OK sign. It is an insult.

*Appropriate Attire:* Professional women can wear a suit or a jacket and skirt. Men should wear the typical business attire. Never comment on someone's clothes.

*View of Women:* There is a large female work force in Denmark. Women will have no trouble being accepted.

*Gift Giving:* If you are invited to a home, never go empty-handed. Bring chocolates or a small gift of something made in the United States. If you want to give flowers, send them in advance of your arrival. Always stay for conversation after the meal. Conversation should avoid one's personal life.

*Dining:* Be warned that there are not many places to go out and have lunch in Denmark. If the area you are visiting is not in a major city, you may have to drive fifty miles to find a good restaurant. If your host invites you to lunch at a company cafeteria, accept.

## INTERESTING INFORMATION

The Danes have a profound sense of destiny and believe that everyone has a specific purpose in life and cannot change who he is meant to be. This is not the same as fatalism, in which no matter how one behaves, things will happen as they will. The Danish sense of destiny is more of a framework for living on earth. Danes believe people relate to the world through the abilities they were given at birth. One's responsibility and sense of joy are to live according to one's abilities and aptitudes. People are not consumed with trying to be better than someone else or trying to achieve goals that are unattainable.

## STRICTLY BUSINESS

You have been in a morning meeting which has come to its logical end near lunchtime. You do not ask for an immediate decision or set a deadline. At this point you don't ask your host to have lunch with you. Wait to see if the host will ask you to lunch at the cafeteria. If the church or business you are visiting is not in a major city, you may have to drive fifty miles to find a good restaurant. Most companies have very good cafeterias. If your host asks you to lunch at the cafeteria, do accept.

During lunch eat continental style. Don't direct all your conversation to highest manager. Engage everyone in conversation Managers usually socialize with those they manage. Everyone's place in society is respected. You are doing what you were born to do. All are equal and important, so talk to everyone in the group. Incomes do not separate people very much. Since the tax structure reduces a high salary to moderate levels, everyone makes more or less a comparable income.

### DENMARK COUNTRY SUMMARY

- Comfort and convenience are extremely important to the Danes.
- The Danes are direct in their style of communication.
- Do not compare your standard of living with others.
- Do not refer to the Danes as Scandinavians.
- The Danes have a great sense of destiny.

# Country Profile: Norway

## (Culture Position: Individualist)

### RELIGIOUS FACTORS

Norwegian Lutheranism and the Nordic brand of Protestantism is the primary religion. The southern and western areas are more fundamental in their approach than people in Oslo. The Lutheran doctrine extends into society as a whole. Norwegian Lutheran ethics encourage conformity for the society.

## Communication Characteristics

*Transaction Communication Characteristics:* Norway does not have an obvious power hierarchy, but one does exist. Norwegians place a great deal of emphasis on individual achievement. They believe that one's achievement is more important than status. The Norwegian believes that self-determination is his highest responsibility and expects others to exhibit competence and self-determination. Problems are solved in a rational manner.

*Interaction Communication Characteristics:* Norwegians are direct, with strong opinions. Individual Norwegians will feel superior to some people and envious of others. They learn best with detailed text and graphics. Punctuality is important. Plans and schedules are detailed. Change does not come easily.

---

### INTERACTION ALERT

In Norwegian culture there are deep roots in the ideal that the individual is most important.

---

## Protocol & Etiquette

*Forms of Address:* Use professional title, especially among older people. Younger people do not always use titles. Take your cue from the introduction. Clergymen and attorneys do not use titles.

*Greetings:* The official greeting is "morn." Do not speak loudly. This is considered rude. Set a time limit on meetings, or they will go on for many hours. Avoid discussing personal family topics. You may talk about politics, sports, and travel.

*Handshakes:* The handshake is the same as it is in the United States.

*Gestures:* It is not necessary to rise when someone comes into a room unless you are being introduced to the person. Do not put your hands in your pockets when speaking to someone. To beckon someone, you can make a toss of your head.

*Appropriate Attire:* Norwegians dress more informally than Americans; however, as a visitor you need to dress more conservatively. Women may wear slacks but not jeans.

*View of Women:* There is a view of equality for women. Norwegian women are strong in educational and political arenas.

*Gift Giving:* Do not give white flowers. Avoid giving carnations and lilies—these are funeral flowers. Chocolate is an acceptable gift. Make sure your gift is wrapped in quality paper.

*Dining:* Learn to eat continental style. Do not expect to be invited out to dine. Restaurants are very expensive. Dinner is served around 5:30 p.m. There will be no small talk before the meal. Hors d'oeuvres are not served. After the meal there will be lengthy conversation, so expect to stay a couple of hours.

## Interesting Information

In Norway, as in most of Europe, the correct way is to write a date is to put the day first, then the month, then the year. For example, August 11, 2005, is written 11 August, 2005.

## Strictly Business

Arrive at the office punctually. Introduce yourself to the manager of operations using your whole name. He introduces himself as Carl Lund, and you shake hands firmly. Thereafter you refer to him as Carl. First names are acceptable, but it is generally more proper in any Western culture to wait until you are invited to use a first name. This very well may happen during the first meeting.

After you are invited to sit down, and after a brief discussion of winter sports, you move on to your presentation. Your approach could be: "My colleague, who by the way is Norwegian and studied in Trondheim, convinced our ministry that the material I distributed would be of great value in Norway."

Norwegians are not interested in what Americans think. Try to find a Norwegian opinion to present to them.

## Country Summary

- Norwegians are continually trying to assert themselves as an important national identity.
- An enormous tax burden influences Norwegian culture.
- There is no rich upper class. Who you know is important.
- This is a culture with deep roots in the ideal that the individual is most important, even though the sense of equality has been legislated into inequality of conformity.
- Norwegians are not interested in what Americans think.
- History defines Norwegians as completely honest and obstinate.

## Sweden Supplemental Data

Similar to Denmark and Norway, Sweden has turned its natural sense of independence and equality into a legislated equality by economic conformity. Swedes are strongly capitalistic and not as protective as Norwegians.

Swedes, along with Danes and Norwegians, highly value intelligence and education. Shake hands when meeting and leaving. Upper-class Swedes address each other in the third person: "How is Mr. Wade today?" instead of "How are you?"

Unlike the Norwegians, Swedes have a history of strong and adventurous monarchs. Sweden historically looked to the East, while Norway looked to the past. The power hierarchy is stronger than in Norway, but not as strong as in Germany.

# Country Profile: England

## (Cultural Position: Family/Clan)

Note: It is as important to know that Great Britain includes England, Scotland, and Wales. The United Kingdom is Great Britain and Northern Ireland.

Scotland and Wales are not part of England.

### Religious Factors

When England split from the Roman Catholic Church during the reign of Henry VIII, it formed the Anglican Church, sometimes referred to as the Church of England.

---

**《 TRANSACTION ALERT 》**

Pose benefits of your service project as improvements to the functioning and well-being of the group. Appeal to tradition.

---

At one time, the Church of England had political power. It does not now. The Roman Catholic Church, Presbyterian, and Methodist denominations and the Jewish faith all are represented in England.

### Communication Characteristics

*Transaction Communication Characteristics:* There is a power hierarchy in all areas of activities. In business there is little movement up the ladder. The British work best behind closed doors. They uphold tradition and seek to benefit the greater good, putting form and deference first and competence last. Problems are delegated but ultimately addressed. Decisions can take a long time.

*Interaction Communication Characteristics:* The British are formal, reserved, and gracious. They are honest but civil, and will word negative feedback so that it is not offensive. England is a nation of cultural interests. The British can feel inwardly superior but will be outwardly gracious. They are strongly verbal, therefore they learn best with verbose conversation. Punctuality is important. Schedules and plans are adhered to and precise. Change is resisted. The English value the past more than the present or the future.

---

### INTERACTION ALERT

Show humility. Defer to Britons' superior knowledge of decorum.

---

## PROTOCOL & ETIQUETTE

*Forms of Address:* Always use Mr. or Mrs. with the family name. If a hyphenated name is given, use both names. When you introduce someone or are introduced with a title, use that title when you address that person. Titles can be confusing. Doctors, clergy, barons, etc., are introduced by their title and last name. Surgeons are introduced by Mr., Mrs., or Miss. When you introduce yourself, give your full name, such as Susan Lee Prescott or Dr. Karol Horn. When you are introduced, respond by saying, "How do you do?" instead of "Nice to meet you." In less formal settings, the British will address you by your first name. Wait until they use your first name to call them by theirs.

*Handshakes:* A handshake is the acceptable greeting when visiting in a home. In social settings, the handshake is not always proper. In a professional setting, the handshake is light. Women do not always shake hands; wait until a woman extends her hand first. The British will shake hands when greeting, but not necessarily when taking leave. When they do not shake hands when taking leave, it means that they want to keep the door open for further discussions.

*Gestures:* Control of your body means you are in control mentally and emotionally. Try not to use gestures. Sit upright with legs together or crossed, one knee over the other knee, never an ankle at the knee. Keep your hands still. Use your head to point, not your finger. Do not touch others. Tap your nose to indicate a secret or confidentiality.

*Appropriate Attire:* Dress conservatively. Choose subdued, dark colors. Women may wear tailored dresses. Men do not wear ties with stripes. Each school has its own color. Do not wear button-down collar shirts. Carry an umbrella; you will need it. When you go into a room, leave your umbrella in the stand by the door.

*Language Differences:* If a Briton tells you something is "quite good," you have not been given a compliment. Quite good means not so good. Also if you are asked to "table" an item on your agenda, this means to discuss it first. There are many words that have different meanings than they do in the United States. It is best to consult a local British usage book before spending time there.

Do not make the "V" for victory sign with your palms facing inward. This is the highest insult you can give. Make the sign with the palm of your hands facing outward.

*View of Women:* The British are cautious when working with women. A woman needs to be self-assured, confident, and project a professional attitude.

*Gift Giving:* The British are not a gift-giving society. When you go to someone's home, take flowers, but not lilies. Nor should you take chocolates. It is proper to send a written thank-you note to your host within twenty-four hours. It is considerate to send it by courier.

*Dining:* Do not use your fingers to pick up food, not even a hamburger. Use your knife and fork. Raise your hand to call a waiter. Eat continental style. Keep your wrists on the table and not in your lap. Do not ask to sample someone else's food. Pass food to your left.

History is a good conversation starter, but only if you know your own American and regional history. The British are history buffs and will note any mistakes you make. You may ask someone what town they are from originally, but you will show ignorance if you ask if they might be a Scot or a Welshman.

The guest initiates the close of the dinner hour, not the host.

## Interesting Information

*English Tea Time:* Tea is served loose in a common pot. Allow your host to pour. You should place the tea strainer across your cup to catch loose leaves. Use the sugar provided, which is often colored. Do not pull a packet of sugar substitute from your pocket. Use milk, never cream.

## Strictly Business

When contacting a church or company, your first letter to the company or church should be detailed so that the right person to handle your request is assigned to reply. When you receive a positive reply, it is proper to call the person to confirm the meeting and to be sure you get to the right area of responsibility. Remember, first impressions are hard to change.

Either your contact or his secretary will greet you. Shake hands using a slightly firm grip. The secretary will introduce you or you should introduce yourself. Use your full name.

Wait to be invited to sit down. It is not necessary in business to rise when a female secretary enters the room. Do rise whenever someone new enters, and introduce yourself. Always stand for women in social settings.

When the meeting starts, your opening remarks need to be small talk about the weather or the office view. The visitor should be the one to get down to business after an initial icebreaker.

Make sure your presentation is organized. Give your contact a professional looking document supporting your proposal. Use a moderate voice.

Keep your body in control. This indicates to your hosts that you are in control mentally and emotionally as well. Do not use gestures. Sit upright with legs together or crossed, one knee over the other knee, never an ankle at the knee. Keep your hands still. Use good eye contact.

Coffee may be served in a morning meeting. Do not ask for it if it is not offered. An afternoon appointment may run into tea time. Knowing you are American, they will probably offer coffee, but be prepared for tea.

The guest initiates leaving. Do not sit waiting for your host to conclude the meeting. When you are finished, summarize your remarks and confirm action items. Present your business card before leaving. The English do not shake hands when leaving, but your counterpart may know that Americans do. Let him offer his hand first. If a morning meeting concludes anytime after 11:30, invite your contact to lunch. If your counterpart is upper management, make a reservation at a good restaurant before your meeting. If not, ask him to suggest a restaurant, which will probably be a local pub.

The British do not like the concept of selling. It seems undignified. Do not sell them, reason with them. Managers will be looking for the wisdom in your proposal. What you propose must be solid, reliable, and conservative in approach. They will not take risks with their stewardship. Novelty is not exciting to them. There must be a good reason to make a change. Try to relate the idea of using your product to some element of tradition. Talk security, tradition, low impact, and low risk. Reserve some noncritical information for an opportunity to follow up several days later. When taking leave of your contact, do not shake hands unless he does, say you enjoyed meeting him, and you look forward to his reply to your proposal.

Do not say, "Have a nice day."

## Country Summary

- Give a compliment by elevating a Briton's self worth, perhaps something about one's family power. Compliments or comments about one's stature, world, or financial status are very rude. Personal compliments in general should be avoided.

- Use decorum, and do not consider the British your equal. You, an American, are a poor relation, with no social standing. Image is everything to the British. They take pleasure in crossing up Americans in the area of etiquette. The British are so detailed and precise in their knowledge that you will have a hard time keeping up.
- Do not brag about the United States or anything else. The British enjoy tradition and ritual more than Americans and they are more reserved than Americans.
- The British use sarcasm to make fun of themselves, but not others. Royalty is a subject rarely discussed.

# Country Profile: France

## (Cultural Position: Family/Clan in the South; Individualistic in the North)

### Religious Factors

The Celtic influence was enormously significant in shaping the behavior of the French. Equally so was the influence of the Roman Empire and the Catholic Church. Indeed, the seat of the pope was Avignon rather than Rome from 1309 to 1378. Today, France is thought of as a secular Catholic country. Most believe that religion is for the poor. Only about 8 percent of France's population is religious. There is little participation at Mass except at Easter and Christmas. The second most prevalent religion is Islam. There are small percentages of Protestants, Jews, and Buddhists.

## COMMUNICATION CHARACTERISTICS

*Transaction Communication Characteristics:* There is a strong hierarchy, but it is well camouflaged. The French do not like responsibility; however, they expect you to take responsibility seriously. They believe when they reach their goals with little stress and accountability in the process, it is a sense of accomplishment. The French expect antagonism. They also expect you to know your place in society. Solutions are discussed rationally; however, implementation is a problem because this suggests accountability. Decisions are based on rational process as well as power implication.

---

### ≺ TRANSACTION ALERT ≻

French society is organized to stress the importance of the individual in some aspects; however, there also is a strong power hierarchy that tends to be based on seniority and influence, not merit.

---

*Interaction Communication Characteristics:* The French feel superior to others. They are formal, closed, and adversarial. They find it a hardship to deal with foreigners. When the French give feedback internally, they are critical; however, criticism is withheld in negotiations. In a working relationship, criticism will be direct. The French learn best by logic and detailed text. Punctuality is important. Schedules are maintained and plans are implemented. Change is not welcomed. The French have an historical perspective about time. Taking time is prudent. Stability over time impresses them.

## PROTOCOL & ETIQUETTE

*Forms of Address:* Friends and close colleagues use first names. Monsieur and Madame are the correct titles to use. Mademoiselle is used for women under eighteen years of age.

*Greetings:* Greet the French with *Bonjour* ("Good day") and "*Comment allez-vous*?" The more informal greeting is *Ça va?* ("How are you?") Young people may greet each other with *Salut.* They also use this when parting. When entering a room, greet everyone. Be careful not to speak or laugh loudly. The French speak more quietly than Americans. The familiar greeting is *tu* and the formal greeting is *vous.*

*Handshakes:* Women are customarily kissed on each cheek by both males and females. Men kiss each other's cheeks only if they are close friends or relatives. When one receives a kiss on the cheeks, it is a light touch, more of an air kiss. The number of kisses one receives ranges from two to four depending on the region.

An aggressive handshake is considered impolite. The French handshake is light and is done with one pump. The man waits for the woman to offer her hand.

*Gestures:* The most vulgar sign you can use is slapping your palm over a closed fist. The French are discreet about their personal habits. You must be discreet about sneezing, blowing your nose, and so on. Do not comb your hair, use toothpicks, or chew gum in public. Keep your hands out of your pockets. Every move should be subdued. While the French themselves gesture, we suggest you employ very little gesturing; use your face to express meaning. Respect a person's private space. Stand at a reasonable distance.

---

### PROTOCOL ALERT

The French disdain the concept of selling. Even in your mission work, negotiate rather than sell your ideas.

---

*Appropriate Attire:* How you dress is important. You must not be trendy, just chic. In southern France, the dress code is less formal but not sloppy. Parisians dress the most formally. In the winter, men should wear black.

*View of Women:* Women are more accepted in the north than in the south of France. Men may treat a woman flirtatiously, but not condescendingly. Businesswomen should give special attention to their attire. One must be fashionable and elegant.

*Gift Giving:* The French are interested in gifts that have some intellectual or aesthetic merit. Do not give a gift that could be perceived as cheap. Gifts carrying commercial logos should be avoided. Do not give a gift until you have met with someone several times.

When you are invited to a party, bring chocolates or flowers. Present them when you arrive. Make sure the flowers are not chrysanthemums or roses. A basket of fruit can be sent the next day, along with a thank-you note.

*Dining:* The French eat continental style, using the knife as a pusher and inserting the fork in your mouth with tines facing down. Lunches and dinners can last up to two hours. Do not rush the process. You may be served up to twelve courses. When dining in a home, people usually rest ten to fifteen minutes between courses.

Men may rest their wrists on the table's edge. Women may rest their forearms on the table's edge. In France, it is rude to cut lettuce. The proper etiquette is to fold the lettuce until you have a neat package. Do this by securing the lettuce with your fork, using the knife to fold. When eating fruit, peel and cut it with a knife and eat it with a fork. Place your bread on the table next to your plate. There are no bread plates.

Culinary cuisine and food preparation knowledge are important to the French. Be sure to compliment their choices of food and the manner in which they serve it. During the meal, make your conversation positive and not argumentative. Linger awhile after the meal. Send a proper, handwritten thank-you note the next day.

## Strictly Business

You met a French diplomat of some stature who gave you an introduction to a company outside of Paris. A meeting and lunch were scheduled. Some appropriate concerns are: 1) that the person you are meeting might not be the right person in the organization; 2) There was no job title attached to his name; 3) that he might be of a higher level, one far above your relative status; and 4) who pays for lunch.

It is difficult to learn a person's functional responsibility. Try to get information through an affiliate or from your intermediary. The question of status is difficult. If he has invited you to lunch, he, as the host, will pay. You may wish to reciprocate at a later time. Do not give gifts. They are considered a personal expression, which is inappropriate.

When you arrived in Paris, you reconfirmed the meeting. You arrive at the office right on time. The secretary asks you to wait. You take a seat near her desk. After twenty minutes, you practice patience, knowing that it will probably be another twenty minutes.

To the French, time is not money; time is power. It is an element of control. Some think French executives are just disorganized. This is not so. They understand the value of time in their own terms.

When your host finally appears, you rise and wait for him to offer his hand.

It would seem natural to extend your hand but this is France. He may not want to shake your hand. This is another technique to humble you, and otherwise throw you off-balance. If he does offer his hand, shake it moderately and with a slight nod of your head if he is very much your senior. If there are others in attendance, you need only give your card to the host.

Break the ice with some conversation about France, nothing personal, and nothing about yourself. If an interpreter is needed, look at the person you are addressing and who is addressing you, not the interpreter.

When making presentations, use the same organized, professional, detailed presentation outlined elsewhere for other northern European countries. Stress performance, quality, financial benefits, and low risk.

To you it may seem that the French way of expressing opinions can sound critical. Do not become defensive. Try to hear the underlying concern and ignore the negative tone. Respond calmly to challenges of your credibility. Prove your assertions.

When your host expresses interest in your proposal and shakes your hand, you may misinterpret this to mean he is seriously interested. All that is required is management's signature on a contract. Your host may recommend the product or service, but he has no power. There is no telling what the top man will decide. Power is tied to individuals. Decision-making is central and lies with the man in charge. Those who work for him are not necessarily aware of his motivations. To increase your chances for success, involve the highest ranking individuals you can early in the process.

## Interesting Information

The French are insistent on the values of equality and liberty, but they also seem to draw their identity from their family structure. The equality and liberty perspective is found more in the north and identity from family structure is found more in the south.

The major difference between the French and U.S. outlooks on life is the French's pronounced cynicism toward mankind as opposed to the American tendency toward optimism. Do not take their cynicism personally.

## Country Summary

- Show some sophistication.
- The French do not want to relate to you.
- Do not speak or laugh loudly.
- Use detailed data when making presentations.
- The best gifts are intellectual and aesthetic ones.

# Country Profile: The Netherlands

## (Cultural Position: Individualistic)

### Religious Factors

The Netherlands is a bourgeois country, a country of the middle class. They are thrifty and practical. The Dutch are said to worship reality. Although more than 30 percent are Roman Catholic, they are anti-authoritarian, and believe in self-determination.

### Communication Characteristics

*Transaction Characteristics:* The Dutch are open to individuals, but privacy is important. They do not have a strong power hierarchy. Management can be horizontal. The Dutch expect to be productive, and want to reach their goals. They respect others' rights, but expect equal treatment and consideration, and self-control is mandatory. They like honesty and practicality. They respect everyone as equals. They are more relaxed than most Europeans, but they appreciate good manners. To the Dutch, problem solving is a cooperative effort. They are realistic and deal with problems straight on. A strong work ethic and appreciation of culture are important to the Dutch.

*Interaction Communication Characteristics:* The Dutch are direct and respectful. They are honest and blunt when they give feedback, but they are not contentious. The Dutch are ready to accept foreigners. They learn best by text and graphics and independent analysis. Punctuality, precise planning, and scheduling are very important. Change is not threatening. New ideas will be absorbed into a study and implemented if necessary. The Dutch are outward looking and enjoy new ideas and personal expression. Do not be confrontational.

## Protocol & Etiquette

*Greetings:* The normal greeting in Dutch is *Gueydan* (Good day). Women greet each other with kisses on the cheeks.

*Handshakes:* The handshake is quick and light in pressure.

*Gestures:* It is rude to talk with your hands in your pockets. It is rude to talk with food, gum, or toothpick in your mouth. The Dutch avoid pointing with their index finger.

*Appropriate Attire:* The Dutch are well dressed. Casual attire is worn only among families in a home setting.

*View of Women:* The Dutch have a conservative view of women, but they are tolerant.

*Dining:* The main meal is served around six or seven in the evening. Meals are social and cultural events. It is rude to leave food on your plate and to refuse a second helping.

## Western Dutch: Belgium Supplemental Data

- Belgians value tact and diplomacy over blunt honesty.
- Do not discuss language differences.
- Shake hands on meeting and leaving. Shake quickly with a light pressure. When being introduced, repeat your name. Be sure to shake hands with secretaries when arriving and leaving.
- At a large party, let your host introduce you to others. You do not have to shake hands with everyone.
- If you translate your materials, provide both French and Dutch.
- The first meeting is usually for getting acquainted. Belgians lean to the family/clan side on this point; in the Flemish north, this will not always be the case.
- Do not suggest a dinner meeting. Belgians like to spend the evening with their families.

### STRICTLY BUSINESS

Depending on whether you are on the French side or Dutch side of Belgium, you would use the protocol from the respective countries. Belgium is a transition country, combining both French and Dutch influence, with Dutch predominant in the north. Brussels is more French in its culture.

### COUNTRY SUMMARY

- Shake hands on meeting and leaving. Shake quickly with a light pressure. When being introduced, repeat your name.
- Be sure to shake hands with secretaries when arriving and leaving.
- At a large party, let your host introduce you. You don't have to shake hands with everyone.
- Belgians value tact and diplomacy over blunt honesty.
- Don't discuss language differences in Belgium.
- If you translate your materials, do so in both French and Flemish.
- The first meeting is usually for getting acquainted. Belgians lean to the family/clan position in this. In the Flemish north, this will not always be the case.
- Schedule business entertaining for lunchtime. Belgians like to be with their family in the evening.

## Country Profile: Italy

## (Cultural Position: Family Clan/Individualistic)

### RELIGIOUS FACTORS

Roman Catholicism is predominant in Italy. It may be surprising to note that the Catholic Church does not play a significant social or even political role in Italy. Vatican City is an independent nation and is not part of Rome or Italy.

## Communication Characteristics

*Transaction Communication Characteristics:* There are more levels of hierarchy in northern Italy than in southern Italy. Northern Italians are more formal and southern Italians less formal in their communication style. In northern Italy, achievement and status are important while in southern Italy, making friends and being relaxed are more important. In northern Italy, problems will be solved immediately; in southern Italy, it will take some time.

*Interaction Communication Characteristics:* Northern Italians are more formal and respectful of protocol and etiquette in their communication style than southern Italians. It is better for the foreigner to err on the formal side until you get to know the people in both regions and a relationship has been established. Most Italians will give feedback in a direct and specific manner. They will want to know something about you before they begin to communicate with you or your group. More educated Italians will want data. In northern Italy time is very important; in southern Italy, it is less so. The Italians expect change to occur.

---

### « INTERACTION ALERT »

Highly educated Italians will use facts over feelings. They can be very argumentative.

---

## Protocol & Etiquette

*Forms of Address:* Do not use first names unless you are invited to do so. Titles are used both in speaking and in writing.

*Greetings:* The eldest or most senior person will be introduced first.

The greeting *Ciao* is a hello or good-bye and is an informal greeting. The more formal greetings are *Buongiorno* for good morning and *Buonasera* for good afternoon or good evening. In the south you may experience more touching when greeting, such as a hand on the shoulder.

*Handshakes:* Handshakes are appropriate. Often, people one will grasp the person's other arm with their hand. Do not cross over other people when shaking hands.

In southern Italy, the Italians kiss on both cheeks of family members when they greet. Women kiss other women on the cheeks. Males greet old friends in an embrace and a slap on the back. Shake hands when you are introduced and when you take leave.

*Gestures:* Italians talk with their hands a lot. Do not assume your gestures will be appreciated. Thumbing your nose means defiance. When angry, the Italian will quickly stroke his fingertips under his chin.

*Gift Giving:* Small gifts like homemade crafts, pens, clocks, or travel books are acceptable. When invited to someone's home, bring flowers or gift-wrapped chocolates. Make sure they are not an even number. Never give chrysanthemums, handkerchiefs, or knives. Each represents a funeral or sadness.

*Appropriate Attire:* Appearance is important to the Italians. Older women wear dresses. Good clothes represent your status in life. Even casual dress is chic. Stylish shoes are a must.

*View of Women:* Women are taken seriously in business and in society. But even in professional settings, men will flirt with women.

*Dining:* Dining is the highlight of the day. As in all European countries, the Italians eat continental style. Make sure to keep your hands above the table while dining. When eating spaghetti, do not cut it or twirl it against a spoon. Twirl it against the side of the dish. Pasta is followed by a meat course. There are hundreds of types of cheese in Italy. Salad is almost always served with oil and vinegar dressing with little or no spices in the dressing. Do not ask for anything else. When you have invited people to a restaurant, there will be fighting over the check. You must insist on paying. A businesswoman has almost no chance of picking up the bill unless payment is arranged ahead and she explains that the company or church has paid.

---

### ❮ PROTOCOL & ETIQUETTE ALERT ❯

Italians consider social interaction to be very important. Do not turn down invitations.

---

## Strictly Business

In northern Italy, use German protocol with slightly less formality. Dress can be more fashionable. Be sparing with your gestures. In southern Italy, you will find a more relaxed atmosphere, but it is wise to continue a degree of formality. Remember, you are still in Europe.

## Country Summary

- Shake hands when meeting and leaving. Exchange business cards with anyone you haven't met previously.
- In the south you may encounter more physical contact during meetings, such as a hand on the shoulder.
- When eating spaghetti, don't cut or twirl it against a spoon.
- When you invite a businessman to a meal, ask which colleagues should be included.
- The phones are not reliable in Italy.

# Country Profile: Spain

## (Cultural Position: Family/Clan)

### RELIGIOUS FACTORS

Spain's religious history is dominated by Roman, Islamic, and Catholic rule. Each of these has resided for centuries. The strong authoritarian power structures reflect man's separateness from God. In early history the people thought they could only react to the whims of the gods. Over 99 percent of the people are baptized Catholic but few think of themselves as religious.

### COMMUNICATION CHARACTERISTICS

*Transaction Communication Characteristics:* There are strong power hierarchies, and there is a great distinction between the lower and upper classes. There is a strong allegiance to the family group. If a Spaniard has wealth and status, he feels he has accomplished a lot in life. The Spaniard expects the foreigner to protect the Spaniard's interests. The Spanish tend to do nothing and wait for solutions to develop; everything resolves itself in time. Decisions can be subjective and based on emotion or hidden agendas.

*Interaction Communication Characteristics:* Spaniards are always courteous but cautious, giving feedback indirectly. Body language and attitude may communicate opinion. They avoid conflict and accountability. The Spanish may appear to be outgoing to foreigners, but they are very protective of themselves and their culture. Cause and effect must be clearly shown. Use visual representation and analogy. Time moves forward, but not necessarily in a linear fashion. Plans tend to be general, and schedules advisory. They resist change and have a low tolerance for the unknown.

---

## « PROTOCOL ALERT »

Spain is a poor nation compared to many of its European neighbors. This is a sensitive subject. Do not compare Spain to other nations.

---

### PROTOCOL & ETIQUETTE

*Forms of Address:* Only young people use first names. You must use proper names. The Spaniard way to address someone is by (*tú*), the familiar form, or (*Usted*) for the formal. Older people and people of higher status may address you by your first name. Do not interpret this as a signal to use their first name; use the other person's surname until invited to do otherwise. If an older person asks you to use his first name, precede it by Don as a sign of respect.

*Handshakes:* The handshake is appropriate. Men who are friends will add a pat on the back and possibly a hug to the handshake. Women will embrace and touch the cheeks.

*Greetings:* A name is given like this: first name, father's family name, and mother's maiden name—Carlos Garcia Mendez. Address him as Señor Garcia. When parting, women will embrace each other.

*Gestures:* the rudest gesture you can give is the American OK gesture. The Spaniards gesture a lot. The meaning varies from region to region. Have a reasonable knowledge of what the gestures mean, but do not try to copy them.

When calling someone, turn your palm down and wiggle your fingers.

To make a point, slap your palm downward.

*Appropriate Attire:* Women will dress more stylishly and men will dress more conservatively in Spain, where status is important and clothing reflects this emphasis. Businesswomen must project a professional image. Dress elegantly, but conservatively. Do not be flirtatious in any way.

*View of Women:* There is a strong distinction between the male and female. The male is to be the protector and the woman is to be the sympathizer and in charge of the children. Only about one-third of the work force is female.

*Gift Giving:* Wait until you form a relationship before you exchange gifts. Status is important to the Spaniards and they appreciate name brand gifts of high quality. They should be eloquently wrapped. When presented with a gift, unwrap it immediately. Never give thirteen flowers, chrysanthemums, or dahlias. Art work representative of your home state is an appropriate gift.

*Dining:* The Spaniards will eat continental style. They will be more relaxed in their dining. Your manners should be slightly formal, but not subdued.

## INTERESTING INFORMATION

Historically in Spain, power was derived was derived from one's family's possessions and wealth. This is a form of materialism not rooted in personal satisfaction but in its symbol of family stature. How one's family appears to others is important. It defines the pecking order in society. There is little trust between the family/clans, and therefore the more power one had, the more certain the survival of the clan. All members of the group were dedicated to its survival, because each drew identity from membership in the group.

## STRICTLY BUSINESS

You have a meeting with someone who can help your church or mission. Where you hold your first meeting depends on the level of the person you are meeting. If he is a top executive, a fine restaurant is in order. If he is middle or lower management, he will feel uncomfortable in a fancy restaurant. Remember that people do not move into position of authority by merit. These are posts reserved for members of the social elite.

At the first meeting, your goal is to let the Spaniard find out the kind of person you are. This is not the best time to establish an agenda.

First meetings almost never accomplish any purpose in an American's terms. In the Spaniard's perspective, he is accomplishing a great deal. The only way one can be assured of performance in this culture is if there is an element of friendship. He must be sure his position is safe before exposing what he thinks during negotiations.

If you ended up at a restaurant, you notice everyone eats continental style. Table manners are not extremely important, but you should dine in good taste. Your manners are slightly formal. But do not be subdued; it would be assumed you are uninterested.

First impressions are important, so these are some considerations:

1. Shake hands firmly when introduced.
2. Address Carlos Garcia Mendez as Senor Garcia.
3. Avoid talking about your business.
4. Wear a good quality suit and black leather shoes.

Always be on time for appointments, but never expect a Spaniard to be. If you are very important, he will not keep you waiting long. And when you do meet, wait for him to initiate the discussion about the matter at hand.

When asked to make your presentation, highlight the benefits for the Spaniard. Your manners are formal, but not stiff. You use your body, especially your hands, to emphasize points. You speak forcefully and with animation to project sincerity. You make good eye contact.

There will be interruptions, and your host may tend to get off-track. Gently guide the discussion back to your presentation.

Be very clear in your presentation. Use visual aids and repetition. Emphasize the most important points. If your presentation is somewhat complicated, it would be wise to have another person in the meeting. The reason for this is that Spaniards will not admit that they don't understand something. They don't want to appear unintelligent. Even if you encourage questions, you may not get honest feedback. The danger is that your proposal might fail if it is not clearly understood. Try to anticipate problem areas. Tell your prospective partner that others usually are confused about (something technical), or that you are often asked about (some detail). If another person from his organization is present, that person may be able to work out the confusion in private, or your contact may be able to say the other person didn't understand and ask questions that way.

You don't push for closure on the deal, but instead suggest meeting again the next day. This gives your host the opportunity to digest your presentation and figure out how your proposal fits into his own priorities. Business lunches are not done until after a few meetings. The next day you return to the office on time.

Several things happen that indicate you are being successful: he doesn't keep you waiting as long this time; he puts a hand on your shoulder when shaking hands; he sits closer to you during discussions. After negotiations are complete, he shakes your hand in agreement and suggests you both have lunch. What do you expect will happen next? He will let you know the head of the company's final decision at some later date.

Remember, all decisions are made at the top. You are halfway there, but anything can happen during the decision process. The handshake is not considered binding, as it is in Denmark and parts of Latin America. Enjoy lunch. Continue building rapport, but talk only about personal matters if your host brings something up for discussion. Consider this leg of your trip a success.

## Country Summary

- Shake hands when meeting and leaving.
- Older people and people of high rank may address you by your first name. Don't take this as a signal to use theirs. Use their surname until invited to do otherwise. If a person of high rank asks you to use his first name, precede it by Don as a sign of respect.
- Beware of casual U.S. gestures. Some of them are offensive. Use the whole hand, not the fingers, to gesture.

- Dressing well at all times gives the impression of accomplishment.
- Businesswomen must project a professional air. Dress elegantly, but conservatively. Don't be flirtatious in any way. Men may make comments to women as they walk by. Be sure not to react or acknowledge them in any way. If you return the gaze of a man, he will think you are interested in him.
- Correspond with a Spanish company in formal English. Do not have letters translated into Spanish. The translation will probably not be sufficiently formal, flowery, and poetic, and might offend.
- Be careful in gift giving. Wait until you have formed a relationship. Products or artwork representative of your home state are appropriate gifts.

# Country Profile: Portugal

## (Cultural Position: Family/Clan)

### Religious Factors

Portugal is primarily Roman Catholic. People from around the world visit the holy site, Fatima. It is claimed that the Virgin Mary appears. A small percentage of Christians reside in Portugal, and some non-Christian religions are also practiced.

### Communication Characteristics

*Transaction Communication Characteristics:* There is a strong power hierarchy, with many differences between the rich and poor classes of society. Ties to the family unit are strong; this is a close-knit society. To please the family and to gain status is a sign of accomplishment. The

Portuguese expect others to value their unique culture and not to make comparisons. There is resistance to handling problems.

Some say the Portuguese are a more subdued version of the Spanish, but they do not like to be thought of in this way.

*Interaction Communication Characteristics:* Members of the upper class will be aloof and formal in their communication style, while the underclass people will be friendly and accepting. Feedback will be decided within the group and if there is blame, the consequences will be severe. In general, the Portuguese will be formal toward the foreigner until a relationship is formed. They learn best by visual aids. Time is not important to the Portuguese, and change will be slow in coming.

---

### ❮ PROTOCOL ALERT ❯

**The Portuguese have traditional ties with England and feel comfortable emulating their behavior.**

---

## PROTOCOL & ETIQUETTE

*Forms of Address:* First names are reserved for friends and family. This sequence of the name is the same as in the United States, first name followed by the last name.

*Handshakes:* Men greet each other with a hello in social situations. The handshake is much like that of Americans, except it is lighter in pressure. Women shake hands when greeting each other in social and more formal situations.

*Greetings:* Touching is a common part of the greeting, because it shows friendship; however, foreigners should not touch the Portuguese.

*Gestures:* Among themselves, the Portuguese use many gestures in conversation, although they are reserved by nature.

*Appropriate Attire:* Clothing should be conservative and not appear worn. Men often wear a hat, vest, and scarf. When one is a widow, it is customary to wear black. Some wear black for the rest of their lives.

*View of Women:* Women take a lesser role in society and are in charge of the family.

*Gift Giving:* Gifts should be in good taste but not extravagant. Fine candy is the preferred gift. It is considered bad luck to give or send thirteen flowers. Roses and chrysanthemums are taboo.

*Dining:* The main meal of the day is lunch. If you are a woman, do not eat alone in a restaurant or you may be approached. The Portuguese eat continental style. Keep your hands in your lap while dining. Finish everything on your plate. Never eat with your hands. Keep your napkin on the table, or you will be offered one continually. *Casas de cha,* tea houses, are popular in Portugal. Do not eat on the street.

## Interesting Information

By the sixteenth century, Portugal had a huge overseas empire. The country has a strong national identity separate from Spain in spite of the proximity and Portugal's smaller size. The Portuguese have traditional ties with England and feel comfortable emulating English behavior. They are certainly a family/clan society, but with modifying influences of England's strong Celtic character.

## Strictly Business

Business procedures are similar to those in Spain in terms of the needs for security and relationship building, but more formal and reserved in style. The best advice is to keep in touch. Contact is very important. Be patient. This is not a society which likes to rush. Do not intrude on their privacy by asking personal questions.

## Country Summary

- Shake hands on meeting and leaving.
- Portuguese tend to be unreliable in meeting deadlines.
- Dinner is always social.
- Finish everything on your plate.
- Never eat with your hands.
- Keep your napkin on the table, or you will be offered one continually.

## Mission Trip Tip

Learn to adapt.
Don't compare.
Slow the pace.
Listen and observe more than you talk.

# 2. Latin America

## (Including: Argentina, Brazil, Chile, Peru, Uruguay, Paraguay, Colombia, Ecuador, Mexico, Venezuela, and Central America)

A family/clan viewpoint is clearly the operating system in South and Central America. These countries have kept the Spanish and Portuguese social system intact for almost 500 years. There is such a remarkable homogeneity of culture spread over a vast area that one might speculate it has remained unchanged due to its isolation from other cultural systems. Mexico, sharing a border with the United States, is perhaps the one society in this region most apt to be affected by proximity to an individualistic culture. This does not, however, mean that Mexico has changed its own cultural style.

Although the similarities among Latin American countries are remarkable, there are also differences. Whereas in Europe the differences are a matter of degree, in Latin America the differences are more a matter of attitude.

We will complete two country profiles in their entirety, Argentina and Mexico. The subtle differences of each of the other countries will be covered by supplemental data that will highlight information necessary for mission workers and travelers to serve fluidly.

## Religious Factors

The legacies of Spain and Portugal's Roman Catholic heritage are found in Latin America. Even today, the church dictates behavior in many of these countries. Because there is a distinct class system among Latin Americans, there is a hierarchy that differentiates the land-owning elite and those who live in poverty. People tend to be satisfied in whatever status they were born because their religion promotes the premise of destiny. Poverty and wealth are destiny and man does not have control to change things to benefit him.

The most important aspect of working with people in this culture is to have an understanding of the family/clan hierarchy. People in positions of power in business are there as a result of their family's power. Family ties determine success. To them, nepotism is logical and moral. It perpetuates their value system. Consequently, the elite class is small and usually made up of direct descendants of European colonists.

In such societies, the highest values and motivating principle are the good of the family or clan. If the economy within the family is stable, they are satisfied. If the government within the family/clan is stable, they are satisfied. If the family/clan is one of the land-owning elite, they are satisfied. Even those who are not part of the elite tend to be satisfied because they accept the premise of destiny. One of the family/clan guiding principles, as stated above, is that man does not have the ability to change things to benefit him. He does not believe in perfectibility and progress.

## Governing Principles

The most important aspect of this culture to a mission worker is the *family/clan hierarchy.* People in positions of power in business are there as a result of their family's power.

Accompanying this perpetuation of family power is the bias against those who have intermarried with the local native culture. To them, the whiter one's skin is, the better the family and and the greater their power. Even in countries such as Bolivia and Paraguay that have a majority population of *mestizos* (European and Indian mix), the business ruling class is still the very small percentage that is of pure European descent.

Those who are the underclass have begun to reject this power balance, if for no other reason than that families are often forced to give up their standard of living when asked to do so by the power elite. This causes hostility when the good of the family is threatened, and this is where the conflicts arise. The solution is often to take what you want. This course of action is programmed into the Hispanic cultures. Their very existence is founded on the model of the conquistadors, the Spanish explorers who simply took what they desired from the local Indians, claimed the land as theirs, and increased the wealth of their family clan back home as a result. To them this was perfectly justifiable. They were acting for the good of their clan. This approach in communication still reigns.

## Protocol & Etiquette Overview

*Forms of Address:* Use titles when addressing a Latin American such as Professor or Doctor. In Spanish, surnames all are:

Mr. = Señor
Mrs. = Señora
Miss = Señorita

Anyone with a college degree may be referred to as *Doctor.* Engineers are *Ingeniero.* Architects are *Arquitecto.* Lawyers are *Abogado.* Teachers are

*Profesor.* Those who do not have professional titles are referred to as Señor or Señora. Hispanic names include the father's and the mother's family names.

*Greetings:* These are some common verbal greetings:

!Buenos dias! (Good morning)
!Buenos tardes! (Good afternoon)
!Buenos noches! (Good evening/night)
¿Como esta? (How are you?)

Announce your full name when greeting: Richard Benjamin Sims.

*Dining:* Latin Americans eat continental style. The hands never leave the table. Wrists, not elbows, should lean against the edge of the table. It is rude to keep even one hand in your lap. There may be certain spices in local food you'll find difficult to eat. Try to taste everything on your plate. It is offensive to leave food on your plate, so finish if you can. Otherwise, make some plausible excuse.

If you are entertaining in a restaurant, do not haggle over the bill, even if you have been invited out. If you want to be certain to win, arrange with the restaurant captain ahead of time for payment. If you are a woman, be sure to do this or you will never be allowed to pay the bill. Explain that your organization or church is the host. Coffee is served at the end of the meal. This is when you begin to discuss business. The Latin Americans may suggest a time to meet again the following day.

# Country Profile: Argentina

## (Cultural Position: Family/Clan)

### Religious Factors

The majority of people are Roman Catholic, but not many Argentines are practicing Catholics, other than having their weddings in the church and baptizing their babies. A small, but growing percentage of Protestants live there, along with a few of Jewish heritage.

### Communication Characteristics

*Transaction Communication Characteristics:* Because of a family/clan mind-set, there is a strong power hierarchy. A person's responsibility is to celebrate his family/clan and protect it at all costs. When an Argentine receives recognition from the outsider or from someone on a higher social status, he feels he has accomplished something in life.

Absolute loyalty is a must within the family/clan. An Argentine expects your complete loyalty and respect. Problems are delegated because blame is assessed. Most decisions are made from an emotional influence. Pride also enters into the picture; Argentines are not always objective.

---

**TRANSACTION ALERT**

Have an interest in opera. Argentina is known for its opera houses, especially the Colón in Buenos Aires.

---

*Interaction Communication Characteristics:* As in all Spanish countries, Argentines will be more formal and aloof with foreigners at first.

After you have built relationships, they will be more welcoming. The Argentine does not like criticism or to be held accountable. Therefore, feedback is subjective and general in nature. When you communicate with the Argentines, use visual aids to support your strong verbal communication skills. Do not present them with abstract ideas. Repetition is helpful, as is coaching. However, do not show any condescension in your voice or manner.

Since Argentines are goal-oriented, time does not translate to money. They enjoy the process and may lose sight of the goal. Do not expect plans and schedules to be detailed. They will be more fluid in their approach. Argentines will resist change in the way things are done. They are not risk takers.

---

### INTERACTION ALERT

An Argentine might make personal observations about you. This just means that the person is comfortable with you.

---

## Protocol & Etiquette

*Forms of Address:* Use the formal title Señor, Señora, or Señorita, followed by the surname. If you are being introduced to an older person, and they ask you to use their first name, do so but precede the name with Don for men and Dona for women. This is a sign of respect.

*Handshakes:* It is customary for men to embrace friends when they meet and for women to kiss cheeks. Handshakes are rather weak. Make sure you shake hands with both men and women.

*Gestures:* Argentines stand close to each other and touch each other and use many hand gestures. Cover your mouth when you yawn. Eye contact is important. Make sure you do not back away when they stand close to you. Do not walk between people when they are in conversation.

Keep your hands out of your pockets. Do not eat walking down a street. Do not put your hands on your hips when you are in conversation.

---

**《 PROTOCOL ALERT 》**

Argentines prefer not to dishonor anyone by refusing a courtesy. They do not like to say no to your face and will seem to be in agreement, only to have a final reply come back negative.

---

*Gift Giving:* Make sure your gift is a high-quality one. Do not bring leather goods. Do not bring knives; this symbolizes severing the friendship. When invited to someone's home, you may bring flowers or chocolates.

*View of Women:* Women are in charge of the family, children, and the finances. Men are in the corporate and working arena. If you are a single woman, you will be flirted with.

*Dining:* The dinner meal is around nine o'clock and may last until midnight.

The Argentines eat continental style. They love to entertain on the weekends. Usually it is a barbecue. They are great cattle producers. Keep your hands above the table and not in your lap. Do not blow your nose at the table, talk with food in your mouth, or clear your throat.

## Important Information

The Latin American finds it hard to defer to another person's culture without feeling as though he has humbled himself and lost power. It is extremely important that you approach a Latin American as a friend; otherwise, he will not have trust in you. You can't get very far without trust. Be patient especially with his view of time. It will be totally different from yours.

## Strictly Business

A well-connected agent has set up a meeting regarding your church or mission. Although you requested a meeting in early February, the agent suggested you wait until March. The seasons are reversed in South America, and many people are on summer vacation in January and February. You would also want to avoid the time around Carnival, occurring a week before Ash Wednesday, which falls in February or early March.

The day before you leave for your trip, call to confirm your meeting. You do this because the person may not have noted the appointment, may have changed the time without notification, or may have agreed to the appointment as a courtesy, never intending to keep it.

Latin Americans never dishonor anyone by refusing a courtesy. They do not like to say no to your face and often will seem to be an agreement, only to have a final reply come back negative. More than likely, the reply will not come at all if it must be negative. Several requests might have been received, and conflicts in schedules arise.

You arrive at a reception and you give your business card to the secretary. The secretary announces you and gives your card to Señor García, the director of the company. You are kept waiting for twenty minutes, and then he greets you. You return his greeting with a formal but friendly handshake, your other hand remaining at your side. You use his professional title, and make good eye contact.

Eye contact is very important. It indicates your sincerity and your self-confidence. A firm grip is fine; but while Latins tend to touch more than North Americans do, they usually keep their distance until the relationship has been formed. Don't force a relationship by your breezy greeting. A low-key, more subdued approach is better, but hands should never be in the pockets. This is considered very rude.

If your host is interested in receiving your proposal, he will escort you to a well-appointed conference room and sit close, but facing you. Positioning himself behind his desk would be defensive. It puts space between the two of you. He is probably not terribly interested in what you have to say. If he is interested in what you are proposing, he is more likely to take you to a conference room, which is more prestigious, unless he has a reception area in his office.

Your protocol challenge will be what to discuss at your meeting. Although the first meeting is to get acquainted, it is all right to introduce your organization, without getting into the specific details of why you are meeting with him. You should point out your position in the organization (the level should match his), the number of employees or volunteers, the area in which you're located, and some specifics about the operation. Try not to sound as if you are bragging; be matter of fact and give general information, so he forms in his mind a picture of your group. You have also turned the conversation to his operation, without asking detailed or pointed questions. You have shared your "families" in a sense.

## Country Summary

- Eighty-five percent of the population is of European descent, including Italian, Spanish, Portuguese, German, English, French, and Russian. Be cognizant of the person's background, even if he speaks Spanish as his first language. There is likely to be a cross-cultural influence.
- Keep your hands still. Many of the gestures we use are offensive or have different meanings.
- Argentines might make personal observations about you. This just means that the person is comfortable with you.
- Opera and sports are good topics of conversation in Argentina.

## Brazil Supplemental Data

- The Brazilians are good at abstract thinking, but can still make decisions based on feelings and personal interests.
- Look for German and Japanese influence in São Paulo, and expect a faster pace.

- The Brazilians' attitude is very light and optimistic. They have good expectations for the future. One does not get this optimism in the other countries of Latin America.
- When thinking, don't absentmindedly rub your fingers under your chin, as some men with beards do. It means you don't know the answer to a question.

## Chile Supplemental Data

- Chile's population is 95 percent European, primarily Spanish, German, and Italian. Use the protocol for not only Latin America but also for Germany and Italy, depending on the people with whom you are working.
- There are more professional women here than in any other Latin American country. This is the best place for a businesswoman to work, although it is still very difficult.
- The northern European influence results in a strong desire for progress and advancement through education. There is a significant middle class.
- Avoid aggressive behavior.
- Don't raise your right fist to head level. This is a communist gesture.
- Gifts are not customary. If someone gives you a gift, open it immediately.

## Peru Supplemental Data

- Peru was the seat of the Incan civilization, overthrown by the Spanish in the sixteenth century. The population is 45 percent Indian, 37 percent mestizo (European and Indian mix), and 15 percent European. The business class is mostly the European minority. There are also a significant number of Japanese and Chinese businesspeople in Peru.

- Unlike other South American countries, men should not cross their legs one knee over the other, but one ankle on the other knee is all right.
- Peruvians use many hand gestures when they speak. Be careful of your own.
- It is best not to discuss ancestry or politics in Peru. There is an extremely strong caste system here, based on ancestry.
- If you are invited to a home, bring the hostess flowers. They must be roses, or you will be seen as cheap. Avoid red, which means love.

## Uruguay Supplemental Data

- Uruguay is the most secular of the Latin American countries. The population is 88 percent European, mostly Spanish and Italian.
- Uruguayans have a reputation for being pessimistic and opinionated.
- There are more professional women than men in Uruguay, yet men still are dominant and women's rights are restricted.
- If you graduated from the University of Chicago, do not announce the fact. While under military rule, their economic advisers trained under Milton Friedman at the University of Chicago. Uruguayans feel that they were an economic experiment that failed.
- It is common to be invited back to someone's home for coffee after dinner in a restaurant. Don't stay very long.

## Paraguay Supplemental Data

- The population is 50 percent Indian, 30 percent mestizo, and 15 percent European.
- *Machismo* is very strong.
- It is permissible to talk business over lunch, but not over dinner.
- Our hand gesture that means so-so—palm down, rocking the hand back and forth—means "no."

### Colombia Supplemental Data

- The population is 58 percent mestizo, 20 percent European, and 22 percent Indian.
- The only professional title that is used is "Doctor."
- Be sure when meeting someone that you drag out the greeting. Don't be in a rush. Chat for a minute.
- Gifts are not opened in front of the giver.
- Women are restricted in some aspects of business.
- Leave small amounts of food on your plate to indicate that you are finished and do not want more.

### Ecuador Supplemental Data

- The population is 65 percent mestizo and 25 percent Indian. There are few pure Europeans, but they are the power elite.
- Business is somewhat less formal here, especially along the coast.
- Ecuador is a more self-centered form of the family/clan mind-set. Citizens show more personal interest.
- There is a strong work ethic, but they are not goal-oriented.
- Do not use head motions to indicate yes or no; use words.

## Country Profile: Mexico

## (Cultural Position: Family/Clan)

### Religious Factors

This is a strong Roman Catholic country with a growing number of evangelical believers.

## Communication Characteristics

*Transaction Communication Characteristics:* The Mexican's responsibility is to support and obey the rules of his family/clan. He expects mutual support and absolute loyalty within the family/clan and from you, the visitor. Admission of the existence of a problem is avoided. There is always someone to whom they delegate the problem. Decisions are made by the people at the top of society and are influenced by personal issues, pride, and emotion rather than by objective merits.

---

### « TRANSACTION ALERT »

You may be kept waiting for an appointment for as long as an hour. When the person finally greets you, note that he is a person of great importance to be kept so busy.

---

*Interaction Communication Characteristics:* Mexicans will be formal and aloof with strangers, but warm and welcoming with those they trust. They avoid criticism and accountability. Feedback is subjective and general in nature. Communication must be visual as well as verbal. Content should be more concrete than abstract. Generalizing data, coaching, and repetition are helpful, but must be done without any condescension. Mexicans are not goal-oriented. Time is not money. They tend to become absorbed in the process while losing sight of the goal. Plans and schedules are not detailed and can become fluid. They are not risk takers.

---

### « INTERACTION ALERT »

Show Mexicans deference by maintaining formality until your hosts choose to relax their style of interaction. Do not treat them casually as you might someone in the United States.

---

## Protocol & Etiquette

*Handshakes:* You should have a firm handshake. It is especially important to maintain good eye contact; looking away implies you have something to hide. Americans may have difficulty maintaining eye contact and standing close during an introduction. It would be a good idea to practice this so you will feel more comfortable. Allow the person to stand close and touch your shoulder, your lapel, or your forearm. Do not back away or you will insult him. Shake hands each time you see someone and when you leave. In a group, shake hands with everyone individually. Women, extend your hand first to the man or he may not shake your hand. When entering a room at a social occasion, bow as you enter and shake hands with everyone.

*Appropriate Attire:* Clothing styles in the cities are much like that of the United States. You will see many colorful costumes at festivals. Men often wear a poncho over the shirt and pants when it is cold weather. In rural areas, people wear a western style of clothing. You should dress in a conservative manner.

*View of Women:* Women are treated as sex objects. A Mexican man may want to fix a visiting man up with a woman, so be prepared to let him know that this is not a part of your lifestyle. When you arrive, show pictures of your family, wife, and children. A single woman needs to wear a fake engagement ring or bring pictures of children. Professional women need to have a senior executive to write to the person with whom they will be meeting to establish their credibility.

*Gift Giving:* When you're invited to a home, it is not necessary to bring a gift. However, a gift of chocolates will be gladly accepted. It is wise to send this ahead. Yellow flowers represent death. Red flowers cast spells and white flowers lift spells. It will be wise not to give any flowers with these colors.

## Interesting Information

The Mexican population is 60 percent mestizo, 30 percent Indian, and 9 percent European.

## STRICTLY BUSINESS

Your Mexican host invites you to lunch. He suggests a very nice restaurant nearby. Your late-morning meeting was brief. You know not to bring up business at lunch unless he does. The conversation turns to *futbol* (soccer). You respond not with, "I never could get interested in that game; now, have you ever watched the Dallas Cowboys play football?" A better response is, "I enjoyed watching the World Cup matches when they played the United States." You may approach other topics of conversation such as the local cultural offerings, the beauty of the country or city, world travel, and the history of his country. Keep it non-controversial. Refrain from using humor. Humor often is cultural based, and the punch line will probably miss its mark.

After coffee is served, your host may suggest a time to meet again the following day.

Either would indicate he has accepted you. With further meetings planned, you might invite him to dinner one evening. Keep in mind that Latin Americans dine late. An invitation from 9:30 p.m. means eating at 11 p.m. Be prepared to linger and stay out easily until 3 a.m. Your project or proposal should not be discussed.

*Etiquette Technique:* The next day, you arrive at his office and greet him, saying

A. "Buenos días, Don Carlos."
B. "Buenos días, Doctor García."

Don't assume that because he has accepted you as a business associate that you are friends. Remain formal and use the greeting, Doctor Garcia, until he suggests otherwise. Even if you are asked to use his first name, if he is your senior, you should address him as Don Carlos. This is a term of respect.

He invites you into his large office and, after a friendly conversation, turns his attention to your proposal. It is a good tactic to have more than one person from your organization at an initial meeting. This gives your Mexican counterpart an option should he want to work with your group, but he doesn't care to do business with you personally.

At the end of the presentation, you ask for feedback. You ask if he agrees with your proposal and will give you a commitment. He says yes. You are being given a brush-off. You have given him no room for consideration; you have not allowed him to consult with others; you have imposed your decision-making time frame on him. When pushed, he will say no by saying yes. Yes means yes only if it is in writing.

Let's consider a different ending: You have finished your presentation. Señor Garcia responds by saying that he will give your proposal to a subordinate to review. This means positive progress. This might sound like a brush-off, but the technical support staff does the real work. Once the head man agrees to do business with you, it is up to the technical people to review and comment on the proposal. The rest of the deal will be worked out between subordinates, with final approval coming from the company head.

## Country Summary

- Power to the Mexican means accomplishment.
- Decisions are based on emotions.
- The Mexican is curious.
- Don't look away when speaking to someone. It implies that you have something to hide.
- Be comfortable with Mexicans standing close to you.

## Venezuela Supplemental Data

- The population is 70 percent mestizo, along with Spanish, Italian, Portuguese, Arab, German, African, and Indian making up the balance.
- A businesswoman going out at night with a businessman will be misconstrued.
- Announce your full name when shaking hands.
- Businesswomen should not give gifts to their male counterparts.

## Central America Supplemental Data

- The smaller nations of Central America have historical ties with the United States, good and bad. The United States has been involved militarily in Nicaragua since their early days as a nation. As a result, there are strong negative sentiments about the United States.
- Costa Rica is unique among Central American countries in its ability to have maintained a fairly stable government and a dynamic capitalism. There is a strong work ethic, although Costa Ricans are not completely goal-oriented. They paradoxically believe in equality, *machismo,* and the class system. The population is 95 percent European, which is unusual for Central America. They are the most punctual of all Latinos. Women tend to be accepted in business.

## Latin America Summary

One the most important things you can remember while in Latin America is the manner in which you converse or make presentations. Everything you say and all your presentations need to be very clear. I cannot stress enough the importance of visual aids and repetition. If your presentation is somewhat complicated, it would be wise to have a person from the country help you with translation. Latin Americans will not admit that they don't understand something. They don't want to appear unintelligent. Even if you encourage questions, you may not get honest feedback. Try to anticipate problem areas.

Anywhere you go in Latin America, soccer is a good topic of conversation (if you avoid violent subplots). Be prepared for this subject. Do a little research.

Another important aspect about Latin Americans is that they would never discredit another person, even in a social context. They won't even criticize you if you ask for their honest opinion. They will find a way around the criticism.

South America gives us the perfect opportunity to point out the merits of the approach presented in this book. Several South American countries have substantial populations of non-Spanish Europeans. There are also large numbers of Japanese in São Paulo, Brazil, and in Peru. The general case that will be used for your travel and mission work in this section must be modified when you know you are dealing with an Italian, German, English, or Japanese person. One set of rules per country does not always work for everyone you will encounter. You must understand the native culture of your counterpart, as well as the culture in which he resides. This book gives you the information necessary to apply protocol strategically in any situation.

### Mission Trip Tip

Expect some cultural shock. Recognize it and turn it into a positive by seeking to gather as much information about people as you can. This can be done by observation, and asking questions at the appropriate time and in a manner that is non-threatening.

# 3. Arab Region

## (including Saudi Arabia, Egypt, Morocco, Tunisia, The Gulf States [Kuwait, Oman, Qatar, United Arab Emirates], Iraq/Jordan, Syria, Lebanon, Turkey, and Pakistan)

Since the culture-based behavior in the Arab world is largely dictated by Islamic beliefs, there is a great deal of similarity in customs among the countries and between Arab and non-Arab Islamic cultures. Therefore, I will profile one Islamic country. This information will be applicable to those countries in the region that are dominated by Islam. Differences in customs will be reported in the supplemental notes.

The terminology used about the Arab region will be different from that encountered in other regions of the world.

- Arab refers to a culture, not a race or religion. There are Christian Arabs, for example.
- In Arab culture, words speak as loudly as, if not louder than, actions. It is the intent that is important.

- Hospitality is a duty and a privilege to an Arab.

---

## « RELIGIOUS TERM ALERT »

Islam is the name of the religion. A Muslim, or Moslem, is a follower of Islam.

---

### Religious Factors

The best way to understand the Arab mind-set is to understand some basics about Islam. *Islam* means "submission to the will of God." *Muslim* means "one who submits." The Koran is the bible of Islam, containing God's laws as revealed through his prophet Muhammad, in the seventh century AD. Like Jews and Christians, their reality is perceived as a separation from God. In Islam, God is in complete control of all events. The individual does not participate in the external workings of the world. Actions are not important. Faith is all that matters.

Arabs are inherently religious. They do not comprehend atheism. Faith is their strongest value. They believe that God *(Allah)* controls everything, and that prayer must be directed only to God, not to an intermediary. This belief is reflected in secular life as well. Society provides many laws. Although obedience is required, nothing is absolute. One can always appeal to a higher power. A well-connected person can make a personal plea to a high official and be able to circumvent cumbersome commercial laws.

The Islamic religion is based on God's laws. This understanding is reflected in an extremely strong social power hierarchy. Since God controls everything, there is a strong sense of fatalism. You are born into a certain class, and you accept your family's position in society. People do not expect to move up or down on the social ladder.

The prophet Muhammad's birthplace was Mecca. *Ramadan* is a month long holy religious observance. During this time, people are expected to give 10 percent of their income to the poor and to fast the entire month between sunrise and sunset.

## Governing Principles

Arab culture is strongly *family/clan society* in nature. The individual finds his identity in the hierarchy of family structure. Perhaps a good way to think of this society is as a mirror. Everyone reflects one another by giving feedback, which must be positive to ensure the good of the individual and therefore the good of the family/clan. They know themselves by looking at others.

One person's behavior toward another is also a reflection of that other person's image. When your behavior is disrespectful, you are telling the other person that he is not worthy of respect.

As a strongly hierarchical culture, society is stratified into a rigid class structure. The ruling families and wealthiest families are at the top. Merchants and landowners form the middle class. The peasants and the poor form the lowest class. Those of the upper class never do manual labor, not even so much as getting another person a glass of water. They are very careful to show their wealth and dress their best whenever they go out in public. Foreign residents are given upper class status. You are expected to behave as such.

---

Never use your left hand for anything—not in passing documents, gesturing, or dining. The left hand is considered unclean.

---

*A Story that Reflects Their Cultural Position:* One American found out how important behavior is in this society in a most surprising exchange. He had been negotiating a speaking engagement and the sale of his book to an Arab enterprise. The two parties had come to terms and were ready to sign a contract. The American left the day before his meeting, dressed for comfort in jeans and tennis shoes. He had packed his formal business clothing in his suitcase. As does happen, his luggage was lost. The man had arrived on a holy day when the shops were closed, so he couldn't buy business clothes. The American knew this was a difficult situation, but since he had established a relationship with the Arab, he felt that if he went to the meeting and explained what had happened, the Arab would overlook it. After the American explained and offered his regrets for his poor dress, the Arab asked for the contract. The American handed it to him. Glancing at it, the Arab tore it in half and said that he never wanted to see him or do business with him again.

What were the American's mistakes?

1. He should have carried the appropriate attire on the plane.
2. He should have never made an appointment on a holy day.

Remember in Arab society the mirror shows an image. It is important to understand that image is everything. How you appear to others is what you are. You are known by your reputation. The motive behind all action in Arab society could be summed up in the question, "What will the neighbors say?" There is great pressure from the family/clan on each member to conform because each individual's reputation affects the reputation of the entire family. If the family/clan unit is discredited, its place in society is severely diminished.

---

### « ARAB PROVERB »

"A sin concealed is two-thirds forgiven."

---

Reputation is so critical that the failure of an individual must not be acknowledged. Arabs choose their own reality. When something they have done is too painful to accept, they simply act as if it didn't happen. They remove it from their consciousness. But when confronted by evidence and accused directly in front of a witness, there is nowhere to hide. Failure has extreme negative repercussions on the family. In ancient times, a person's failure could cause the demise of the entire family/clan.

# Country Profile: Saudi Arabia

## (Cultural Position: Family/Clan [Tribe])

### Religious Factors

Saudi Arabia is the strictest of all Islamic countries. Their lifestyle, as in the entire Arab region, reflects a deeply religious belief. What the neighbors think is important, but it is also important for you to know that to the family/clan Arab there are two kinds of people—neighbors and strangers. Neighbors, or members of other tribes with whom they might come into contact, can reflect and judge their behavior. Strangers are of no consequence. Therefore, while an Arab prides himself on his friendliness, good manners, loyalty, and hospitality, he only behaves this way with his own tribe and neighbors. There is often much pushing and shoving in lines at the airport, and drivers take no note of other cars on the road. If you want to change someone's rude behavior, simply say something to him, such as, "Please don't push me if you can help it." Speaking to him makes you a reality in his social consciousness and he must watch his behavior around you. In general, outside a certain sphere of influence, decorum goes out the window. Arabs visiting America might totally cut loose and behave in ways that would be scandalous at home. But the Americans are outside his sphere of influence and his behavior will not affect his social standing.

## Communication Characteristics

*Transaction Communication Characteristics:* There is a strong vertical hierarchy. The family/clan must come first and make the decisions from the top layer of that professional/social hierarchy. The Arab's obedience to the will of God and to uphold the honor of his family is his primary responsibility in life. His sense of accomplishment comes from his family/clan and the honor they give him. If the feedback from them is positive, it is all he needs to feel he has contributed to society. Of course, social interaction is necessary to maintain this kind of respect. The Arab expects mutual support and courtesy at all times.

The Arab approach to problem solving is first denial and amelioration. If blame must be accepted, the consequences will be harsh. People rarely cause problems. To their way of thinking, it is the will of God. The people at the top of hierarchy make all the decisions, both in secular and professional arenas.

*Interaction Communication Characteristics:* The Arab is warm and personal with those he knows. With strangers, he is offensive and closed. Feedback is always positive, spontaneous, and frequent. Negative feedback is often handled through intermediaries and is always indirect, never fixing blame on a person. Often the Arab has complete disregard for the foreigner and is defensive when approached. People outside the family/clan are not on his list of priorities. The Arab learns through the senses. Use of imagery, analogy, and graphics are extremely helpful. Repetition is important and shows sincerity. Time, for the Arab, is flexible and nonlinear. Schedules are not closely followed. Plans are not detailed and may be altered spontaneously.

## Protocol & Etiquette

*Forms of Address:* Arabic names can be confusing. It is wise to ask your contact person for the correct pronunciation of a name. You address someone with the first name first, followed by the last name. Usually there is a middle name. Be sure to include that when you address someone. Always use a title, for example, Dr. Aziz Muammar Amhad. In Arab names you sometimes will see *bin* in a name. It means "son of."

*Greetings:* When you greet an Arab, after the handshake, say, "Peace be upon you *(As-Salaamu 'Alaykum)*."

A man should always wait for a woman to extend her hand first. She may not offer to shake hands. It is correct to address her directly, but after your greeting, do not direct comments to her. Men always stand when a woman enters a room.

*Handshakes:* A handshake is appropriate. Arabs will shake hands with a fellow Arab. If they have a close relationship or if they are greeting a person with a high rank, the person greeting will place his left hand to the other person's right shoulder. The receiver will do the same. This is usually followed by a kiss to each other's right cheek, then the left cheek. A male will not acknowledge a female who is wearing a veil.

*Personal Space:* Arabs feel most comfortable in groups and in close proximity to others. It gives them a sense of security. Their choice of physical space illustrates this preference. They seem to be attracted to other humans as if they were magnets. When an American enters an elevator that has one person in it, the American will stand at the opposite side of the elevator to give the other person maximum personal space. If an Arab were to enter, he would probably stand right next to or directly in front of the other person. This behavior often confuses and annoys Westerners. Arabs don't like to be alone. The best translation of the English word "privacy" is their word for loneliness. As a result, most homes have communal rooms with few partitions. Offices are open plan. Even the separate offices of high officials do not provide privacy, since they hold conferences with many individuals at one time.

Arabs stand close to each other; in fact, some say so close that you can smell the breath. Do not move back.

*Appropriate Attire:* As a visitor, you must dress conservatively. Women should not wear anything tight or revealing. It is a show of respect to others if you wear a scarf on your head. The headdress for a male is called a *ghutra.* This is usually red check or pure white. It is wrapped with a black braid. The ankle-length skirt, which is worn over pants, is called a *throbe.* The upper body is covered with a cloak, called a *mishla.* The full-length cloak an Arab woman wears is called an *abaaya.* Underneath it, she will wear beautifully tailored dresses. Whether women wear veils to cover their face depends on the region. In certain situations, you'll find that many Arabs wear Western-style clothes.

*View of Women:* It may come as a surprise to you but Arab women exercise a lot of power in the home. They make decisions where their children will be educated and how the finances will be handled. In public life, this is a male-dominated society and women do not take a leading role. As a woman visitor you must be very cautious about being too opinionated, too forward, or too aggressive.

In some Arab countries, a modest liberation of women has begun. Saudi Arabia is the strictest of all Islamic countries and maintains tight restrictions on women, but Iraq, Tunisia, Lebanon, and a few others are experiencing increased literacy rates and are allowing women to work and vote. More women are entering the labor force each year. The women are not especially prepared for liberation, and most are comfortable with their traditional roles, but progress in a Western sense is being made. However, because a woman's misbehavior is seen as doing more damage to the family honor than a man's misbehavior, women are severely restricted in their activities to protect the family's reputation.

In the Arab view, Western women just don't fit into Muslim society. There is no place for them. The Islamic laws forbid them to act in many ways that are necessary for them to conduct business. Most Arab countries acknowledge this and don't require foreign women to obey all Islamic law. If a woman must be alone in the presence of men, she is given the status of *honorary man.*

*Gift Giving:* Gifts are not expected, but it is considerate to bring something such as candy or houseplant. Flowers may be considered too personal and meant for the wife. A coffee-table book of your home state is a nice idea. Gifts for the children are also appreciated. Present gifts with your right hand. Do not expect your host to open gifts in your presence.

---

**Do not compliment an Arab on anything in his home or a piece of jewelry a woman may be wearing. If you do, he will feel obligated to give the item to you—and will expect you to give a gift of the same value. He may even be so bold as to ask that you do so.**

---

*Dining:* Hospitality is a duty and a privilege to an Arab. He must spare nothing for the comfort of his guest. His generosity shows his willingness to provide for his friend, and his ability to provide for his family. His self-worth is enhanced by the guest's acceptance of his largesse. It is the duty of a guest to praise his host.

An invitation to dine will probably be verbal and spontaneous. Never decline hospitality. Expect dinner to be late, between ten and eleven in the evening, and plan to arrive about two hours before the meal. Conversation takes place before the meal.

Generosity to guests is essential for a good reputation. You will be offered many courses. The amount of food may seem overwhelming. It is a compliment to the hostess to take second helpings. This must begin with a ritual refusal by the guest, three times, ending in acceptance. In most places, if you clean your plate, it is an indication that you want more. Leave just a little food on your plate to indicate that you are done. Be sure to eat only with your right hand. Pass food only with your right hand.

After dinner, tea and coffee are served. Conversation continues during coffee until it is time to leave. A tray of ice water is brought around when it is time to leave. On the Arabian Peninsula, incense and perfume may be offered instead of ice water. When you are ready to go, the host will ask you to stay. This is a ritual and may be declined, unless your host protests profusely. Be sure to offer extensive praise and thanks. Reciprocate the hospitality when you can.

## Interesting Information

In the United States, one is proud to admit that he is a self-made man, that his parents were poor immigrants and today he is a multimillionaire. Arabs would give this person low status because his parents were of humble origins. They would not feel comfortable doing business with him. After several generations, perceptions change, and some movement in social class can be made. As an American, it is best not to talk about your family if they were of humble origins. Likewise, it would not help you to discuss your child's drug problem or that your wife divorced you. You are a composite of family behavior. Only show them what you want them to use as evidence of your worthiness. Their own social status is the sole determinant of their success.

## Strictly Business

All business is conducted with friends. You must first be accepted as a friend before an Arab will do business with you. Only friends can be trusted. But more than that, friendship comes with a contract for mutual support and assistance. Once you are accepted as a friend, it is expected that you will give help and do favors to the best of your ability. Your Arab friend will do the same. Etiquette maintains that you must never refuse. But there is a loophole.

In Arab culture, words speak as loudly as—if not louder than—actions. It is the intent and a positive response that is important, not the result. After all, people can't control an outcome, only their intentions for a good outcome. If you don't perform, it won't be mentioned. Your Arab friend would not want to embarrass you by bringing up your failure.

Words have a great deal of power to an Arab, and are often sufficient to preclude action. Arabs may make threats, venting their emotions. But they don't have the need to follow up a threat with action. Saying the words has solved the problem. No action is required.

At the most, you are of little consequence. Arabs are used to seeing their friends frequently. Three days is a very long time between visits. The initiation of business must certainly be done at his office. You must change your status from stranger to neighbor, and then from neighbor to friend. You will not succeed otherwise. Generally, the top managers will speak English and many have been educated in the West. Translation is probably not necessary.

People are of the greatest importance to Arabs. They are the resource that makes up their family/clan structure. Their list of priorities begins with family first, friends second, neighbors third, and work is somewhere further down the list. You may be in a meeting with an Arab executive and be constantly interrupted by his family and friends making requests of him. He will not delay responding to them simply because you traveled from the United States to meet with him. Loyalty to his family will always take precedence.

The Arab concept of time is not linear. People in this culture are not goal-oriented and tend to do many things at the same time. Time is a gift from God, and they savor it. It is interesting to note that the Koran is not arranged chronologically. Cause and effect is difficult to perceive.

Time may also be used as language. Withholding it can mean lack of interest. Delaying can be a power play and tell you that the one who delays time is your superior. It can also be a test of character. Patience and persistence are highly valued. Many Western businessmen have been kept waiting for appointments, not only for hours, but for days or weeks. You may have an appointment, arrive on time, be escorted into a room where others are doing business with the man you have come to meet, and he may never get around to talking with you. You may be asked to come back the next day. This may have nothing to do with his interest in you. There is always tomorrow. Be aware that Thursday and Friday are the Muslim days of rest. There are also many holiday periods that should be avoided. During the extremely hot summer months, most businesspeople are on the Riviera.

The Arab use of language is not highly precise. There is much sensate imagery that is used. The language is very poetic and very spiritual. Rational thought often gives way to emotion. Scientific evidence is not as important as faith. Decisions are made according to human needs and are not necessarily based on the objective merits of the proposal.

One pitfall for Americans is to assume that because an Arab dresses in Western fashion, speaks fluent English, and has been educated in the West, he is like us. He will still think and behave like an Arab. There are certainly Western influences affecting Arab civilization, and some social change has occurred. Remember that Islamic fundamentalist groups have been on the rise in recent years to stem the flow of Western influence on Arab culture. They perceive Western ways to be a threat to their way of life.

Humility shown by a man of stature is well regarded by the Arabs. It shows that you are powerful, yet sensitive to the needs of your family and your friends. It demonstrates that you are a servant of God. There will be many humbling experiences for a Westerner in the Arab culture. What we regard as disrespectful behavior must be tolerated as their way of doing business. The first instance of this is time. There is no concept of wasting a person's time. A person does not own time such that it can be wasted. Appointments cannot even be confirmed until the person is in town.

Our concept of respect includes paying attention to the individual. It is humbling to be ignored, which is exactly what will happen during your group audiences with Arabs. Even though you are admitted into an office, there are many meetings going on at once. Your Arab counterpart may speak with you for a few minutes, then move on to someone else, returning to you at a later time. Whichever topic is of greatest priority to him is where he will focus his attention. Humble yourself to accept this form of interaction. Do not demand to be treated as you would treat others in a society whose virtue is in individuality.

Decisions can take months in coming, with no progress reports. Your needs will not be taken into account. You are completely irrelevant to the decision-making process unless you have become a close friend, with all the duties and obligations the relationship entails. Never try to push for a decision, and never criticize anyone for the way he conducts business.

It is absolutely critical to spend time elevating the Arab's ego. You do this by your behavior as much as with your words. Both are important. Praise and appreciation must be verbalized often. Your own good manners and respectful behavior reflect the quality of the person with whom you are dealing. Your conservative dress indicates your respect for the other person. The better you dress, the greater is your perceived status. This reflects well on the Arab, as it shows to others that he is worthy of attention from a person of high position.

Make your purpose his welfare. Even if you don't, he will. There is no reason to work with you if it doesn't solve a problem for him or make him look better. Find a way to show him how he will benefit, now and in the future. Be careful not to give him expensive gifts as a tactic. It is appropriate to give a gift on first meeting, but keep it small, as a gesture of your desire for friendship.

You have a meeting scheduled for 10 A.M. You are there precisely on time and asked to wait. What follows is a typical Arab business encounter. However, you may be doing business with someone who has adopted the Western style of doing business. It is best to be prepared for the traditional approach. Be careful when encountering what seems to be a Western approach to remember that all aspects of the meeting will be done as in the United States.

## Protocol Challenge

After thirty minutes, you are ushered into an office. As you enter you notice four or five other people having conversations among themselves and with the director. What do you do? You announce yourself, sit down, accept any refreshment that is offered, and wait to be asked about your business.

Remember that at this point you are still a stranger with no standing in the Arab's mind. There are others before you, meetings that might have been spontaneous but granted because a personal request was made. Do not rush your host to receive you, and don't expect privacy during the first meeting. The Arab feels safer in a group. While you are waiting, you may introduce yourself to others in the room and speak quietly. You are being observed, so refrain from appearing agitated. Cultivate patience. Expect to be ignored and it won't come as such a shock.

The director finally comes to you. He says, "I am Rashad Abdullah Asad."

What do you do?

You shake hands with a limp grip and, without pumping, hold the grip throughout the introduction, say good morning, and refer to him by title and first name.

When you shake hands with Arabs, the grip must be non-confrontational. They touch much more than Americans, so be prepared to clasp hands for several minutes while you might be asked about your health and the well-being of your family. You may do the same, but never ask an Arab about his wife. If you do not know someone's professional title, use *Sayed,* which means Mr., along with his first name. The other two names are his father's and grandfather's names. Some countries have required people to use surnames, and Westernized Arabs will use their family name until better acquainted.

When you are sitting or standing, be careful of your posture. Poor posture is disrespectful. Never slouch, drape yourself over a chair, sit on a desk, cross your arms or stand with hands in your pockets. And above all, never ever show the soles of your shoes to anyone. This is a severe insult. Be careful when crossing your legs never to cross an ankle over a knee, exposing the bottom of your foot.

You now have the ear of the man you came to see. What do you expect to accomplish? You may hope to establish a friendship or hope to get a second meeting. It is true that no substantive business will take place until some level of friendship has been established, but that doesn't happen at this first meeting. Your purpose at this point is to give your host enough information to interest him in your proposal. If he is interested, he will grant you a second meeting alone when you can present your proposal in detail.

After a few minutes your host moves on to another supplicant. He has not told you to come back for another meeting. What should you do? Sit down, have more coffee and wait for him to return to you.

Just because he leaves you with no resolution does not mean he is not interested. He puts your words into his mental processor while he greets another businessman. Time and processes are not linear in the Arab world. If he comes to have a good feeling about your proposal, he will return, ask you to come back the next day at a certain time, and will shake your hand. Expect this next meeting to be more formal. You are now free to leave. Shake hands with others you have met as you leave.

At your second meeting shake hands with your host and greet him as you did the previous day. He directs you to a chair, usually to the right of his desk, the seat of honor. You take a seat, and after a few minutes chatting about your health, a servant comes in and serves coffee. At that time, you do not drink your coffee and put your cup down, then begin your presentation. Rather, you drink your coffee and talk about your family, when he asks.

The first choice rushes things too much. You are not taking advantage of your host's hospitality. It is not polite to have less than two cups of coffee or more than three. Business is not discussed until after the refreshments. During this time your host will want to get to know you. We assume that he wants to talk about our education, our profession, and our personal interests. This is not so. He wants to hear about your family. Tell him your roots, unless they are not flattering. He does not want to hear that you endured a difficult childhood and rose to the top. This will not gain his respect. After family has been discussed, subjects of common interest may help form a bond, such as sports. Find out about his local and national sports. Be sure to maintain eye contact while you are conversing.

Always accept an object and hand an object with your right hand. The left hand is used for hygiene. Never eat with your left hand, even if you are left-handed. Coffee is not over until you give the proper signal to the servant. He will continue to refill your cup if you put it down or hand it back to him without first shaking it from side to side. In some places, the signal is to twist the cup quickly a few times in your hand. Beware that the bottom of the cup is full of thick grounds. Sip the coffee slowly, leaving an inch in the bottom of the cup. Note that during the month of Ramadan (approximately September), coffee will not be served. Arabs are required to fast between sunrise and sunset and even displaying a coffee cup in their presence is very rude.

You may now move forward and discuss business, but don't enter the subject too abruptly. The Arab considers good manners to be the best gauge of a person's character. Being sincere is very important. Don't rush the pleasantries.

The best way to present your proposal is a general approach at first, highlighting the human aspects of the proposal. You will use much visual support data, including renderings, graphs, blueprints, and material samples.

The second approach will be the most persuasive. If the benefits are clear, then you will enter further negotiations. Don't expect any sort of decision the first few meetings. You must show a commitment. It is wise not to tell the Arab when you are scheduled to fly home. He may leave things to the last minute, and get concessions from you in your hurry.

Your style of presentation is also important. Speaking with emotion shows your sincere concern for the outcome of your presentation. Repeat yourself often, especially on important points. Otherwise, an Arab will not believe you are telling the truth.

Remember your Arab counterpart's response could be anything from high praise to "changes needed," but he will never say directly that he is not interested or that he doesn't like your proposal. Negative feedback is not polite. On the other hand, a noncommittal reaction might just mean that he needs to get approval from higher up or he doesn't understand something that he wants to talk over with his staff.

You know you have a deal when you sign the contract. Be careful not to offend them by including in the contract every conceivable misunderstanding that might arise, as lawyers in America tend to do. They will think you don't trust them, and may back out of the deal.

## Country Summary

- Saudi Arabia is the strictest of all Islamic countries. Western men will not meet Saudi women.
- Whenever someone enters the room, always rise and shake hands.
- Arabs usually wait to be asked more than once before accepting second helpings of food.
- Whenever something is offered, refuse first, then accept.
- Never send a woman to do business, even as a member of a team. There are strict legal restrictions on women's activities.
- Print business cards in both Arabic and English.
- Present a modest gift after meeting someone two or three times.

## Egypt Supplemental Data

- Do not use first names immediately. Wait for your host to offer.
- Don't take any criticism of the U.S. government personally. Egyptians like Americans, but often criticize the government's policies.
- Do not discuss bad news on a social occasion.
- The U.S. gesture for waving good-bye means "come here."
- Women should avoid direct eye contact with men and avoid crowds, where men may try to touch them.
- Finishing everything on your plate is considered rude. Leaving food indicates the abundance of the host.
- Political contacts do not have the same influence in Egypt as they do in other Arab countries.
- In the cities, women will not have difficulty doing business. Entertain at hotel restaurants that are European style.

## Morocco Supplemental Data

- Women should never make eye contact with men who are strangers. They will interpret it as an invitation.

- Moroccan bureaucracy was patterned after the French. They conduct business formally, as do the French.
- Don't bother to use the telephones. It takes too much time.
- Print business cards in both Arabic and English.
- French is spoken by much of the business class. Use an interpreter.
- Business is never done without serving tea first.
- You will probably be invited to a home dinner. Men and women eat separately. The women get the leftovers.

## Tunisia Supplemental Data

- Tunisia is the most Western of Arab nations because of its long dominance by France.
- When greeting someone in a professional setting for the first time, use the French title Monsieur.
- At a home meal, it is important to wash your hands in front of everyone. The servant will bring a bowl and pitcher.
- Hire a French interpreter.
- Give your business card to the senior man first, and then others.

## Gulf States (Kuwait, Bahrain, Oman, Qatar, United Arab Emirates) Supplemental Data

- When you see someone bowing and kissing someone's hand, do not feel that you must do likewise.
- After any meal, leave when you have finished coffee.
- Suggest that instead of meeting at the man's office that you meet at your hotel lobby. There won't be so many interruptions. Remember that you are now the host and must be generous in your hospitality.
- When meeting with a group from the Arab company, the Arab who sits, listens, and says nothing is usually the decision-maker.
- Your meeting is over when coffee is served again.
- Kuwaitis are very punctual. Don't be even ten minutes late.

- Don't send a woman to do business.
- Never whistle in public.

## Iraq Supplemental Data

- Use first names as soon as you are introduced.
- When offered food or drink, refuse the first time, then accept.
- Iraq is much less formal than other Arab countries.
- Iraqis don't like the excessive praise and flowery language of other Arab nations.
- The best business gift is a book.

## Jordan Supplemental Data

- English is Jordan's second language.
- Address people you don't know well by the English titles Mr., Mrs., and Miss.
- Jordan is much less conservative than other Arab nations. Women may dine out with men.
- Private businessmen are much more straightforward than other Arabs.
- If a woman must do business in Jordan, she is given honorary male status.

## Syria Supplemental Data

- Syria is officially a secular state.
- Educated Syrians are cosmopolitan but conservative.

## Lebanon Supplemental Data

- The Lebanese have had long contact with the West and know their customs. However, they are Arabs and share the perceptions of most Arabs.

- French and English are widely spoken by the educated.

## Turkey Supplemental Data

- Turkey is the bridge between Europe and Asia. It is the home of the former Ottoman Empire, which came to an end after the First World War. It is a democratic, secular state. Ninety percent of the population is Muslim and 85 percent are ethnic Turks.
- Turkey is a tribal nation and, because of Islamic law, shares many customs with Arab nations.
- One difference is that they do not shake hands again when leave-taking.
- The form of address upon introduction is the surname preceded by *Bay* for men and *Bayam* for women.
- Most entertaining is done in restaurants.

## Pakistan Supplemental Data

- Pakistan was established as a separate Muslim state during the British partitioning of India in 1947. The government is a democracy. Urdu and English are the official languages. Note that the Urdu words for yesterday and tomorrow are the same.
- Forms of address are very complicated, since there are many variations on Pakistani names. Ask how they should be addressed.
- The country conforms to Islamic law, so the tribal elements and customs largely remain the same.
- Men should never wear a suit and tie from November through March. A jacket is worn only when seeing government officials.
- Never gesture with a closed fist.
- Women are generally not well-received in business.

## Arab Region Summary

- The term Arab refers to a culture, not a race.
- The Arab region is predominantly Islamic.
- Arabs strongly believe God is in complete control of the person. They are inherent religious.
- Islam means "submission to the will of God."
- The Arab is constantly using others' perceptions of him to reinforce his identity.
- There is a rigid class system among the Arabs.
- What the neighbors think is very important.
- It isn't received well when an outsider states he or she is a self-made person.
- Arabs do many things at once.
- The Arab language is not highly precise.
- It is very important to establish personal contact. Arabs acknowledge others by interacting with them. Bringing them into his consciousness requires interacting with them physically and intellectually. Arabs need to see you, hear you, touch you, smell you, and share food with you. This is the evidence that you are a factor in his life. But he doesn't claim to know you until he knows your family. No one exists apart from his family. You are the product of your father, your grandfather, your mother, and all your other relatives. Your spouse and your children reflect upon you.

## Mission Trip Tip

Learn to listen more. Don't speak without giving thought to what you want to say.

# 4. Asia/Pacific

## (including the People's Republic of China, South Korea, Japan, Taiwan, Thailand, Malaysia, Singapore, Indonesia, the Philippines, and Vietnam)

The Asia/Pacific region is dominated by Chinese culture. The ancient Chinese populated every country in the Far East, including, to some extent, Southeast Asia. The key to understanding the motivations for behavior in these countries is understanding Chinese culture. Thus we begin with an overview of China and that will be the framework for the region. Where the differences among the people in the region are the greatest, they will be discussed in length. Those of more similar cultural leanings will have useful supplemental data.

### Regional Religious Factors

Confucianism is prevalent. Confucianism is not so much a religion as a social doctrine, supporting the belief that there was no self, but there was structure and dualism in the world. Confucian dualism recognizes there is one older, one younger, one stronger, one weaker, one servant, one master. In some of the regions, worship can include elements of Buddhism and Taoism. Ancestor veneration can also seep into worship.

The nations that exhibit the greatest deviation from these common beliefs are Indonesia, Malaysia, the Philippines, and Japan. Indonesia and Malaysia are Muslim countries while the Philippine Islands are Catholic. Christianity and Islam are growing in the region. China is officially atheistic; it's estimated that 3 to 4 percent of the population is Christian and another 1 to 2 percent is Taoist, Buddhist, or Muslim.

## Governing Principles

All original cultures of the Asia/Pacific region, including China, are *group-minded* societies. The guiding principles for this culture are harmony and continuity. These principles are observed in the laws of nature, as the Divine is revealed in the laws of nature. Dualism suggests position and status; consequently, society is organized into a highly structured, stratified organization of the whole. Duality suggests inequality. While people are not equal, all contribute to the good of the whole. What resulted was a strongly authoritarian social structure with mutual cooperation among classes for the good of the group.

For the human being, this means that no one person is significant. The group is the smallest unit that can survive. A person cannot survive in society on his own. He has no definition outside the group. People in this society must conform for the good of the whole. It is as though the individual is a cell within a body. All the cells work together to maintain a healthy body. One bad cell can start a disease. Therefore, all cells must work in harmony. For example, if one fails to follow proper social etiquette (*kata*) in daily behavior, he will be ostracized. There will be no place for that person to go, no place to fit in. He will become an outcast.

*Group identity* is different from a family/clan identity. In family/clan societies, there is the sense of self as a member of the family. It is almost a sense of multi-self, as the entire family enters into one's identity. In group societies, there is a very weak concept of self. One's identity is relative to someone who is older or younger or more or less educated.

This is such a true representation of the perception of the individual that some languages have many variations on the pronoun "I." The people of China refer to themselves in one way if they are talking to an older person, another way if they are addressing a younger person. There are other pronouns for when they meet someone more learned, more powerful, less learned, and less powerful. The list goes on.

Often, when meeting someone for the first time, Asians will ask questions about each other prior to a formal greeting. This is to determine the right pecking order, the proper use of pronouns, and how low one should bow in greeting. Until they know how they compare to someone, their identity and societal value are not pinned down.

The desire for conformity and harmony might suggest that this is a culture that professes equality of all people. That is not the case. All people are important to the group, but some are functionally more important than others. Just as the cells of the brain might be viewed as more important than the cells of the skin, there is a hierarchy of importance in the group society. Whereas the tribal cultures have a power hierarchy, group societies are organized as functional hierarchies. Everyone has his position in society and his job to carry out. Those at the top serve those below, just as those below support the work of the top. There is, of course, recognition that those higher up are more important to the body, and worthy of higher esteem. Those in power do not have free rein to lead the group into ill-advised plans. The position of authority comes with the burden of contribution to the group's well-being.

Each person is born into a certain position in life, but that position is not static. His view of position is similar to his view of time. It is all a continuum, and as future flows into present, which flows into past, so the younger become older and as they do, their stature increases. Identity and position are always relative.

Members of these societies carry with them the concept of improvability, i.e., social standing mobility. While they may not have control over the processes of life, they know that life is always changing and that one's position can improve. There is a reason to strive for a better place. Still, as it is difficult for a skin cell to become a brain cell, it is difficult for a servant to become a leader.

Following the precepts of its underlying belief in the natural order, Confucianism promotes harmony in all aspects of life. To be in harmony with each other is to treat each person with dignity and humility. Conflict avoidance is a must. No one should give negative feedback. Criticism promotes conflict and discord.

It is also necessary to emulate the structure of the natural order by showing respect to those who are superior. The structure of society is maintained by rules of protocol regarding the interaction between superior and subordinate; the same is true between men and women. Women have predetermined functions in society, and governing is not one of them. Men and women are a duality; therefore, they must be separated.

Time is a continuum to the Chinese way of thinking. Past and present are related. The flow of time is unbroken but cyclical in nature, as are the seasons. There is a great reverence for ancestors and for the elderly. They are part of the larger definition of time. To group societies, time is not money; time is harmony.

One of the most significant differences in the beliefs of Confucian societies and those of the more fatalistic family/clan cultures is the concept of improvability. As we saw with the northern European individualistic cultures, the belief in perfectibility, or improvability, is the only impetus one has for hard work. Why should a person work long hours with great effort and take pride in his work if there is no hope of gaining anything by the effort? One can be forced to work, but then the motivation is fear. This motivation is ultimately self-defeating.

Confucianism promoted hard work, but perceived achievement as being valid only in the context of the group. Confucian cultures held education in high esteem as being the best means to foster achievement. However, education in general was viewed as little more than facts.

Everyone learned the same way. There was a rigid requirement of conformity in education as well as in other areas of one's life. Even though a group society values education, it does not promote imaginative thinking. Group cultures contribute best in group efforts, such as large-scale production.

As in family/clan culture, concepts of ethics are relative. Within one's group, traditions of respect, honor, and dignity are upheld. Outside the group, there is little regard for others. If dictates are sent down from power structures that are far removed from the group, they will be disregarded.

# Country Profile: China

## (Cultural Position: Group)

### Religious Factors

China's underlying philosophy is non-theist, they do not believe in a separate, personified god. Reality is therefore seen as a continuum. All things are interrelated. All things are part of a continuous whole. No one thing in nature is of significance. It is the wholeness of nature that is important. This view of reality is portrayed in the language. Individual words or characters do not transmit exact meaning. Characters must be combined in such a way as to paint a picture representative of the intended meaning. Chinese culture has perpetuated these beliefs through the adoption and institution of the philosophy of Confucius.

### Communication Characteristics

*Transaction Communication Characteristics:* There is a rigid functional hierarchy. All contributions to the welfare of the group are highly regarded. To live and work in complete harmony and to have a secure place within the group gives the Chinese a great sense of accomplishment. There is a place for everyone, including outsiders. This does not mean you will be accepted into the group. This simply means after a lengthy time of building a relationship, you will be given a place of honor, figuratively speaking. It is wise to know this going in.

Problems are dealt with by denial and evasiveness. If a problem is not presented as an error but as a change, the Chinese can deal with it logically and efficiently. Decisions are made by consensus. If you, the foreigner, the outsider, are a part of the overall decision-making process, it is beneficial to defer to the entire group and not just to one or two people.

*Interaction Characteristics:* The Chinese are respectful and proper. People outside the group are not worthy of note. This is why it is necessary to build the relationship first. To the Chinese, feedback must be positive. There is no criticism. When attempting to imply a negative, the Chinese most likely will use body language and expressions such as a hissing sound, sucking in the breath.

To the Chinese, foreigners are barbarians. They have no place in the group. That is why it is imperative you slowly build the relationship; that way, you will at least be made an honorary member of the group.

---

To the Chinese, building a relationship is not friendship; it is respect.

---

Humility is a requirement of a Chinese life. One who is powerful shows humility, demonstrating allegiance to the group. Humility also shows the person to be a wise and beneficent leader. It demonstrates that he is ultimately no better than those who might consider themselves inferior. Humility maintains harmony. The humble but powerful person gains respect for his humility and not envy for his power.

## Protocol and Etiquette

*Forms of Address:* If there are no titles, the correct address would be Mr., Mrs., or Miss. It is proper to use *Lao* for an older person and *Xiao* for a younger person instead of titles.

*Greetings:* Greetings must be done in order of seniority. Among the locals, bowing may be done. Do not try to copy this ritual, because there is a definite communication by the depth of the bow. Bow too deeply to the wrong person—or not deeply enough—and you may cause an insult. A Westerner is not expected to know this ritual; a handshake and a nod of the head demonstrate respectful acknowledgement of their custom.

It is preferable to use formal greetings when addressing a Chinese. One such greeting is *Ni hao ma* (How do you do?).

*Handshakes:* The Chinese bow when they greet instead of giving a handshake. Men keep their hands to their sides, palms turned inward. Women bow holding the hands waist-level with fingers touching. Again, do not attempt to copy this ritual or you might bow too deeply to the wrong person or not deeply enough. This may cause an insult. Keep to a handshake and a nod of the head. The handshake is light in pressure. Do not give strong eye contact. Direct eye contact is too confrontational to the Chinese.

*Gestures:* Posture represents a person's self-control. If the body is controlled, the mind is disciplined. One should refrain from crossing the legs. Posture should be almost rigid. One should never touch the head of another person, which is the most sacred part of the body, nor should the soles of the feet be revealed, as they are the least sacred part of the body. Yawning is particularly offensive and should be stifled, and not just covered.

It is important that the hands are visible and calm. Fingers are not to be used to point or to gesticulate. Try clasping your hands loosely in front of you, so they are visible yet still. Never rest with your hands in your pockets.

---

### ❮ PROTOCOL ALERT ❯

Graciously reject any compliments you receive—with sincere modesty.

---

*Appropriate Attire:* Dress conservatively. Some Chinese wear Western styles, particularly in cities. Women in urban areas are more likely to wear dresses, not slacks. In the countryside, women are more likely to wear simple, functional clothing.

*View of Women:* In China, each person, including a woman, has a specific function within the group. Historical doctrines have taught them that men and women are different and must be separated. The men are dominant and women are subservient.

A Western woman is viewed as someone outside of the group. They are unknown. Western women do not meet the definition of women in the Asian culture. Asian men do not know where to position Western women in social rank and role. As a result, an Asian man does not know how to behave in her presence; he is confused and uncomfortable. Chinese men perceive women in their own culture as equal but very different from the man; therefore, he is skeptical of her ability.

*Gift Giving:* In some parts of China, it is illegal to receive a gift. In the areas where gift giving is legal, make sure your gift is not extravagant or showy. A gift of food, except when you've been invited to dine with your host, is an acceptable gift. Hair accessories and stamps representing your region are also good choices. Make sure you have small gifts for everyone. Wrap your gift in bright red, a lucky color, or pink or yellow, which is cheerful, but never use white. White denotes death. When presenting a gift, present it with both hands. Do not be surprised if the gift is refused three times. This is a show of humility and non-expectation. Eventually, they will accept your offering. Be sure to thank them when they accept.

*Dining:* Tea is usually served before the meal. When a group enters the dining room, the guest of honor should be allowed to go first. The guest of honor is seated to the left of the host in the middle of the table, facing the door if possible. Proximity to the center of the table is by descending order of rank. Group-minded cultures tend to use bowls for serving food. The guest of honor or the eldest person is given the honor of eating first. This honor is declined at first, then accepted. Use both hands to eat.

---

### ❮ ETIQUETTE ALERT ❯

When sipping tea, place your left hand under the cup and your right hand to the right of the cup. Hold the cup close to your mouth until you rest the cup. This will take practice if you are left-handed.

---

## Interesting Information

In this society, a person's self-worth is relative to his position in the group. Special attention goes to those who are older and those with advanced degrees. A teacher is more important than a doctor in most Asian cultures. When in doubt, defer to another person's knowledge.

Never compliment a person directly. This alienates him from others in his group and makes him feel uncomfortable. Be extra careful not to praise someone in front of his superiors. This threatens his relative position in society. It causes a subtle challenge to lines of authority and respect. Address his welfare by addressing the welfare of his group.

## Strictly Business

A person's strength is in his group. It is almost impossible to get the attention of a businessperson in this culture if you are not present. Personal relationships are necessary before business can be done. This relationship does not necessarily mean friendship. The Chinese must have some perception of you as a person. They will try to place you in a position relative to their society to establish your social standing. They will not deal with someone who is deemed unworthy of them.

The visitor must show humility as a sign of respect while maintaining his image of influence. If the sense of humility combined with influence is not presented, the resident leadership will not perceive him as a person worthy of their business. Humility must be demonstrated primarily by accepting their values of harmony, respect, and social structure. Applying an individualistic concept of time as money and objective decision-making will cause conflict and dismissal. Humility will gain you an invitation into their orbit.

It is always necessary for the *group* to improve their position. Improvability and progress are basic values. Be prepared. They are adept at determining your motivations and primary focus. They will use these to make gains in areas away from the main subject of discussion.

You arrive at the office punctually and after reaching the reception area, you nod respectfully to the receptionist, giving her your name. She asks you to wait. After about twenty minutes, she escorts you into your host's office.

Males and females are not treated equally. Touching people of the opposite sex is taboo. If a woman is westernized, she may extend her hand, in which case it is proper to shake gently. Notice that you are expected to be on time to appointments, but your host may leave you waiting. This often is not gamesmanship, but the predicament of an overworked executive. If your business is not deemed vital to his interests, you will not receive top priority.

You may be escorted into a conference room instead of an office, particularly if your presentation is technical. Many functional experts will likely be present. Let us assume this is the case. As you enter the room you determine who the chief executive is and approach him first to greet. If you are the senior person in your delegation, you make the initial greeting. You shake hands with a medium-firm grip and add a nod of the head. Your eye contact should be at throat level. You address him by his first name, which is his family name and yourself only by your last name.

As the senior member of your delegation, you are responsible for all communication. Your team should follow your lead and defer to you at all times. Otherwise, you will appear weak. Introduce yourself by your last name to relieve them of the effort in determining which name they should use. Begin introducing yourself with the most important information first:

- your company name,
- followed by your title,
- then your family name.

For example: AMG Publishing, Acquisitions Editor, Penwell.

The next required act is the exchange of business cards.

After greeting your host, you present your business card by taking one card from your pocket at a time, and presenting it with your right hand with a slight bow, even if you're left-handed.

You have had your cards printed in English on one side and in the language of your host on the other side. Present the card with the side of their language facing your host so he can read it.

In America, we distribute cards as a reminder of how to spell our names at a future date. In the Far East, the exchange of business cards is a symbolic ritual. A business card is an extension of the person presenting it. Your position on your team as an individual is not well-defined on his own. Your card helps determine this. On his card is information about the group and the person's place in that group. His name, his title, his degrees, and his corporate responsibility will all be on that card. Yours needs to reflect the same.

When you receive his card, treat it with great respect. Study it and remark on the education of the bearer. Never write on it or put it away in his presence. Keep business cards in a traditional gold card case in your left breast pocket.

By regarding your own card in the same way, you have a great opportunity to garner their respect. Be sure to include your academic degrees and your functional title on your card. When listing a functional title, be sure to research uses of business titles in the country you are visiting. A director in America may be a top executive, but in some places, a director is a lower echelon manager. Never inflate your title to impress them. If you are discovered the deception will not be tolerated. Be sure to use high-quality printing and card stock paper.

A staff member arrives and offers you a cup of green tea. You accept the tea.

Hospitality is important to the Asian. The culture is very ritualistic and hospitality is part of the ritual. Always accept an offer of hospitality. When it includes invitations, be sure to reciprocate as soon as possible. Reciprocity of hospitality is important as it demonstrates mutual support and respect. Accept the tea and spend a few minutes chatting.

## Country Summary

- Establish contacts before you go. The U.S. Department of Commerce can help. Everything shuts down between noon and 2 P.M. Avoid colors in your presentation. Colors have symbolic meaning. Bring at least twenty copies of your proposal. You will meet with many groups.
- Relationships are important before a dialogue is closed. At the end of a meeting, leave before the Chinese.
- Reciprocate banquets, but never outdo your host in lavishness. Spouses may be invited to banquets and guests arrive on time. Wait for the host to eat or drink. The host offers the first toast. If you are greeted by applause, you applaud back.
- Never put your hands in your mouth.
- Gift giving is technically illegal. Do not give anything expensive in front of others. A gift from your company to the Chinese organization is acceptable. When giving or receiving a gift, use both hands. The gift is not opened in the presence of the giver. Chinese will decline a gift three times to appear humble. Keep insisting.

Never give a clock. It is associated with death. Do not give gifts until all business is concluded.

# Country Profile: South Korea

## (Cultural Position: Group)

### Religious Factors

Confucianism is dominant in South Korea. Ancestry worship and reverence is an active ritual. Even Christians in South Korea practice cultural rites for the dead. While about 50 percent of Koreans are Christian, Confucianism is followed.

### Communication Characteristics

*Transaction Characteristics:* Koreans expect detailed information. They will ask many questions and often the same question many times. They expect you to act in a reserved manner and to be punctual. Patience is a virtue to Koreans.

*Interaction Characteristics:* Relationship building is a must with Koreans. Although they present a firm approach they are easily embarrassed. They do not favor bragging on what you've accomplished. Learn something about their cultural heritage so as to make interesting conversation. You will not see male and female Koreans exchanging public embraces.

### Protocol & Etiquette

*Forms of Address:* Address the person by his family name, which comes first, along with his title or Mr.

When writing, use the greeting "To my respected..." with the title and *full* name. Relationships and hospitality are important, but Koreans are most familiar with Western practices. Westerners generally perceive that they are less ethnocentric, less xenophobic, and less chauvinistic.

*Greetings:* Wait to be introduced.

The younger person will initiate the greeting followed by the senior person.

Because senior people are well respected greet them first. Have a few niceties to say.

*Handshakes:* Shake hands with a moderate grip and add a slight bow. To indicate added respect, support your right forearm with your left hand. The younger person should initiate the greeting and be the first to bow. The senior person will extend his hand first. Women do not commonly shake hands.

*Gestures:* Physical contact in public is considered rude.

Make sure your feet do not touch another person. Feet are considered unclean.

Never make the mistake of putting your arm around someone's shoulder.

Eye contact, which is unusual in Asian culture, shows sincerity and attentiveness to the speaker.

It is rude to blow your nose in public.

*Appropriate Dress:* Dress conservatively. Do not wear anything revealing or too bold.

Do not wear yellow or pink. It is frowned on when young people wear shorts.

*View of Women:* Women are more accepted in Korean culture than some other Asian countries.

*Gift Giving:* When giving or receiving gifts, use both hands. Do not open the gift in the presence of the giver. Expect the gift to be refused at first. This is good manners. Reciprocate gifts and hospitality. If you admire an object of theirs, they will feel obligated to give it to you.

Do not bring gifts from Japan to Korea.

When invited to someone's home, it isn't necessary to bring a gift. If you are guests in their home for several days, a gift would be appropriate.

*Dining:* At the end of a meal, there may be singing. Music is very important to the Koreans, and you should not refuse to join when asked. Have a short tune prepared. Singing expresses harmony in a symbolic, extra-dimensional way. It is a form of controlled, emotional release.

When eating, do not finish everything on your plate. This indicates that the host did not provide enough food and you are still hungry. Always refuse food twice before accepting.

Support your right wrist with left hand when passing food or when tea is poured.

## Interesting Information

Although harmony is very important to Asian societies, Koreans are the most likely to express emotion and to be direct and even somewhat aggressive during conversation. You, however, should remain calm.

Koreans are more likely than other Asians to say "no" and mean it. However, they will still avoid it when possible.

Do not write a person's name in red ink. It means the person is deceased.

## Strictly Business

Be punctual for all appointments. Koreans often hold one-on-one meetings or gatherings. This does not contradict their *group society* nature. The person you meet acts as an intermediary who must present your purpose to the entire group. It is important to establish a good relationship with this person.

Offer your business or calling card with your right hand. Treat it with dignity. Do not place a person's card in your wallet, and then put the wallet in your back pocket. Place all the cards you receive in your left hand with the most senior person's card on top and the others behind in rank order. Hold them there until you get to the meeting table, then place them on the table in front of you in rank order. If you are not going to a meeting and you must put a card away, slowly remove your card case from your breast pocket, open it, and slowly place the card in it. Do not rush to snap the case. Women need to wear a jacket with a side pocket so she can place her card case there and not in a briefcase or bag. Do not write on a card. This is like taking an ink pen and writing on the face.

Do not use triangle shapes in your presentation. They have a negative connotation. Remember, this is a culture that uses symbolism.

Silence can be a clue that you were not understood. Do allow some silence for thought, but follow up by rephrasing your last point.

During the meeting, if the Koreans return to social small talk, it is an indication that they are through discussing the business or program for the day. Meetings begin and end with a bow. If the ending bow is deeper and longer than the opening bow, it is an indication that the meeting went well.

If you do not have the answer to a question, say something to this effect: "The question the group posed has many interesting facets. We would like to honor the question with supplying you with a complete and thorough report. We will have that prepared for our afternoon meeting."

Entertaining is done at night. Do not talk business over a meal unless your host does.

## SUPPLEMENTAL DATA

Koreans may laugh when embarrassed.

Koreans are proud of their culture and do not like to be compared to other Asian societies. Their self-image is directly related to their cultural roots.

Koreans are very formal and expect you to be.

To lose face in Korean society brings much shame to them.

Four is an unlucky number in Korea.

# Country Profile: Japan

## (Cultural Position: Group)

### Religious Factors

The two main religious beliefs in Japan are Buddhism and Shinto. Buddha spoke words of peace and inner and outer calm, but with no recognition of God. Buddhism is a practice, not a religion.

Shinto is practiced as The Way of God, better known as *Kami.* For simplification purposes, *Kami* means power that can be noble, base, strong, weak, good, or bad. It can be a tree, rock, man, or animal of unnatural quality.

### Communication Characteristics

*Transaction Communication Characteristics:* A person's responsibility is to be a part of the group. Accomplishment for the Japanese is to simply have peace and harmony within the group. The Japanese expect cooperation among group members, for everyone to have their place in the group intact, and to build and maintain harmony within the group. Present a problem as a change, not an error; that way, the problem can be dealt with logically and efficiently. No decisions are made and no efforts executed without a consensus.

The Japanese are positive and noncritical when giving feedback. It may not be the truth. Truthfulness is not as important as harmony. If the feedback is negative, they will use body language in place of words. You will find the Japanese defensive and inattentive until a relationship is established. An outsider cannot rush the process. The Japanese communicate best when given facts and details and when they are shown rather than told. It helps to make your points by presenting related anecdotes. As in all of Japanese society, harmony is the key word. Time is harmony; therefore, punctuality is a must.

Project an attitude of quiet reserve. Graciously reject any compliments with sincere modesty. Show others respect; take care not to hurt anyone's feelings. Any act of deference to you as an honored visitor, such as taking a seat of honor or going through a door first, should be refused at least once before being accepted.

## Protocol & Etiquette

*Forms of Address:* Japanese are formal in every approach. Address the Japanese in a formal manner. They will state their last name first followed by *san.* You would address them as Mr. Okada. Foreigners do not use *san* after the last name. It is too personal. First names are reserved for family and close friends.

*Greetings and Presentation Style:* The Japanese have very stylized, formal greeting. They will form a line as they greet you, with the highest-ranked or the eldest person first. Arrange your group members to do likewise. The most senior person will greet the most senior person on your team and then introduce you to the next person. Follow suit. Continue in this manner four people deep after which the remaining people introduce themselves to the person in front of them. Allow the Japanese to begin.

When it is time to begin your presentation, speak softly while directing your comments to each person. Important remarks or initial speeches should be directed to the most senior person.

Models, demonstrations, and interesting graphics are highly recommended. Novelty is greatly appreciated. Beyond the visual effect, the content must be heavy on facts and data. Abstract concepts and vague remarks will miss their audience. Use a highly rational approach. Separate information by function, so the chief marketing person gets only marketing data on a separate piece of paper, the chief accountant gets a separate paper with only economic data, etc. Use visual aids whenever possible. This does not mean text on an overhead projector, but symbolic presentation: drawings and diagrams.

*Handshakes:* The Japanese probably bow more than any other Asian society. You do not need to return the bow. A nod of the head in acceptance of the bow is all that is expected.

The Japanese are well informed about Western culture. They know our protocol and are aware of the American handshake; therefore, they will likely extend their hand for a handshake along with the bow.

When accepting the handshake, do not use a firm grip and do not make strong eye contact. Both are too confrontational for their culture.

*Gestures:* Keep gestures small. Do not touch except to shake hands. Refrain from public affection with a spouse or companion. Put more distance between you and the other person than you would in the United States. The Japanese believe the person in control of the body is in control of his mind.

*Appropriate Attire:* Err on the formal side. Women never wear yellow. This color is reserved for royalty. Women do not wear navy or black suits with white blouses. This is the Japanese woman's working uniform, not that of a professional.

Make sure your shoes are in good repair. Carry good-quality handbags, attaché case, purses, and so forth.

Wear slip-on shoes because you will be removing them frequently. Slippers are provided for guests when entering a home and in some restaurants. Be aware that there are special slippers to be worn in the bathroom. Change your slippers going in, and do not forget to change coming out. Doing so might be walking around with a pair of slippers that say "toilet" on them. If an occasion arises for which you will be wearing a kimono, or kimono-style wrap clothing, always wrap left over right. Only corpses are wrapped right over left.

*View of Women:* In this culture, men are dominant and women are subservient. Japanese men do not know where to position a woman outside their group socially or professionally.

*Gift Giving:* The Japanese are one of the most gift-exchanging cultures in the world. They believed gift giving strengthens relationships between two parties.

There are two major gift-giving seasons.

- *Ochugen:* midyear in July to thank people for help received thus far and to indicate desire to continue the association
- *Oseibo:* end of December to thank people for favors throughout the year

Some appropriate gifts include food items, such as fruitcakes or local specialties from your area; coffee table books; or anything Western with a cowboy influence. Avoid flowers. They have too many symbols for you to remember. Wrap your gifts in a solid color or simple pattern. Do not use bows. Use cords. Do not attempt to wrap your gift in formal Japanese styles. If you wish to do so, have someone locally wrap your gift. Present your gift with both hands at the end of all your meetings with this comment: "This is just a small token." Do not expect your gift to be opened in your presence and do not open your gift in their presence. Remember every gift is a payment for, or in anticipation of, a flavor.

*Dining:* The meal is a ritual. Do not rush the process. Presentation is as important as the food. At the beginning of the meal, you will be brought a hot towel to wipe your hands. Men may use the towel to wash their face and neck. Women wash only their hands. When finished, roll it or fold it. The host orders the meal. A waiter will appear the moment you sit down. If you need more time say, *"Chotto matte kudasa."* Try to use the chopsticks. (Practice at home before you go.) When not eating, place the chopsticks across top of plate or bowl, or lay them on the chopsticks rest. If the chopsticks are wooden, place them in the paper wrapper at the end of the meal.

Noodles and soup are meant to be slurped. The louder the noise, the more your host knows how much you like it. Place the bowl in your left hand. Mix the soup around with your chopsticks. Inhale as you suck the noodles into your mouth. Bring the bowl to your mouth and drink.

Rice is served as a last course except at lunch. It is served in a small bowl and placed to your left. Pick up the bowl in your left hand. Do not pour soy sauce over the rice. Do not stand the chopsticks straight up in rice. This is a symbol for the dead.

Business entertaining is important and expected. Lavish dinners or banquets are the norm. Let your hotel make the arrangements. They know what is expected. It is usually assumed that women will not be invited. Keep in mind that business is never discussed at a dinner. It is often acceptable at lunch, but only at the end of a meal.

Bills will be brought to the table as soon as the order has been taken. Usually bills are paid at the door upon leaving. Japanese rarely haggle over a bill because it disrupts harmony.

## Strictly Business

*Protocol Challenge:* During negotiations, your hosts appear to dismiss a key point. You note this and . . .

A. restate the point.
B. let it go.

B. is correct. Negotiations do not necessarily follow a linear path. Your hosts may have chosen not to deal with that issue at the logical point in the discussion. Remember, they have their own strategy which might include making key points appear insignificant.

*Protocol Challenge:* During negotiations, you request feedback. Your counterparts smile and nod their heads. This means . . .

A. They agree.
B. They do not have a clue what you mean.

A general rule of thumb is the bigger the smile, the deeper the trouble. Negative feedback must not be given. Usually a smile means lack of understanding, but a "yes" could mean anything from "yes" to "absolutely not." It usually means, "Yes, I understand you," not, "Yes, I'll do it." A quick sucking in of air through clenched teeth is a very distressing signal.

Let us assume they agree.

*Protocol Challenge:* What happens after you reach agreement on all issues?

A. If the chief executive is present, a contract will be offered.
B. You wait.

The answer is B. Most Asian countries need approval of major transactions from the public sector. Business deals must be consistent with the direction of the state. It is useful at this point to have a person of status on your side to bring the project to high-level attention. This person should not be used to interfere with or unduly influence an official, but things move slowly at the public level.

After a long wait and another trip across the Pacific, approval has finally come. In keeping with their language and approach to life, the contract they propose will be vague by our standards. A written contract is a guideline to further negotiations. Be sure to specify critical responsibilities, but do not overload it with detail; you will appear distrustful. The best recourse you have is detailed meeting notes. Make the effort to take detailed notes, marking the date and time of key points of agreement, as well as who spoke.

## Country Summary

- The Japanese language is very subtle. There is much left unspoken, but to Japanese, all is understood. Use of an interpreter is recommended, even if the Japanese say they speak English. Provide your own interpreter. The two languages require completely different thought processes. When they respond to your remarks with a big smile, they have not understood.
- Numbers should always be written on a piece of paper for clarity.
- Be punctual for business meetings. For social engagements, be somewhat late.
- Greet someone with a weak handshake and a nod of the head. Cast your eyes down. Men, put your hands against your sides; women, put your hands on top of the thighs.

- Present business or calling cards after shaking hands.
- Address the person by his last name. Foreigners should not use the honor term *san* after the name.
- The smallest gesture may have great meaning. Keep your hands and face quiet. Do not blow your nose in public, and never use a cloth handkerchief. Use a disposable one. Gestures indicating a negative response can be fanning the right hand in front of the face and sucking air. This might be used in a case of an insult or a business recommendation not being accepted. Maintain greater distance between people when conversing than is normal in the United States.

# Country Profile: Taiwan

## (Cultural Position: Group)

### Religious Factors

As in most Asian countries, there is a mixture of Confucianism, Buddhism, and Taoism which is a religion as well as a philosophy. It promotes the yin and yang concepts of dark and light. Dark represents the male and light represents the female. You will find the yin and yang analogy used in food (sweet and sour), in color, in strength, and many other cultural nuances.

Another component of Taoism is that rest comes before motion, with tranquility and emptiness.

There are various Christian denominations in Taiwan but they represent less than 5 percent of the population.

## Taiwan Supplemental Data

- Have written materials translated by a Taiwanese expert. Chinese characters are different than in China.
- In a group, sit according to rank, with the most important member at the center, the next important to his right, third important to his left, and so on. Greet someone with a slight bow and light handshake. If someone asks you if you have eaten, the correct response is yes, even if you have not.
- Use the person's title or Mister or Madam, with the family name, which comes first. Do not point with the index finger; use your whole hand. Taiwanese indicate themselves by pointing to their nose instead of their chest as Americans do.
- Gifts may be given on the first trip. If offered a gift, always decline three times before accepting. Avoid giving clocks, or anything that cuts like a letter opener. Avoid the colors white, black, or blue.
- Evening business entertainment is very important. The guest samples the food first. Eat lightly, leaving a small amount of food in the bowl. There may be as many as twenty courses. If your bowl is empty, it will be refilled.

## Thailand Supplemental Data

- Thailand is ruled by a cooperative yet competitive triumvirate of bureaucracy, military, and commercial elite. The ethnic Chinese make up most of the business community. Ethnic Thais are more likely to be found in government positions. Local influence is necessary to accomplish anything.
- Theravada Buddhists comprise the largest segment of religious followers. They believe that Buddha was a man and not a god or creator and was not myth or legend. Thus Buddha experienced birth, aging, sorrow and stress, and dying.
- The greeting in Thailand is the *wa,* pronounced "why." It is done by pressing your hands together as if in prayer, pointing the fingers

outward. Elbows are close to the body. One lowers his head toward his hands. The higher the hands are placed, the greater the respect. Westerners may shake hands, but Thais appreciate the effort of the bow.

- Titles are very important. Use titles plus the person's first name.
- Thais are very proud their country never came under European rule. Thai means "free."
- Be punctual.
- Entertaining is done in the evening. If you are hosting, you may invite your host's wife to a dinner. Some evening entertainment is for men only. Do not bring your spouse unless specifically invited.
- Thais eat semi-continental style. They use a fork and spoon, instead of a fork and knife. Cut with the spoon. It is an honor to be offered the last bit of food on a serving dish. Refuse several times before accepting.
- Dress well as a sign of status, but avoid wearing a black suit which is reserved for funerals.
- The first meeting is to get acquainted, but you should eventually restate your intentions so the Thais can determine who should be at the next meeting, if there is one.
- Thais hesitate to ask questions. It implies that someone is a poor presenter. Public criticism is a form of violence.

## Malaysia Supplemental Data

- According to the constitution, a Malay is someone who speaks the Malay language, professes Islam, and practices Malay customs. Holy days of rest are Thursday and Friday (this varies in different parts of Malaysia). Ethnic Malays are primarily Muslims; Taoism, Hinduism, Buddhism, Sikh, and Christianity also are practiced.
- The overlay of Islamic and Arab culture shows in the necessity for praise and self-esteem. Credit is lavished on the smallest successes.

Status and power are not just organizing principles; they must be demonstrated.

- Do not invite a Muslim to lunch during the month of Ramadan (in the fall; the dates vary). He will be fasting.
- Use a very light handclasp which may be held for ten seconds. Do not rush the greeting. At one time, ethnic Malays had no family name. Use the first name. This is also used for ethnic Chinese. It is acceptable to ask them the proper form of address. When you explain how they should address you, match their level of formality.
- There is a significant Indian population in Malaysia.
- Reciprocity and public recognition facilitate decision-making. Cash is not commonly used to speed up decisions.
- Economic control lies with the Chinese minority.
- Gifts should not be given on the first meeting. Never give trivial or token gifts. Avoid giving any gift that might be construed as a bribe.
- Dress for hot weather keeping in mind that white long sleeved shirts are a mark of prestige. Dress formally until you determine the degree of informality that is accepted by the people you are meeting. A "lounge suit" refers to a dark business suit.
- Do not host a social event until you have been invited as a guest. Let your host make the first invitation.

## Singapore Supplemental Data

- These religious beliefs are practiced in Singapore: Buddhism, Confucianism, Hinduism, Christianity, Islam, Judaism, and Taoism. You will find temples of all these beliefs situated next to each other.
- Capitalism reigns in Singapore, and the ethnic Chinese are in control, representing 76 percent of the population. Singapore is the closest thing to a meritocracy in the Far East. Few people get ahead without long hours and hard work.

- Even though they appear Western in their work ethic and meritocracy, all other protocol is generally along the Chinese model. Communication and feedback is not direct, saving face is important, relationships are a must.
- Be punctual.
- Singaporeans laugh as a sign of anxiety or embarrassment, not levity.
- Use a limp handclasp as a greeting. Use the person's title and first name which is usually the family name, or the appropriate given name, if the person is a Muslim Malay.
- Singapore prides itself on being the least corrupt state in Asia. Gifts are given only to friends. Decline a gift three times and do not open it in the presence of the giver.
- Business moves fairly quickly by Asian standards. Communication channels are usually clear. After an initial meeting of about forty-five minutes, the visitor should initiate leaving.
- An invitation to one of Singapore's private clubs confers prestige. Refusing hospitality indicates bad manners.

## Indonesia Supplemental Data

- Indonesia has the largest Muslim population in the world. Eighty-eight percent are Muslims; other religions practiced include Christianity, Hinduism, and Buddhism.
- Much of Arabic protocol is appropriate here. However, Indonesia is naturally a group culture with Islamic culture overlaid. Hierarchies tend to be more authoritarian. And, remember that a majority of Indonesian businesspeople are ethnic Chinese.
- In the Bahasa Indonesia language, it is difficult to converse with a person until you know his status relative to yours. Pronouns depend on relative status.
- At social gatherings, those of lesser status should arrive first. An invitation may tell you when to arrive. If you are asked to arrive early, you can be sure you are not the most important guest.

- Indonesians follow the Arab concept of time, whereas Chinese expect punctuality.
- The response, "yes, but . . ." means "no."
- Facts are "degrees of probability." Compromise and accommodation are always in order.
- Decisions require consensus.
- Indonesians do not like to be singled out in a group. Compliment the group, not an individual.
- Shake hands only upon initial introduction and before and after a long separation. Use a weak handclasp. Do not rush the greeting.
- Naming conventions are not standardized. Some people have one name, some have several. Ask how to address the person. If he is Chinese, use the first name.
- Gifts are given often. Any small occasion is appropriate, even when someone comes to serve. They need not be expensive. Do not open gifts in the presence of the giver. Refuse the gift three times before accepting.
- A dinner guest should wait to begin eating or drinking until asked to do so. If you are the guest of honor, refuse the honor several times before accepting.
- Be careful not to invite a Muslim to lunch during the month of Ramadan. He will be fasting.

## The Philippines Supplemental Data

- The Philippines is a predominantly Catholic country. The Christian culture overlies an inherent group base. About 5 percent of the population is Muslim, and conflict between Muslims and Christians is not uncommon.
- The country operates under a system of "guided free enterprise." Power is ultimately held in the government. Entry into the Philippine market will require a local agent, one who knows the fine line between legal and illegal.

- Interaction is a process and decisions are not made on factual input. People factors are most important.
- Greet the Filipino with a firm handshake, but not with much pumping.
- Titles should be used along with the surname. Many names are Spanish, as the Philippines was colonized by Spain. Therefore, the proper surname would be the next to the last name, the name of the father's family.
- The culture exhibits its family/clan behavior by encouraging praise and building self-esteem through compliments, unlike most of Asia. This is a country that learned machismo from its Spanish ancestors.
- A confrontational style is not appropriate in negotiations. Harmony should prevail. The presenter should plan a multimedia presentation. Filipinos prefer to see the big picture and not the details.
- Filipinos run on Latin time. Unlike the group cultures of their region, they are not punctual. They do expect you to be on time, though. Waiting is often a status game.
- Dinner invitations are the sign of a good relationship. Entertainment will be lavish. Dinners are social affairs and may include wives. Reciprocate invitations.
- The visitor should project an air of importance and subtle power. Wealth and social status are important.
- At the end of any meeting, invite your counterpart and associates to dinner. You may have to ask several times whenever issuing an invitation, since an invitation may be offered casually as a polite gesture.
- Social events may end with dancing and singing. Be prepared to sing if asked.
- Dress conservatively until you know how casually the people with whom you are meeting will be dressed.

## Vietnam Supplemental Data

- One misconception about Vietnam is that they hate Americans. This is not so. They are now eager to become friends with us.
- Buddhism is the predominant religion; Christianity is on the rise. As in most Asian societies, worship and prayers for the dead are prevalent. You will find in temples, pagodas, and homes displays of fruit and flower with incense to burn in honor of the dead.
- The typical group pattern is followed: group meetings, greeting every person at the meeting, accepting hospitality, discussing any business only when the host is ready, and establishing trust and friendship first.
- Unlike in other parts of the world, the Vietnamese should be addressed using his given name, which happens to come last. For example, address Phan Talla as Talla. Talla is the given name and Phan is the family name.
- Make your presentations very clear. Start with basics. Do not assume the Vietnamese will fill in the blanks.
- The government is socialist and is very directly involved in private business.
- The Vietnamese will offer you a handshake. There is about a three feet distance between people when they greet. Do not touch anyone's head. It is the spiritual space. Do not summon a person with your forefinger; rather, wiggle four fingers in a downward position.
- Use both hands to pass something.
- Pick up your bowl to eat your rice. It is improper to eat with the bowl resting on the table. Do not take the last portion of the food in a bowl.
- When giving gifts, make sure you have gifts for everyone.

## Asia/Pacific Summary

- Learn Asian protocol. Most of the region practices this method of interaction with all people.

- There are many religious views in this region. Be knowledgeable about those practiced in the area in which you will go.
- Group behavior influences everything.
- Harmony oils the society and gives it continuity.
- Women have predetermined functions in Asian culture.
- Gifts are refused three times.
- Hospitality is an important part of Asian society.
- Learn the greeting and business card exchange. Practice before you leave American soil.

## Mission Trip Tip

- Don't travel alone. Be patient. Don't demand to be on your time table.
- Get names and titles right. Don't use first names unless invited to do so. Learn how to say thanks in their language.

# 5. Central and Eastern Europe

## (Including Russian, Belarus, Ukraine, Romania, Bulgaria, Croatia, Hungary, Slovakia, Czech Republic, Poland, and Lithuania)

The remnants of communism still have an effect on cultural attitudes today. We will use Russia as our guide for serving in this region. The other countries will be addressed in the supplemental data. First, we must look at the effects of Communism on the entire region.

1. Communism imposed nameless, faceless conformity onto its members. Communism forced group cultural behavior onto family/clan people. The extended family group was no longer the building block of society. Family identities were lost. People became non-people. Thus, a crisis of identity developed.

In family/clan societies, elevating the person is important, since he derives his self-worth from others in the group. Without a system of rewards, without positive feedback and praise, the self-worth and motivation of the individual suffered. The equality that Communism promoted was an equality of conformity. It became an equality of suspicion, an equality of disdain.

2. The subject of age must be stressed. In all these countries that were under communist domination for forty or more years, there is a huge generation gap. The older generation was been well trained in the communist ways and was conditioned to secrecy, distrust, and fear. They are not the driving force behind the new economy. The younger generation is eager to make the transition from a closed society to a free one. The behavior of the younger person will be very different from those of the older generation. The younger generation will be more open and relaxed in dealing with Westerners. But do not make the mistake of presuming too much. Attitude is one thing, performance is another.

What is happening now is the re-emergence of the family/clan. The family is the only unit of security. No one else is trusted. People now are motivated to support their families as they were never motivated to support the group.

Be aware that the style of democracy and capitalism that is evolving will reflect the inherent progressive family/clan type, and will not eventually become just like the United States. The possible exceptions to this are Estonia, Latvia, and the former East Germany. These are all individualistic cultures. Estonia and Latvia have had strong bonds with Denmark, Germany, and Sweden over the centuries. The Western Germans are finding out the effects of Communism on their strongly individualistic culture. It is taking much longer to reunite the two Germanys than had originally been imagined. An entire generation has been trained in the communist way, and it will take more than a few years to return them to their natural behavior.

# Eastern and Central Europe Overview

## Religious Factors

This region's religious factors were founded with the basic perception of the divine in nature. The people personified this divinity as someone who benevolently provides for them through the power of nature. Mother Nature or Mother Earth rewarded their work. They were separate from God. There was a sponsor-provider relationship. They worked, and they were provided for. Their society was a blend of hierarchy and common equality, but not in the sense of the group society. This group of people personified God and was separate from the deity. There was a sense of conformity within a hierarchical structure, but their ultimate focus was outward. Their clan, or family work group, was very important. They derived their identity from the family group, but there was an external consciousness that gave them direction.

The concept of a consensus vs. absolute leadership is an interesting differentiator between Central and Eastern Europe. The argument finds a perfect analogy, or reflection, in the religions of the area. There is division in thought between the Roman Catholic areas and Eastern Orthodox regions, with two major philosophical dividing points between the two Christian religions. One regards the nature of the Trinity, which we won't get into here, although it does have some bearing on the perception of hierarchy. The other major contentious issue is in the organizational structure of thc Church.

The Roman Catholic Church has a strong vertical power hierarchy—patristic in nature with power concentrated at the top. The Orthodox Church has a less vertical hierarchy, with power distributed horizontally to a group of archbishops. They, along with the Holy Synod, are the decision-making body of the Orthodox religion. Decision-making is by consensus. This model of power accurately reflects the perception of divine/human reality of native Eastern European culture. Central

Europe, which was under the domination of the Hapsburg dynasty and the Austro-Hungarian Empire for many centuries, held strictly to Roman Catholicism by the Hapsburg monarchy. One can expect their business institutions to exhibit a more patristic, vertical structure. It will be interesting to see if these cultures gravitate back to original perceptions, or if the influence from the West will now tend to shape their institutional behavior.

## GOVERNING PRINCIPLES

This culture should be classified as *family/clan,* but it varies from the family/clan forms of Latin America, the Mediterranean, and the Middle East. It is what we shall call *progressive family/clan.* This means that the family group is not the entire reason, or justification, or validation for existence. The group has an outward responsibility. The major manifestation of this difference is in the work ethic. The productivity, in a Western sense, of progressive family/clan cultures is greater than that of purely family/clan cultures.

As in all family/clan societies, a person's identity is relative to his family group. Self-esteem is derived from the respect that others show for one's achievements. Achievements are measured relative to the group. Honor and pride are motivating factors because validation does not come from within. The identity group was one's focus in life. It was the foundation from which people drew their identity and their protection.

# Country Profile: Russia

## (Cultural Position: Progressive Family/Clan)

### RELIGIOUS FACTORS

Before Communism, Christianity was the state's religion. Communism discouraged any show of religion worship of belief. Today, the Russian Orthodox Church is the dominant religion, with a smattering of Islamic and Jewish groups and some Buddhists and Muslims.

### GOVERNING PRINCIPLES

Russians have a deep connection to the land. It is the most important organizing principle in society. The physical extremes of climate and cycles of sunlight and seasons shape Russians' sense of physical reality and physical security. Mother Nature takes care of them. God's presence is revealed to them through the physical world. Nature is a powerful force. With its cycles and extremes of climate, it defines their lives.

The act of personification indicates a separation from God, which is indicative of a family/clan mind-set. But the pure family/clan culture is modified by the strong influence of God in nature. The focus is turned more outward. This results in a lessened power hierarchy. The vertical strength of the family/clan hierarchy is muted somewhat and social ties beyond the group become more important. There is more of a sense of equality than in a purely family/clan culture. There is a sense of equality of contributions, but not exactly the equality of uniformity that is the group frame of mind.

### COMMUNICATION CHARACTERISTICS

*Transaction Characteristics:* There is a loose hierarchical structure in all sectors. Functionality is important. To contribute beyond the group is an important responsibility. Contributions and care for the family/group is important too. Improving themselves and their family life gives people a great sense of accomplishment. People in this region expect mutual support, sharing, family royalty, and honesty. Whatever happens is absorbed into the process. Problems are thought of as change of orders. Bad news is changed to neutral news. This society is reactive by nature. People in this region are not accustomed to being responsible. Decisions are difficult because issues are likely to be made from a consensus of experts.

*Interaction Characteristics:* People in this region assume equality of all participants. Deference is not shown at first. You will find the people are modest in their interactions. One must build a relationship before there is trust enough to interact openly. Feedback is sparse and vague so as not to be disruptive or held accountable. This changes as fear of reprisal diminishes. You will find people in this region reticent with strangers. When they feel there is no threat to them, you are treated with warm hospitality. People work from the general to the specific, and relate abstracts concepts to concrete knowledge. Physical analogies and visual description are best to use when interacting with them. Time is not linear. There is not much regard for keeping to schedules. There is no association between time and money. They are process-oriented, and may become absorbed in process at the expense of a schedule. Change can be accepted if it isn't disruptive. New information can be absorbed into the process.

## Protocol & Etiquette

*Forms of Address:* Address your host by last name. Do not use the term, "comrade." When you become friendly, it may be suggested you call them by any variety of nicknames. A respectful way to refer to someone with whom you are on familiar terms is to use the first name and the second name, which is a patronymic (indicating "son of so-and-so"). Women add an "a" to their surname. Observe age and rank, and adjust your protocol to honor these.

*Greetings:* Common greetings are:

*Zdravstyuyte:* Hello
*Dobrpoye utro:* Good morning
*Kak dela:* How are you?
*Gospodi:* Male
*Gospoxha:* Female

*Handshakes:* Shake hands coming and going and when introduced. Use a firm shake. Never shake hands with gloves on, and do not shake hands across a threshold.

*Appropriate Attire:* Dress is conservative and fashions tend to lag behind the West. Try not to appear too affluent. It would be wise to buy a pair of Russian shoes, because thieves can easily spot a Westerner by their shoes. Save your good shoes for business meetings.

*View of Women:* Businesswomen are respected in Russia. There will be no risk of harassment.

*Gift Giving:* Token gifts are often exchanged when you first meet. Be prepared to give a lot of gifts, and bring an extra bag for the ones they will give you. Reciprocity of gift giving is very important. Gift giving indicates sharing, respect, interest in the person, and generosity—all the values one would want in a friend.

*Dining:* If you are invited to someone's home, which is rare, bring an odd number of flowers. Even numbers are for funerals. Very few people stop for lunch, except in Moscow. There are a limited number of restaurants. The continental style of dining is used.

## Important Information

The spiritual and physical reality of the culture causes definite culture-based perceptions. Some of these are:

*Time:* For this culture, time is more cyclic, like the rhythms of nature. Events are controlled by natural forces. People do not control time or events. Something happens, they react.

*Control:* There is not a strong "take charge" mentality. It is more of a "do what is asked" mentality. To completely take control of a project and define each step in great detail with lines of communication clarified and a precise schedule to follow would not be expected.

*Risks:* If a person does not feel that he has the personal power to shape events, to initiate action, or to change the course of troubled projects, he will not put himself in a position to fail. This person's sense of physical and professional security must be maintained to reduce stress.

*Space:* The Russians' sense of physical space borders on infinite, but their social distance is more communal. In effect, their comfort distance for personal interaction should be greater than family/clan, but closer than pluralist. They have more of a sense of the physical than group societies and so touching, as in handshakes, is to be expected. Closeness affords a greater sense of physical security.

*Power:* Their concept of power is abstract, lying in a loosely personified force. On a human level, power is not so much power in the sense of supremacy as it is authority. Those in the clan who have the authority to lead the group do not necessarily have power as they perceive natural power. In the family/clan group it would seem natural that those in authority would be one's parents or the group elders. We should expect the people of this culture to take direction from their parents at home and from older figures of authority in business. They most likely will defer to age.

*Self-Awareness:* The people in this culture exhibit self-awareness as an extension of their family or clan. All members of the group are transient, as is all life on earth. However, the group survives. A form of self-awareness in group and family/clan cultures is the veneration of ancestors. The ancestor is retained as a permanent part of the group even after his physical death. No one person may be singled out and held in high esteem during his lifetime. They must maintain equality of conformity. But after someone dies, leaving the group, a method of retaining these individuals in the group is to continue to recognize them after their death.

*Pride and Honor:* The person's self-esteem is rooted in the respect given him by others and not by his internal sense of self-satisfaction. Achievements are made relative to other individuals in the group. We should expect relationship building to be an important factor in business, as well as the values of sharing and cooperation.

One aspect of personal achievement is highly valued, and that is achievement in the arts. This is because the physical expression of humanity through visual, performing, and practical arts is sacred to all in the society. It represents the fundamental spirit of all members of the culture.

*Responsibility:* Since cultural attitudes toward work are strongly influenced by the concept of personal responsibility, one can expect the businesspeople to be good at teamwork. Their cultural background supports a tendency toward reaction vs. action, but it also requires them to work for what they need. Expect that these people will work well and productively in groups when guided by unambiguous management.

## Strictly Business

*Strategic Plan:* This culture forms closed groups for mutual support and security. They will definitely feel more comfortable remaining on their own turf. They are wary of strangers, especially foreigners who appear more powerful than they are. Your goal is to communicate that you seek mutual benefits.

Relationships are exceedingly important in this society. To minimize any perceived threat from you and to open the way for relationship-building, you must approach with an introduction. A professional yet impersonal introduction will be accepted because Russians regard competence highly, which is attested to by a professional reference. These people are not so suspicious of strangers that they will let their fears get in the way of a clear benefit, yet the form of a congenial relationship is necessary before substantive talks can begin.

Humility is the recognition of and respect for their brand of conformity and modesty. Some helpful guidelines are:

- Do not dress in an ostentatious or expensive manner.
- Do not entertain lavishly.
- Do not assert American values of personal gain to motivate them.
- Accept their way of doing things and their group accomplishments. All family/clan players feel an obligation to better the position of their group. All need to demonstrate their competence by receiving value from the outsider. However, this culture believes in the value of mutual support and sharing.

*Value of Relationship:* Valuing the person is valuing the relationship. Focus on the shared respect you have for each other and your enthusiasm for the new relationship that is being forged. The person's prime identity is through his family group. Showing respect and concern for his family is a great compliment to them. Always be sincere, since honesty is highly valued.

Let's say you have entered Russia with a referral from the country's embassy trade mission to the United States. That's a good start. Now, how do you initiate contact with the company to which you were referred?

You follow up the letter of introduction with a letter stating your hopes of doing business with them, your ideas for a cooperative effort, and a request for a meeting.

Courier the letter to be sure it arrives safely. Be sure to have the document translated into Russian to speed up the process. Be direct, clear, and brief as to your proposition. Make clear what the other party will gain and what you would like to receive in return. Clearly state the purpose for an introductory meeting. Make reference to the letter of introduction from the embassy. Provide an estimated timeline, but not a detailed schedule. Tell them you are very willing to travel to their offices. Formally request a meeting and let them know the most appropriate medium for response: fax, e-mail, or courier. Your tone should be friendly but professional. Do not use first names. Use titles and family names. Do not send a massive brochure about your project.

Be patient in waiting for a response. Let's assume that you receive an invitation.

You have received an invitation to talk. How do you respond? You write back, sending your response via courier, accepting the meeting, and offering several possible dates. State how many people you will be bringing, who they are, and their function.

The Russian's response finally comes with a date set for your meeting. You confirm by writing to confirm time, date, and place. You request any necessary help in obtaining a visa.

You are now ready to move on to the first meeting. Your strategic objective is to establish trust and mutual respect, and to open communications.

Choose to wear a conservative business suit to your first meeting, formal yet not too severe. Colors of accessories are muted. Clothing is clean and neatly pressed. You realize that people in this culture feel more comfortable blending in and conforming to the group.

You and your two associates have been announced and led into a large conference room. Four people walk in the door, three men and one woman. You are the leader of your team. When they enter the room, you wisely stand and wait for a leader among them to emerge. He or she will introduce him/herself, to you, the team leader. You then introduce your associates to the leader. Then he will introduce his people to you.

In individualistic business societies, all meeting participants are equal until they get down to business. An American would naturally introduce himself to anyone at the meeting. But in a family/clan/group society, position is recognized. In purely family/clan cultures the leader would be recognized because of the strong power hierarchy and the need to maintain distinctions within the hierarchy. In group cultures, the leader is the representative of the group. He is equal to every member of the group, so if you have met the leader you have met the group. This culture is a mixed family/clan/group society. The hierarchy is not strong, but leaders are the focal point of the group.

After both sides have been introduced, you stand and talk for a few minutes. Non-individualistic societies need to form relationships before getting down to business. They aren't sure they even want to do business until they find out what sort of person you are.

Introductory conversation should be limited to your appreciation for their invitation and your interest in their country and culture. Depending on their experience with Westerners, they may choose to get down to business by directing you to the meeting table. Don't prolong or monopolize the preliminary conversations just to have them learn something about you. They may prefer to do this over a longer period of time. Let your host set the pace.

Your host presents you with what looks like a contract, called an agreement of cooperation. You take the contract and pleasantly and matter-of-factly look it over (along with an interpreter, if it is not translated) and heartily agree to such friendly cooperation and sign it.

Your pre-trip study of national commercial law indicated that contracts are vague and largely unenforceable. Contracts primarily set forth intent to begin a business relationship. Any contract they propose should not be assumed to have much detailed substance. It is the spoken agreement that carries more weight. Specific terms of any substantive contract should be discussed at great length and accepted by both sides as mutually beneficial.

You have been asked to proceed with your remarks. You open your presentation with a discussion of their capabilities as you perceive them, your need for their capabilities, and the potential should the two of you agree to work together. The Russians will be looking for the benefit to their group. Get their attention up front by giving them the information that is most important to them.

When making a presentation, your voice should be moderate and relaxed. Some emotion may be effective. Never allow your voice to become stern or commanding. However, maintain formality in your speech. Keep good eye contact with all members of the group. Address most important remarks, or emphasis, to the leader.

Now you are ready to move on to their part of the information exchange—their qualifications to do the work. You ask the Russians to discuss their key personnel's experience. When soliciting information, do not ask questions that can be answered yes or no. That is all the answer you will receive. They will not elaborate or volunteer information as they will not anticipate a need for it. Ask precise questions that are process oriented. Use hypothetical questions to learn their thought process and problem-solving approach. Steer them toward the subjects you want to discuss. Encourage input from the entire group.

You and your associates are in agreement that you would like to work with this company. You thank them for the information, being positive in assessing the possibility of working together. Then you invite them all to lunch at a nearby restaurant. You take a central location and ask your guest of honor, the head person, to sit to your right.

You want the seating to be less confrontational. You are trying to break down barriers. If the local etiquette is uncertain, do what is graceful and practical, and by all means use it to accomplish what you want—in this case, getting the person of most importance next to you.

When you are the host it is polite to order, or indicate that you are considering ordering, one of the more expensive items. This gives your guests permission to choose something in that price range. If you are a guest, never order something that is significantly more expensive than your host has ordered. Be generous, but not extravagant. Extravagance in a culture whose standard of living is considerably lower than your own may be taken as an affront. In a purely family/clan society, lavish entertaining may be appropriate to show respect for another, but when there is a group influence, any ostentatious behavior is not appropriate.

What is the appropriate method of eating? Eating behavior is highly localized in less-developed parts of the world. Western countries have more or less standardized formal dining protocol and etiquette, but even the United States varies remarkably. Here are a few clues:

- Observe the place setting. Are there knives, forks, and spoons in the familiar places? If so, you can assume a continental method, which is summarized in Chapter Nine. If there are no utensils or only a spoon, the proper etiquette may be to eat with your hands. If there are chopsticks, use these as your utensils, except as common sense will dictate.

- Observe the natives. As host, they may expect you to begin first. You might pick up a utensil and approach the food, which is usually the signal to begin. Then pause to observe what others are doing. If they all slurp their soup, slurp your soup.
- Note that cultures with less intense power hierarchies have less interest in a formalized etiquette. Do what seems proper, and look at the list of universal etiquette before you go.

You know that you are dealing here with a loosely family/clan/group, and originally agrarian culture. You reason that their approach to eating might be more communal, with common serving bowls, passing bread and condiments, and serving each other.

Keep the conversation social. Your objective is bonding. Find out about their families. They are probably a lot like yours. Just to be safe, do not ask about their wives or daughters unless information is volunteered. Note similarities wherever you can. Another good subject is education, and particularly, their experiences at the university. Professional people love to talk about their universities. Use this time to assess their attitude toward you. Do they seem interested in forming a relationship, business or otherwise? You may have decided to do business with them, but they may not want to do business with you.

At the end of the meal you say to your counterpart, "I would like to ask for the check . . ." as you look for the waiter. There are many different customs for flagging down a waiter for the bill. Most of these will be offensive to someone else. The most inconspicuous manner is always the best. Your comment might elicit help from your guest. Do not use hand gestures if at all possible. Wait until the waiter is nearby and look him down, if you don't get any other help.

Walking back to the office, where you have left your briefcase (but taken valuables with you), you say to the person in charge, "I feel that our meeting this morning was very valuable. I would recommend that we both consider the comments made and reconvene tomorrow to discuss our next step. I would like to take a minute to write down a few summary notes for both of us, if I may." This gets you all the cooperation you ask for. You return to the meeting room and make a brief list of key points. You follow this with a brief list of action items. Be simple and specific. Take nothing for granted. Guide them through the thought process. They tend to be nonlinear and respond best to concrete communication. Upon leaving, shake hands again.

Even though business could have been concluded that day, it is necessary to allow them the time to confer, to develop a consensus, and receive direction from above. Allow it all to sink in. You may also take some of this time to continue the bonding process.

You return to the office the next day at 10:00 A.M. You shake hands with your host again, and begin your second meeting. You discuss the action items listed the previous day. The Russians indicate that they are in agreement with you and you begin to discuss a contract. You use a form that you have brought with you.

The following should NOT be included in your proposed contract:

- an estimate of the time frame for achieving certain milestones, as well as a more detailed schedule
- elements of the Russian commercial code
- a complete description of the deliverables
- standards to be used in performing the work
- a provision for arbitration instead of court ruling on subjects in dispute
- simple language instead of American legalese
- a detailed work plan showing the job tasks and decision points

Any contract the Russians propose will be vague. You must provide clarity, especially on critical points. Don't make it so complex that they cannot understand it or get lost in the paperwork. Give explanations of your intent as you review each topic. Be sure they understand each point.

After discussing each point, allow them time to consult with others before signing the contract. Russians have difficulty saying no, giving negative feedback, or admitting that they do not understand something. Give them an out. Arrange a later time to pick up a signed document.

Try to have the document signed by both parties during this trip, but don't push the time element.

Your good strategy blasts you ahead to your last step: establishing a working relationship. This is the toughest part of the game because it can be full of obstacles representing key cultural differences. You will face:

1. loose organizational structure. Clear this obstacle by establishing a clear hierarchy with job descriptions.
2. non-accountability. Clear this by explaining your system of accountability, and indicating consequences.
3. fear of taking risks. Clear this by encouraging openness and setting up a safe structure for creative thinking. Reward creative contributions and improvements.
4. the culture gap: Clear this by fostering a family atmosphere. Show mutual support. Share results. Include them in your group by keeping them informed of your office happenings. Bridge the gap by visiting as often as is feasible.

## Country Summary

- Russians have an affinity for Americans. This may be because both are used to life on a broad canvas. Their nations' territories are extensive, and there is much the two peoples have in common.
- Don't hire an expatriate Russian to represent you in Russia.
- Russians believe, and those who know Russia agree, that Russia has a "soul." Russians feel that they must take their own path and not copy the West.
- Russians see themselves as rational and conscious realists. They are also romantic and sentimental.
- Private business is done on trust. This makes relationships very important to doing business. Initial contacts should be made through a trusted third-party.
- European manners are used. Keep your hands out of your pockets,

use good posture, don't cross your ankle over the opposite knee, and remember that whistling indoors brings bad financial luck.

- Be punctual. They may not be.
- You will probably need an interpreter. But the presence of an interpreter doesn't mean they do not understand English. Avoid making off-the-cuff comments in English. Translate written materials into Russian, especially sample contracts, to save time in translation.
- Bring many business cards, printed in English and Russian. There are few telephone books, so people collect cards. They may not have a good supply themselves. Keep a list of meeting participants and their phone numbers.
- Business will begin soon after a bit of conversation. They may ask you to sign an agreement of cooperation, which is not a contract to work together, but to express mutual interest.
- Be clear of your intentions for this first meeting. If it is merely exploratory, say so.
- The Russian negotiating team will usually have specialists with different interests. The head of the team will do the most talking and you should direct most of your remarks to him.
- If you want to make a big impression on them, invite them to come visit you in America. You will be responsible for their expenses in the United States, but they will pay the airfare.
- Negotiations may take time. Time is not money. Time is wisdom.
- Management skills are often lacking. Don't leave anything unsaid. Don't assume they will fill in the blanks properly.
- Presentations should be concrete, visual, and factual, with detailed specifications.
- Decisions are often made subjectively, based on emotion.
- They are not afraid to express emotion, and use it as a tool. Sometimes they will storm out of a meeting, only to return later. Don't lose your temper.

## Belarus Supplemental Data

- Family/clan affiliation is especially important in Belarus because of their weak national identity. Belarus has been dominated by Poland, Lithuania, and Russia throughout much of its history.
- Western business practices are not generally understood. Explain everything.
- Shake hands with a firm grip while stating your last name. Men and women shake hands with each other.
- Small gifts are appreciated.
- Dress conservatively.
- Accept hospitality, whether invited to a restaurant or to a home. Expect substantial drinking, but if business is discussed you will be held to what you say.

## Ukraine Supplemental Data

- Ukrainians are independent thinkers who are capable of both objective analysis and subjective decision-making. Their emotions often take precedence over logic.
- The Ukrainian Orthodox Church provides a focal point for the progressive family/clan culture.
- Beware of both "yes" and "no" during decision-making. Both are used tactically, either to stall talks until more information has arrived or to keep you talking when you seem to be losing interest. Nothing is certain until the contract is signed.
- Negotiations may become emotional. Play hardball.
- Ukrainians are generally more easygoing than are Russians. Otherwise, many business and social customs are similar.

## Romania Supplemental Data

- The early history of Romania was dominated by the Roman Empire, of which Romania was a province. Its proximity to the subsequent Byzantine Empire along with its progressive family/clan nature resulted in a predominantly Orthodox Christian state. After World War II, Romania came under the influence of the Soviet Union. Today, Romania is a democratic republic, and one of the poorest countries in Europe.

- The people distrust authority, and are reverting to insular family/clan structure.
- They have very weak business management skills.
- The more educated the person, the more objective he is in decision-making.
- The current priority for all Romanians is to feed and house their families.
- Opinions and emotions are freely expressed.
- Send letters in English. They give higher priority to English language documents. A letter that must be translated is more respected.
- Distrust makes it difficult to make contacts. Use local representatives. Once you are accepted, the relationship will be a strong bond.
- Romanians are status conscious. Stay in the best hotel. Have your title and degrees printed on business cards.
- Small gifts are appreciated at the first meeting.
- Shake hands often, each time you see someone in a day and when you are introduced. Use a firm grip. Use last names and professional titles.
- Romanians gesture a lot with their hands. You should not, since many United States gestures can be seriously misunderstood.
- Eat continental style.
- Use European manners.

## Bulgaria Supplemental Data

- The Ottoman Turks dominated Bulgaria until World War I. The country was on Germany's side during World War II and then came under Soviet influence. Currently, Bulgaria is privatizing industry and returning group farmland.

- The Bulgarians admire the United States and Western Europe. They admire the entrepreneurial spirit and apply it in a family/clan sense.
- They have a strong work ethic.
- They respect openness, strength, competence, honesty, and loyalty.
- Management skills are lacking.
- European manners are used. Respectful behavior towards other is important.
- The head gestures Americans use for "yes" and "no" are reversed in Bulgaria.

## Croatia Supplemental Data

- Croatia was ruled by the Hapsburg dynasty for centuries. After the fall of the Austro-Hungarian Empire following World War I, Croatia, Slovenia, Bosnia, and Serbia were held together in a federation known as Yugoslavia. After the fall of the Soviet Union, nationalism and ethnicity separated these countries. Strong family/clan identity now operates.
- Croatians are primarily Roman Catholic. Expect a stronger power hierarchy, and centralized decision-making.
- Croats value kinship bonds, education, and a good career.
- European manners are used.
- It is acceptable to express emotion and opinions.

## Hungary Supplemental Data

- Hungary developed a high level of culture during the Renaissance. They came under the influence of the Hapsburg dynasty in the sixteenth century, and in 1867 a dual monarchy was declared, beginning the Austro-Hungarian Empire that lasted until the end of World War I. After World War II, Hungary fell under the influence of Soviet Union, though the people chafed under the control. Hungary is now a democracy, and is one of the most prosperous Eastern European nations.

- The country is two-thirds Roman Catholic, a result of the Austrian association, and one-quarter Protestant. Religion is not a big part of their lives.
- Vertical hierarchy is preferred, but consensus decision-making may prevail until greater confidence in business is achieved.
- Hungarians value family, education, job security, private property, and travel.
- They admire professionals and intellectuals over the merely wealthy.
- Intentions, feelings, and opinions may be directly expressed. Deviousness is not respected.
- Your host will probably entertain you. Hospitality is important to the Hungarians. At the end of negotiations, you should host a cocktail party or dinner at a good hotel.
- A firm handshake is used when meeting and leaving. Use family names until invited to use first names. In Hungary, the family name precedes the given name.
- When visiting a company, bring many small gifts for everyone you meet.

## Slovakia Supplemental Data

- Until World War I, Slovakia was under Hungarian rule for a thousand years. After World War I, it was united with the Czech Republic as Czechoslovakia, a democratic republic. In 1948, the country came under communist domination. The Czech Republic and Slovakia again became separate nations in 1993.
- Slovakians are proud of their peasant roots and peasant values.

- They view entrepreneurs as greedy.
- They do not value aggressiveness and individualistic self-confidence.
- Education is valued above wealth.
- Use titles when greeting people. Print your titles and degrees on your business card.
- Many hand gestures are used. Avoid using American gestures as some of them are offensive.
- European manners are appropriate.

## Czech Republic Supplemental Data

- During the fifteenth century, Prague was a center of the Protestant Reformation. In the sixteenth century, the Czech Republic (the former Bohemian Empire), came under the rule of the Austrian Empire, which reasserted Roman Catholicism. Today, 40 percent are Roman Catholic, with a similar number professing atheism.
- Cooperation and contribution are valued over individual accomplishments. The family unit is considered in all decision-making.
- The most important values are education, social standing, modesty, and cleverness.
- European manners are followed.
- Translation of material into Czech will impress them, but English is acceptable.
- Czechs are detail-oriented, and will study all aspects of an agreement. Expect negotiations to move slowly.
- Present information clearly, highlighting major points and using visual aids when possible.
- Don't get down to business too abruptly. Relationship is important and slow to form.
- Dinner entertainment is more common than lunches. Do not discuss business during a meal.
- Greet someone with a firm but brief handshake. Use the last name,

which is the family name. Use professional titles when they are known. Wait to be introduced if there are more than two people present.
- Avoid using your index finger, waving or beckoning.
- Dress conservatively.
- Be aware that the Czechs shake their heads up and down in agreement. This can be very confusing for people who speak English.

## Poland Supplemental Data

- Poland has been a Roman Catholic country for over a thousand years.
- In 1791, Poland adopted a constitution modeled after the United States, but retained the monarchy and nobility. In 1795, the country was partitioned by Prussia, Austria, and Russia, and no longer existed as a nation. The Polish identity was maintained through the Roman Catholic Church. In 1948, Poland came under Soviet control. The country is now democratic.
- Poles value punctuality, skill and intelligence, privacy, family, and loyalty to the Polish nation. Still, they are critical of themselves and their institutions.
- They have a strong work ethic.
- Direct communication is preferred.
- Facts are more important than emotions in decision-making, but relationships are more important than laws.
- Poland has strong power hierarchies and is a male-dominated society.
- Translate materials into Polish.
- Business lunches and dinners are popular. Expect to stay out late.
- Shake hands to meet, greet, and say good-bye. Use last names.
- Avoid loud behavior in public.
- Polish men have more traditional views of women. A woman should not talk to a strange man, or it will be considered flirting.

- A gift is appropriate at the first meeting.
- Dress conservatively.

## Lithuania Supplemental Data

- Lithuania and Poland have had close ties for centuries, including their Roman Catholic faith. They developed along the same lines until they were partitioned in 1795. Lithuania then came under Russian rule until 1920, when it regained independence briefly. In 1940, the country again was annexed by Russia; in 1990, it declared independence.
- Customs and protocol are similar to Poland.

## Central and Eastern European Summary

- This culture forms closed groups for mutual support and security. They will definitely feel more comfortable remaining on their own turf. Members are wary of strangers, especially foreigners who appear more powerful than they.
- Relationships are exceedingly important in business. To minimize any perceived threat from you and to open the way for relationship-building, you must approach with an introduction. A professional yet impersonal introduction will be accepted because members of this culture regard competence highly.
- It is important for you to recognize and respect this culture's brand of conformity and modesty. You should not exceed these people's ability to provide material goods. This means one should not dress in an ostentatious or expensive manner. One should not entertain lavishly. One should not assert American values of personal gain in order to motivate them. Show that you respectfully propose business that will benefit the group in their terms. This means for the good of the group. For a progressive family/clan culture, this group is both family and state.

- All family/clan players feel an obligation to better the position of their group. All need to demonstrate their competence by receiving value from the outsider. However, this culture believes in the value of mutual support and sharing. They are win-win players, as are most Americans, and will negotiate for the good of both parties once their group is taken care of. Be prepared to give them a guaranteed gain in exchange for equal value. Minimize risk to them in what they are to receive and in what they are to give.
- To value the person is to value the relationship. Focus on the shared respect you have for each other, and your enthusiasm for the new relationship that is being forged.
- Central and Eastern European countries share not only a common recent history of communist domination, but a common past in their Slavic heritage. This fundamental unifying factor is important in understanding how their culture was affected by Communism, how they behave in business today, and how they will change in the future.

## Mission Trip Tip

- Consider the culture variances.
- Have clear perceptions.
- Consider target country's basic needs/interest.
- Come to wise and enduring resolution.
- Forget little inconveniences. Focus on people and the relationship. Learn to enjoy cross-cultural interaction. If you are more task-oriented, stretch yourself to become more comfortable with relationship building.

# 6. Africa

## (Cultural Position: Family/Clan)

Africa is a continent of diversity. Many cultures are represented; the climate and geography are different, and the population of over 250 million people is astounding. Africa is situated between the Mediterranean Sea and the Cape of Good Hope and contains fifty-four countries. There are immense possibilities for those who are in the business of spreading the gospel through witnessing, teaching, and discipling individuals who do not know Christ.

This book divides the continent into five regions: North Africa, West Africa, East Africa (including the Horn of Africa), Central Africa, and Southern Africa. We will provide some general information regarding each region with a discussion of a representative country from that section.

# West Africa

## (Nigeria is the representative country to illustrate West Africa)

West Africa has an arid climate to the north. To the south the climate is more suited for farming. There are many ethnic groups in Sahel region. West Africa is noted for its historical slave trade which so dominated the region it caused a lessening of their influence in the world. Timbuktu was the exception. It was an ancient commercial center and a seat of renowned learning. It is believed that the majority of West Africans are descendants of slaves from West Africa.

### Religious Factors

A number of the countries in West Africa are predominantly Muslim, so the information presented in the Arab section regarding protocol and etiquette would apply to many parts of Africa as well.

### Cultural Position: Family/Clan

The social structure which governs this society is the family. The male is head of the household and this lineage is passed from generation to generation. The extended family is the community. There are governing principles and guidelines for every facet of society, every individual. This close-knit relationship goes beyond the nuclear family, but extends to the entire village and sometimes beyond.

A distinctive feature of the entire African continent is the explosion of hundreds of tribal groups. The three main tribes are the Hausa-Fulani, the Yoruba, and the Igo. The Hausa-Fulani, as practicing Muslims, are very religious. The Yoruba tribe is more outgoing, festive in spirit, and enjoys feasting and celebrating. The Igo (Igbo) are resourceful merchants, conscientious, and hard working.

## Protocol and Etiquette

*Forms of Address:* Use of titles is important, such as Doctor, Director, or Chief. Seniority and age is respected so an older brother may be addressed as "N'de Joseph" and an older sister as "N'se Alice." Always use sir and ma'am when speaking to anyone in authority and an older individual.

*Greetings:* Maintain a degree of formality. Never use first names. This is reserved for friends.

*Handshakes:* A simple handshake is a most common greeting, although men, who are close friends, do not shake hands. Women often hug other women friends. It is considered rude not to shake someone's hand or to acknowledge his presence when he enters a room. After being formally introduced, one shakes hands again, and upon departure.

*Appropriate Attire:* There is no formal dress code. Men are expected to wear a suit and tie and women a dress.

*Gestures:* Personal space is closer in Africa than in Western society. Don't back away when someone stands close to you.

*View of Women:* Women in West Africa, especially in Nigeria, play an important role in commerce and are more independent than other Muslim women. The male is still the family head. It is wise for foreign women to be reserved and take a non-aggressive posture.

*Gift Giving:* Receive and accept gifts with both hands.

*Dining:* The food will be hot and spicy. Do not pass food with your left hand. The Nigerians like to extend their hospitality to the home.

## Strictly Business

The initial meeting may be more formal and conducted in the office. Once a personal rapport has been established, longer, more substantive meetings may be conducted in a restaurant or at a Nigerian counterpart's home. Business can take on a celebratory attitude. There will be greetings and personal conversation before business is discussed.

Business will be conducted at a slower pace. If there is a long pause after you've posed a question, it could mean that the person in charge did not know the answer and does not want to be embarrassed. Be comfortable with silence.

One must build trust and friendship if one is to succeed in business or any endeavor in Africa. Friendship is so important that you must establish it first, and maintain it throughout your involvement. This friendship is not only maintained in a business setting but also beyond the negotiating table. You will find the Africans warm and friendly to strangers.

## North Africa

North Africa lies between the Sahara Desert and the Nile. Arabs and Berbers are primarily the inhabitants of North Africa, originally called Moors by Europeans. People in North Africa have both African and Middle Eastern roots. They were also influenced by ancient European civilizations. It was Rome that brought Islam to the area. Today an increased interest in Islam is the result. Refer to the Arab Region for protocol and etiquette specifics.

## East Africa Supplemental Data

- Global forces created the Great Rift Valley, hosting Mount Kilimanjaro and Mount Kenya, the two largest peaks in Africa. This region is known for its wildlife, national parks, and game reserves.
- East Africa exhibits the strong influences of Arab traders and European colonization.
- In 1963 East Africans broke away from British Rule, after which Kenya grew to be the most prosperous and political stable African state. Other countries in the region, called the Horn of Africa, include Djibouti, Eritrea, Ethiopia, Somalia, and Sudan.
- There is freedom of worship in East Africa, with many religious denominations and sects.

- The followers of the Christian faith are the majority. Islam is the main religion for most of the communities along the coast and the Somali community. The Asian community is mainly Hindi. Some Kenyans observe traditional methods of worship.
- There are more than forty ethnic tribes in the East Africa and three main linguistic groups: Bantu, Nilotic, and Cushitic, although many languages are spoken. The two most familiar are Swahili and Zulu.
- East Africa also supports Indian, Arab, and European (primarily British) communities.
- Address East Africans by their titles. Be well acquainted with an individual before using their first name. Be prepared for lengthy conversation about your family and country.
- Women do not look men directly in the eye.
- You may encounter a variety of handshakes. Some may be long, extended ones, or a brief, customary handshake.
- A suit is the standard dress in Nairobi, the capital, and a more casual look is acceptable in the outlying or coastal areas. Men wear a jacket and tie to dinner and women a dress or skirt. Although Kenyans appreciate foreigners who wear traditional Kenyan clothes, they must be worn correctly. When not sure, don't.
- Women in business are on the increase. Foreign women who go to Kenya on business should use tact and present a serious approach. If a husband can accompany her, it is better.

## Central Africa Supplemental Data

- Central Africa is comprised of desert land and lush rain forests. It is rich in natural resources. Central Africa is known as Middle Africa. Slave trade has heavily influenced the development of this region. Competition between France and Briton to develop this region and the spread of Islam has left a powerful legacy.
- The cultural foundation, as in all of Africa is the family, and the same strong influence of the tribe.

- English and French are the official languages. Besides the official languages there are over 200 tribes, each with their own native tongue.
- The south is both Catholic and Protestants with twice the number of Catholics than Protestants. In the north about 40 percent of the population are Muslim. Indigenous African religions are also practiced.
- People in this region of Africa are warm and welcoming. Handshakes are the norm when greeting, although some tribes may offer more elaborate greetings and handshakes. Men and women may embrace one another, but only after they are well acquainted.
- Standard business attire is acceptable for both men and women. For less formal occasion, because Cameroon is located near the equator, a more comfortable, casual look with open-collar shirt and shorts is acceptable.
- Women are accepted and generally welcomed.

## Southern Africa Supplemental Data

- This is a diverse country located on the southern tip of the continent. Seventy-five percent of the population is native black African with about 15 percent designated as white (European extraction).
- Although most South Africans speak English and Afrikaans (derived from Dutch Settlers), Bantu languages comprise the majority of the country's eleven official languages.
- Following years of apartheid, a policy of legal racial segregation, South Africa is working to recover from the devastating effects of that practice.
- The Dutch Reformed Church has had profound influence in South Africa and today it is nearly 70 percent Christian.
- Titles such as doctor, professor, and advocate (lawyer) should be used appropriately, as well as Mister, Mrs., and others. First names

are to be used only after the South African uses yours. In the initial meeting, avoid discussing marital status or the particulars regarding one's family situation.

- The standard greeting in South Africa is the typical handshake. You may see more elaborate handshakes between two blacks or a white South African when they greet each other. This elaborate handshake involves the thumbs and fingers that are cupped and clasped. Generally speaking, if two whites greet, they would perform the standard ritual. Male friends hug and women will kiss one another on the cheek.
- General Western business attire is acceptable with a more casual look of khaki shirt and Bermuda shorts when your meeting dictates.
- South African women are dominated by men.
- South Africans admire punctuality, efficiency, and dependability. Thus, meetings are expected to start and conclude in timely manner.
- Like in other regions there is a period of getting acquainted before discussing business. Business lunches and dinners at restaurants occur frequently, but they are generally social events. You may be invited to someone's home where you may enjoy a picnic.

In a manner similar to other African countries, trust and friendship is a must.

## Mission Trip Tip

- Deal with cultural differences. Don't focus on cultural stereotypes.
- Do not think all of Africa is alike. Each region is vastly different.

# 7. Other Nations of Note:

## Australia, Canada, Greece, India, and Israel

Additional countries of interest have not been covered within the major regions in the previous sections. This is because each country in this section is significantly different from those around it, by reason of religion or ethnic background. In all cases, the governing principles are different from those of nearby cultures. For example, Australia is technically located in the Asia/Pacific. Yet to discuss its culture at the same time as those of China and Japan and every group society of the Far East would not be logical. The primary inhabitants of Australia are of British descent, making their cultural background unique to Asia.

Similarly, Israel has been extracted because it is not an Arab culture, yet it is a significant global player. Religion is not the only factor that distinguishes it from its neighbors. Its unique culture is a mixture of Northern European and Mediterranean cultures.

India stands in close proximity to two strong cultural systems: Islam to the west and east, and Confucianism / Buddhism to the north. Yet it maintains its own religious beliefs and mode of operation as representative of those perceptions.

Canada houses two very distinct cultures that must be addressed separately. It is very important for people in the United States to make the distinction between themselves and Canadians.

# Country Profile: Australia

## (Cultural Position: Individualistic)

Australia is an independent member of the British Commonwealth, and as such, one would expect the Australians to be similar to the English in many ways. England is a family/clan culture, as discussed in the Western European game, but Australia is not. Australia is individualistic. It is easy to see the evolution from family/clan ancestry to individualists' culture when looking at the founding of Australia.

### Religious Factors

Anglicans, Roman Catholics, and other Protestants each comprise about 25 percent of the population. Due to an influx of immigrants, there are now Australians who practice Hinduism, Taoism, and Buddhism, with a very small number of Jews. Religion is not a daily practice but reserved for celebration of special occasion.

---

To an Australian, no man is his master and no man is his servant. Arrogance is the worst sin, followed by deference.

---

## Governing Principles

Australia's cultural position is *individualistic.* Its early inhabitants were almost exclusively male. The family was not the group from which identity was derived, but from the male "club." Men formed strong bonds that continue as a major social institution today. Men feel that their friendships with other men are more important than their relationships with their wives. The man has very little to do with household affairs, yet he is the symbolic head of the family. The society fosters a very strong masculine stereotype.

Part of this stereotype is the strong, independent, tough individual. It is an identity of strong individualism but at the same time, it is an identity of conformity. The concept of "masculine" is well-defined, and the group is easily threatened by any deviance by a member such as over-sensitivity to the needs of others, long hair, and wearing jewelry.

This makes the Australian very difficult to classify. He behaves as a strong individualist who is self-directed and equal to any man, yet he is defined by the identity of the group. This group identity appears to be family/clan because of the element of self-awareness, unlike the group member who seems to have no identity apart from the group. Yet he is not truly family/clan because his sense of identity is not related to a family or hierarchical structure. If you are a member of the identity group—that is, male—you are equal to every member. So we have an independent individual who is defined by his conformity with the group, but who is self-aware within the group. These conflicting cultural identities are evident to those who study the country. The inhabitants of Australia are, by international survey, the happiest people on earth. At the same time, they have one of the highest suicide rates in the world. They are easy to get to know, friendly, and generous—and, just below the surface, aggressive and violent. Much of this aggression is expressed relatively harmlessly through the attention given to sports, especially contact sports.

The Australian wholeheartedly believes that one man is as good as another. Until recently, tipping in restaurants was unheard of because it suggested a servile relationship between guest and waiter. The original self-concept of Australians was of a nation of the working class. Now, with greater affluence and education, it is a nation of the middle class. There is a strong desire for competition and drive for material wealth, but there is also the attitude that if one exceeds the success of the group or if one sticks his neck up above the crowd, he should be cut down to size. This behavior of acting out against anyone who puts himself above the group is a mechanism for cultural stability.

This is not to suggest there is not an upper class in Australia. The upper class is small, and made up of a few land-owning families and those with great industrial wealth. It is less an upper class of the British model than it is of the American model. There is mobility among classes. One does not accept one's station in life. There is the possibility of entry, mostly through acquisition of wealth. One can gain access to the upper crust not only through heredity but through self-improvement. The existence of the upper class is not supported by cultural behavior. They may have more, but they are not due more respect. There is not a strong inner drive to make one's way up the social or professional ladder, as there is in the United States.

Because of the belief that one makes one's own station in life, and the fact that there is social and occupational mobility, this culture should primarily be classified individualists; however, keep in mind the strong equalizing forces of conformity.

## Communication Characteristics

*Transaction Communication Characteristics:* Privacy is important. Power hierarchy is based on achievement, but Australians are strongly antiauthoritarian. To maintain individual independence and enjoy life gives Australians a sense of accomplishment. Australians expect equal treatment. Problems are assessed objectively, but a bit casually. There is a slightly carefree approach to life and work. Decisions are based on objective facts and policy, not on emotions and friendship bonds.

*Interaction Communication Characteristics:* Australians are open and friendly. They are very informal. First names are used almost immediately. Feedback is direct, specific, and objective. Australians are not afraid to say no. They are friendly and not defensive. Foreigners are held separate from the group if their culture is very different. Australians are intolerant of different behavior. They learn best when presented with detailed data, facts, and concepts, and empirical and theoretical knowledge. Problems are assessed objectively, but a bit casually. There is a slightly carefree attitude when presented with problems. Schedules and plans are precise and important to those responsible for them. They are moderately adaptable to change.

## PROTOCOL & ETIQUETTE

*Forms of Address:* The correct way to address someone in more formal situations is with the surname and last name: *Mrs. Greene.* In informal settings, first names are appropriate. Never address someone by last name only.

*Greetings:* "G'day" is the most usual greeting. In formal settings, the greeting would be, "Hello, how are you?" When people greet from a distance, they usually wave.

*Handshakes:* The appropriate handshake is warm and heartfelt, not stiff and formal. Often, women will hug and kiss the other's cheek.

*Gestures:* It is inappropriate to stand too close or touch an Australian. Do not point. This is considered rude. Do everything you can to stifle a yawn. If you must yawn, turn your face away from the other person and cover your mouth with your hand.

*Appropriate Attire:* Australians dress casually. Make sure your sense of casual is not sloppy. In business, a suit is required for men; women can wear a long sleeved blouse and skirt.

*View of Women:* Women are highly respected. They are well educated, make similar wages, and are considered equal to men.

*Gift Giving:* Food items can be an appropriate gift. Make sure it is in a bottle or can or it may not pass customs. Books are appreciated, especially illustrated ones. When going to someone's home, take a small bouquet of flowers.

*Dining:* Australians eat continental style. There will be some ethnic variations to dining etiquette. Do not put your elbows on the table. As a guest, one must wait to be asked for a second helping of food. In restaurants, side dishes are served in separate plates. In homes, the food is usually put on the table for people to serve themselves. Do not leave the table until everyone leaves.

## INTERESTING INFORMATION

Australians are very proud of their country and their unique culture. They do not want to be thought of as a "little" United States. Any display of superiority will turn them away. Equality and antiauthoritarianism are their strongest values. Treat them as equals.

It is important not to overlook New Zealand as a separate nation. The European development of New Zealand came from colonization by Australia. The prison colony at Sydney spawned a group of fortune-hunting men who colonized New Zealand for their own profit, using prison labor. In the early 1800s, New Zealand was a frontier of Australia. The local residents, the Maoris, were pressed into service on land and on trading ships and whaling vessels.

Later, the English sent settlers to colonize the new land. They were largely cultivated representatives of English county families and their retinue. New Zealanders are more British in behavior than the Australians, yet they remain more like the Australians than like their English ancestors.

## STRICTLY BUSINESS

It is important to show interest in Australians and their country by physically going there. Follow-up can be done by phone, but visits should take place at least twice a year. Because of the distance involved, it would be wise to keep a local representative on staff. He can keep up on local developments and keep your name prominent. Initiating a business contact can be done by phone, but it is always better to have a letter of introduction. Bargaining over price is a waste of time. Give your business card at the introduction, but understand that your counterpart may not give you one. Cards are not very important in Australia. Business dress is conservative, and not overly elegant. Leave the gold chain and other ostentatious jewelry at home. It is too showy and considered not "masculine."

Decision-making can occur at lower levels, but things still take longer than in the United States.

## AUSTRALIA SUPPLEMENTAL DATA

- One way Australians express equality is through their informality. Accept this and do not make your manner of behavior overly formal. Australians appreciate consideration, but dislike stuffy, stiff formality. Do not be offended if they use your first name. Also, do not assume that if they do, it indicates friendship. Use of first names is a way to mutually disarm and equalize the relationship.
- An Australian's self-worth is based on his feelings of equality and masculinity. Deference and compliments will not give the desired effect. Acting in a way that acknowledges ability and one's independent reasoning is the best form of communication. Validate their importance to you in what you are hoping to achieve for mutual benefit.

---

No man is a servant, and no man is a master. Be sure to structure your presentation to emphasize the equality of the two participants.

---

- Australians have a strong personal interest in their own performance. Help to identify and offer solutions to any problems.
- Gifts are not given, unless you are invited to someone's home.

- Don't fill your presentation with hype or glitz. A simple, direct presentation is more effective. Get to the point.
- The Australians make a clear distinction between work and play. Sports are an excellent topic of conversation. Learn something about Australian football and rugby. When discussing sports, do not use the term "root" as in "root for the home team." It means something obscene.
- There is a difference between "afternoon tea" and "tea." "Tea" is the meal served between 6 and 8 P.M.
- Women are legally equal but socially an underclass, although men may not admit it.

# Country Profile: Canada

## (Cultural Position: Family/Clan, Individualistic)

Americans often ignore the importance of learning the customs of our English-speaking neighbors. Don't let the language fool you. They are not Americans and do not wish to be thought of as Americans. In fact, many Canadians fear U.S. dominance and believe that given the chance, the United States would annex their country.

For a cultural understanding of Canada, one should really think of it as three countries:

1. French-speaking Quebec
2. English-speaking Ontario
3. the western provinces

The major difference between America and Canada is that America tends to assimilate diverse cultures into one system. Canada holds ethnic groups separate, due to the fact that most of Canada is family/clan.

*French Canadians:* The French Canadians in Quebec are fiercely battling against being assimilated. Their language is the most obvious differentiating factor, and is actually a symbol of their culture. When they are forced to speak English, they feel they are losing their identity. The French Canadians are perhaps more family/clan than the French in France. France, as we discussed earlier, exhibits a combination of pluralist and family/clan tendencies. The French Canadians exhibit more of the family/clan culture, especially in their exclusion of outside cultures and their need for identity as a member of the group.

*Ontario:* Ontario is also family/clan. This is the most British part of North America. During the American Revolutionary War, a large number of people loyal to the king fled to Canada. They are respectful of authority, function best in a strong cultural hierarchy, and believe in the need for state control. Compared to U.S. residents, Ontarians are more elitist, less achievement-oriented, and more socialistic. Power is centralized and tightly held. Although they are an exclusionary society, there is social mobility, although not as much as in the United States, and social status is not offered to immigrants. They are ethnocentric.

*Western Provinces:* The upward mobility of the ethnic cultures that have come to reside in the western provinces is due largely to American businesses that came into the area. Because of the greater American influence and the pioneering psychology of the Western inhabitants, this region tends to be more individualistic.

## Religious Factors

Forty-six percent of Canadians are Roman Catholic, with Protestants comprising 36 percent. Because of emigration, Hinduism, Judaism, and Islam also are found in Canada.

## Governing Principles

The cultural position is both *family/clan* and *individualistic.* The family/clan French Canadians are not the same as the family/clan English-speaking Canadians, and they all differ from the western provinces. The best approach is to use a modified French approach in Quebec, a modified English approach in Ontario, and the general individualists' approach for the provinces.

*The French Modified Plan:* The French protocol plan is modified to reflect a more relaxed and pragmatic approach to business. French Canadians are somewhat less cynical than the French, but are focused on their fight to preserve their culture.

- All presentation materials should be printed in both French and English. Assume that you will be speaking French or using an interpreter.
- French Canadians are less reserved than the English-speaking Canadians. They tend to use more gesturing. They may touch you while conversing.
- Use a reasonably firm handshake, and shake upon a first meeting, greetings, and departures.
- Use last names until your host switches to first. He may go back and forth.
- Eat continental style.

*English Modified Plan:* The modifications to the English approach generally remove some of the strictness of the social hierarchy. Canadians are less formal than Britons, but not as casual as the Americans. More emphasis is placed on one's ability and education. There is a greater sense of equality, but this is limited to the English-speaking majority.

## Important Information

A family/clan cultural approach should be followed for eastern Canada, and a more individualists' approach should be taken in the west. Crossing the cultural divide requires a plan made specific to the person with whom you will be meeting and the area in which he resides. Refer to the English and French profile for the needed approach. Alter your strategy slightly to reflect a more egalitarian social structure. In the west, self-interest will be more of a factor, as opposed to a group attitude. Be aware there are many other ethnic groups in Canada. There is a large group of Chinese from Hong Kong in Vancouver. Certainly, one should devise a plan that most suits the person with whom you will be meeting.

### Strictly Business

In business situations, maintain good posture. One can be more relaxed in social settings. Business gifts should be modest. Gifts are opened immediately. An invitation to a restaurant is considered a gift. Business meals are common. At dinner, wait for your host to bring up business.

### Supplemental Data

- Handshakes are firm. Shake upon greeting and introduction, but not upon leaving.
- Use last names when introduced. First names will be used very soon thereafter. Wait for your host to initiate this.
- English-Canadians are not comfortable touching or speaking at close range.
- Privacy is important.
- Eat continental style.

# Country Profile: Greece

## (Cultural Position: Family/Clan)

The major difference between this family/clan culture and other family/clan cultures of the Northern Mediterranean is its rejection of Rome as the seat of its religious allegiance. The factor that makes it different from Central European cultures is it is not Slavic and has not been dominated by Communism.

## Religious Factors

Greece is a traditional family/clan culture with a basic belief in the separation and personification of God. It is a predominantly Christian country, supporting the Greek Orthodox Church. But Greeks stand somewhere between the more abstract Latin interpretations of the relationship of man to God, and the more concrete and personalized expression of this relationship found in Orthodox Christianity.

## Governing Principles

Greeks tend to share behavioral traits with their Mediterranean neighbors, such as their tendency to act from emotion and subjectivity, greater use of nonverbal language as in hand gestures, their self-praise, their emphasis on hospitality, and a lax notion of time. They are more closely related to their northern *progressive family/clan* neighbors in their preference for a consensus power hierarchy, and not for strong authoritarianism as is the patristic Latin model. They value education and work. They are hard-working, yet are not pressured by time.

As a *family/clan culture,* Greece shares these basic social requirements with all family/clan cultures:

1. obligation to family
2. loyalty to friends and family
3. traditions that reinforce the social framework

## Important Information

Although throughout history Greece has been besieged by foreign invaders—from the Romans and Ottomans to Hitler and the threat of Communism—the country has always maintained its unique cultural identity and always returned to the guiding principle of democracy.

## Strictly Business

- Business cards should be printed in both Greek and English. Hand the card Greek side up, being sure that the writing is right side up.
- Dress conservatively.
- Presentations should include a variety of presentation techniques, many visual.
- Treat the senior member in a group with respect. Authority usually rests with him, although there is a need for consensus in decision-making groups.
- Expect to bargain and make quick decisions. Patience is important in negotiations, but be prepared to move quickly on a moment's notice.

## Greece Supplemental Data

- Relationship building is important, and friendship comes with obligation.
- Be punctual, even though your Greek counterpart will not be.
- Shake hands with a firm grip, and don't break away too quickly.
- Use last names and titles when introduced, showing special respect for older people.
- Language is often exaggerated and emotional.
- Meetings are often done over a cup of coffee. Informal meetings may be held in a coffeehouse.
- Lunch is the main meal of the day. Dinner is small and is served late.
- The communal approach is followed in some restaurants, where diners share several dishes.
- The head gestures indicating yes and no can be confusing because they are traditionally reversed in Greece.
- A smile can mean anger as well as pleasure.
- Don't give gifts at the first meeting.

# Country Profile: India

## (Cultural Position: Family/Clan, Group)

### Religious Factors

India must be understood in context with its religious beliefs. Hinduism is followed by more than 80 percent of the population, over 800 million people. Let's look at the governing principles for India by summarizing their religious beliefs.

The Indian perception of reality is quite mystical. Spirit is the true nature of reality. Matter exists as a result of spirit. It has no absolute existence on its own. The physical world exists solely as a medium in which the soul can improve itself and attain higher levels, eventually attaining oneness with God through absorption into Him.

The goal of human existence is liberation from suffering on earth. Suffering is caused by metaphysical ignorance, or not understanding the true spiritual nature of one's existence. Through an extensive series of reincarnated lives, the soul gains greater knowledge until finally it achieves the necessary knowledge of selflessness and is absorbed into the primordial oneness. The law of karma directs each successive life on earth. What you do or do not do in one life is accounted for in the next. One can progress as a result of actions, but one can also regress. The outward, physical evidence of a soul's level of advancement is the caste into which it is born.

Castes are a hierarchical arrangement of society, very similar to the rigid class systems of family/clan and group societies. Originally, there were four castes, and those who are below the castes are the outcasts or untouchables. Through the centuries, many subcastes were recognized. The original four castes parallel the Confucian system of a four-class society.

Liberation from suffering is possible at any level through the practice of yoga, in which the spirit learns its true nature. Lord Krishna guides and intercedes, allowing release by his grace. There is a belief in perfectibility, but its focus is on improvement of the soul, and not of one's physical condition. This is why we find the Indian culture to devalue physical life. One cannot change one's physical conditions, only one's spiritual condition. Spiritual concerns are more important than one's daily work. People's souls are more important than money. Power and authority are accepted as a privileged person's right.

## Governing Principles

India's culture is a blend of *family/clan* and group influences. The extended family is the most important unit of survival. This can be a very large group, bordering on a group. The strong sense of separateness in the family/clan cultures, resulting in a strong power hierarchy, is somewhat muted in India. There is also a sense of oneness and long-term perspective that is more a part of the holistic, group communities. In either case, one's identity is formed relative to the group. An appropriate term for a unit of the social structure is the "family/clan/group." Relative status is important, especially with regard to age. Indians defer to elders. The oldest member of the extended family is its head.

The British dominated India for 200 years. During this time, they transferred their system of etiquette to the upper castes. When dealing with top-ranking and professional Indians, English standards will be appropriate. One element, the use of time, raises some problems for the Indian. Their perceptions result in a nonlinear cyclical apprehension of time. The British system stresses punctuality, and this is right for business appointments. However, do not assume this sense of punctuality extends to the maintenance of schedules and development of plans.

## Communication Characteristics

*Transaction Characteristics:* Space is at a premium. Status is conferred by the servants or staff you have working for you and by a private dwelling or office space. Indians are hierarchical in their cultural approach. Contribution to the family group and spiritual awareness is where their greatest responsibility lies. An Indian believes that to do his work to benefit his family is a great accomplishment. Another requirement is a passive approach to the law of karma. The Indians place great emphasis on mutual support from the group and on those from other countries who come to serve and conduct business. Problems are embarrassing, negatives are minimized, and blame is not assigned. Solutions are approached by group support. When making decisions, the Indian will take a subjective approach over an objective one.

*Interaction Communication Characteristics:* The Indian communication style is similar to the British model with more formal dialogue; however, they tend to be friendlier and more interested in people. Indians do not like to say no and will say "I'll try" instead. The Indian needs to know where the foreigner fits into the social fabric. Once the person is identified relative to the group, he is not a threat.

Presentations should be visual as well as verbal. Content should be more concrete than abstract. The more educated the person is, the more analytically he thinks. Time is nonlinear. Schedules are not always followed because planning may be lax. The Indian appears adaptable to change because it happens so often. Plans must be adjusted to account for present conditions.

## PROTOCOL & ETIQUETTE

*Forms of Address:* Use titles when appropriate. Address someone in the formal manner using surname and last name.

Mr. is *Shri*
Mrs. is *Shreemati*
Miss is *Kumari*

*Greetings:* The traditional greeting in India is *Namaste.* Indians who are equals greet each other with "Hi" or "Hello."

*Handshakes:* When you greet an Indian, you will receive a short bow along with the palms together, fingers up, with palms close to the chin.

*Gestures:* Do not touch people with your hands or your feet. Do not use expansive gestures. Do not whistle.

*Appropriate Attire:* Traditional clothing is appropriate for the foreigner. Do not wear or carry leather accessories. The cow is sacred in India.

*View of Women:* Indian women today have made progress but in general, women still do not have the status that men do in society.

*Gift Giving:* Do not give anything made of leather. Chocolates or flowers are appropriate gifts when invited to a home. Make sure the flowers are not frangipani. These are considered funeral flowers. Do not bring anything that represents a dog because Indian Muslims consider dogs unclean. Do not wrap gifts in black and white. Wrap packages in primary colors. Do not open presents in front of the giver or expect him to open yours immediately.

*Dining:* You will find a mixture of dining habits including Western style. Some Indians eat their food using their right hand. To indicate you do not want any more food, place your palms, with fingers touching, under your chin and give a slight nod of the head.

## Interesting Information

Family structure figures prominently in Indian business. There are four types of private businesses: the affiliates of multinational companies; "large houses," major companies each controlled by a family; smaller family-run businesses; and companies set up by a partnership of technical professionals. In the family-owned and operated companies, the head of the family is usually the head of the company. Decisions are made at this level.

## Strictly Business

The Indian attitude favors the personal over the commercial. It is always important in family/clan and group societies to meet face to face. This lessens his resistance to you, and shows that you value the interaction. It is important to maintain contact with your Indian counterpart when you have returned home. Although Hindi is an official language, English is used in business. You need not translate your materials.

High-level businesspeople require some sort of reference before granting an appointment. It is important for these Indians to know your status and the status of your company. The best references come from banks, embassies, or professionals with whom they are acquainted. A personal introduction is the best way to get into a company.

Indians are modest and humble. Matching this demeanor is the best tactic. Respect is shown by the use of good manners, as defined by the British model. Formality of dress is also an indication of respect. Don't be ostentatious in dress or accessories. The Indian is not excessively materialistic and may be turned off.

Do not try to speed things up by any hint of a bribe or by demands and threats. Often the government is involved if the deal involves a significant amount of money, and dealing with the government takes time. Family-owned businesses move faster, but not as fast as American business. Don't expect results from the first meeting.

Bargaining is not common in India. The price offered should be close to the final deal. There should be some room for movement, but don't expect extended price negotiations. Other issues may require negotiation. Be prepared to respond to requests for secondary concessions.

The Indian's pride is usually derived from his education and occupation. These should be the focus for complimentary observations. Use academic titles when appropriate. Since Indians are not particularly materialistic, the benefits of making the deal should appeal to his sense of group involvement. He will be looking for business that will benefit his company, especially if you are dealing with one of the private, family-run businesses. Ultimately, this benefits his family/clan group.

## India Supplemental Data

- A medium-firm handshake is the proper greeting for business. You may see people greeting each other with the *namaste (Nah-mah-STAY),* which one does by placing the hands together as if in prayer, fingers pointing up, and bowing the head slightly.

- Use the last name, along with "Mr." It is not appropriate for a foreigner to use the term *sahib.*
- Don't shake a woman's hand unless she offers it. Men generally do not touch women in public. It is polite to refer to women as "ladies."
- A business card printed in English should be provided. Your card should have your title, academic degrees, and professional affiliations included. This will help the Indian position you in his universe.
- Be punctual. Your host may not be.
- Relationship is important, but the Indian will get down to business fairly quickly.
- Accept any hospitality offered.
- Social distance may be close, but touching is not common in conversation.
- British manners prevail. Be subdued. Self-control is favored over impulsiveness. A quietly self-confident aura breeds trust and respect. However, one should be friendly and communicative.
- Indians are tolerant of others. Be cautious in giving criticism. They take offense easily.
- Use the right hand when passing papers and objects, and when eating.
- Keep shoes and feet on the floor.
- Whistling is considered rude.
- Your first meeting should include the head of the company, who will probably make the final decision on your proposal. Always try to match the status of meeting participants. If you send your chief technical person, make your appointment with a technical person. Speak to the secretary of your targeted person to be sure you are contacting the right person at the appropriate level.
- A business lunch is appropriate after an interest in your business has been established. It is acceptable to talk business over the meal. Dinner invitations should be offered only after some sort of relationship has been established. Entertaining is usually done in

private clubs or in restaurants. The guest of honor should be seated to the right of the host. There is no toasting ritual. The traditional manner of eating is by using the right hand and no utensils. Hindis do not eat beef.

- Gifts are a sign of friendship. They should be modest and reserved for later meetings.
- There is a significant Muslim population, especially in the northern section of the country. Study the Arab Region section of this book for proper interaction with a Muslim.
- The caste system was legally abolished but it is so much a part of the Indian belief system that inequality is rarely challenged. Women, except in the highest caste, have had no power. They are legally equal, and if they choose to enter business, they are allowed to compete. Yet many women do not choose to work in business.

# Country Profile: Israel

## (Cultural Position: Family/Clan, Group)

Israel is perfectly suited as a model for our methodology of determining protocol. In the late nineteenth century, Theodor Herzl, an Austrian, began the Zionist movement, encouraging Jews to return to their spiritual homeland in Palestine. Modern Israel was created in 1948. Although held together by a shared religion—80 percent are Jewish—Israel's inhabitants came from many cultural backgrounds. Only 60 percent of the population is native to Israel. Business practices may be North American, Russian, European, or Mediterranean. Review the cultural profile of these regions before you venture to Israel.

Jews are usually divided into two ethnic heritages. Sephardic Jews come from the Mediterranean area, Northern Africa, and the Middle

East. Ashkenazic Jews come from Europe. The Ashkenazic Jews are dominant in politics and religion, and the Sephardic Jews are more present in government and business.

In terms of global protocol, the Ashkenazic Jews tend to show strong pluralist tendencies, while the Sephardic Jews are family/clan. The Jewish religion promotes, or rather, reflects, a family/clan perception. Even though some Ashkenazic Jews come from strong pluralist countries such as Germany and the Netherlands, their culture has always maintained the family/clan hierarchy. Protocol and etiquette support the needs of the family over the needs of the individual.

About 50 percent of the Jews in Israel are Orthodox Jews. It is interesting to note that they share many customs with Muslims. There are many strict laws about eating, general behavior, interaction between men and women, and details of appearance.

It is difficult to develop a player portrait that applies in general to an Israeli businessperson. The approach to Israel would be to study general family/clan culture and the discussions in this book about the Arab, Russian and Central European, and European cultures.

The plan for a Sephardic contact is similar to that of the Arab position. Things happen slowly. There is not much regard for time. People and their problems and concerns are more important than striking a deal. It will take many meetings to complete a deal. Spatial attitude is also similar to the Arab. People stand close together and touch to emphasize a point. Israelis put a high regard on hosting, as do Arabs. Coffee is served at the end of a business meeting, as in Muslim countries. Control of the body in posture and gestures is similar to the Arab game plan.

The plan to use for Ashkenazic contacts is more European in style. Punctuality is important. Formality and reserve are noted. People tend to get down to business faster. But don't disregard the family/clan tendencies of this group. They still maintain strong hierarchical structure and must come to trust a person before doing business with them.

The major differences in business customs between Israel and other Middle Eastern countries are the following:

- Israel is a democratic and egalitarian culture that values competition.
- The Israeli negotiating style is much more confrontational. They love to argue and debate.
- Women are legally equal in status and even serve in the military. Men still dominate, as in all family/clan societies.
- The security of the state is taken into consideration when making major decisions.
- The holy days are Friday and Saturday each week. Judaism and Islam both use lunar calendars. Israelis are used to thinking in twenty-eight-day months.
- Use engraved business cards. Print them in both English and Hebrew (Arabic, if you are visiting an Israeli Arab).
- Businesswomen should not extend their hand to greet an Orthodox Jewish male. His religion has laws against touching women. She should also never hand something directly to him, but put it next to him so he can pick it up. Orthodox Jews can usually be identified by their yarmulkes, or skullcaps. Half of Israel's Jews are considered secular and do not observe these rituals.
- The common greeting is to shake hands and address the person using a courtesy title plus the surname. *Shalom,* which means peace, is said when greeting and leaving.
- Conservative business suits are appropriate, and in general, modest dress is required.
- The continental style of eating is most widely used.
- Pointing at someone with the index finger is rude, as in most of the world beyond America.

## Mission Trip Tip

- Watch your jargon.
- Have a strategy for each mission trip.
- Allow yourself plenty of time and then some.

# 8. International Dining Guide in Detail

## Dining with Finesse

The objective of dining finesse is not merely to eat. If it were, we would all simply fill our stomachs and leave the table without a word to anyone. No, dining is definitely an art form. The greater the differences between your culture and that of your dining partner, the more exciting and challenging the activity will be.

Even among people of the same culture, dining is about position, skill, and honor. These three elements are evident in every group dining experience.

1. Position refers to where one sits and the importance derived from that location. Most cultures have some sort of seating hierarchy that places the most important person in the seat of honor relative to the host or hostess.

2. Skill comes into play in the method of eating: the utensils used and the use of the hands and body. It is important to be skillful so as not to be perceived as inexperienced.
3. Honor is the interplay of giving and receiving hospitality. Some cultures require much gamesmanship in the interaction of host and guest.

The purpose of dining protocol is the same as the purpose of any culture-based protocol: to promote and protect the basic beliefs of that culture. Dining protocol in each of the three major cultures—family/clan, group, and individualist—reflects the underlying value system.

- The family/clan dining method reflects the communal aspects of the culture.
- The group approach stresses symbolism and ritual.
- The individualistic method is more pragmatic and egalitarian.

Protocol also has a purpose, and that is to communicate information about the people with whom you interact and to show respect and define limits within the relationship. So we are back to the original three rules of global finesse:

1. Never judge. Show respect.
2. Never try to become like someone else (define limits), or try to make him become like you (trust).
3. Never forget that business is about people. Communicate.

The purpose of eating together when conducting business is not to extend the business meeting through mealtime. It is an opportunity to cross the cultural divide. Two (or more) people who are eager to satisfy different desires come together during a meal with a common goal and interest. They share a general behavior in the utensils they use; they give and take freely among themselves in the giving and receiving of hospitality or the passing of bread and salt. Conversation is no longer at cross purposes, but becomes an enjoyable interchange in association with the pleasure of eating. This is an extension of the depth of a relationship, in communicating equality and respect, and in repairing any overt hostility that may have come out during a meeting. However, if the dining situation is not played according to the rules, more harm may be done than good. Dining protocol is important to your Christian service.

## Importance of Position

The most commonly used seating arrangements in Western society are the French and the British methods. Both arrangements assume that the dining table will be rectangular or oblong, creating two long sides with a head and foot at each end. Social and business seating protocol are different. Let's look at the social arrangement first.

*Seating Arrangements—French Method of Position:* In the French method, the most important people—the host and hostess—sit at the center of each long side, facing each other. The most important male guest sits to the right of the hostess, the most important female guest sits to the right of the host, the next most important male guest sits to the hostess's left, and the second most important female guest sits to the left of the host. Men and women alternate in this way, with the least important guests seated farthest from the hosts. No one sits at the ends of the table.

*Seating Arrangements—British Method of Position:* In the British method, the host and hostess sit at the foot and at the head of the table. The most important male guest sits to the right of the hostess, the second most important male guest to her left. The most important female guest sits to the right of the host, and the second most important female guest sits to his left. Male and female alternate this way, with the least important diners at the center of each side.

Note how important it is to be paired off into couples. A single male or female guest will throw off the whole arrangement. The American objection to the use of such strict arrangements is that inequality of importance is highlighted. When one entertains his boss or wants to show additional respect to an exceptional guest or client, the hierarchical seating arrangement offers the opportunity to communicate respect. But among friends, most Americans drop any strict seating rules.

In business dining, the operative principle is to achieve your goal: honor your important guest and seat him next to you or as close as possible so you can influence and enter into the conversation. In the French method, the hostess is replaced by a co-host or second in command. The side-central seating is maintained, with the most important guest to the right of the primary host. The second most important guest is seated to the right of the co-host. If all goes well, these two pairs will be of similar rank. In the British method, the highest-ranking guest sits to the right of the host and the second-ranking guest sits to the right of the co-host. If the group is small and there is no co-host, the second most important guest should be seated to the host's left in either method.

*Seating Arrangements—Asia Importance of Position:* In Asia, tables are often circular or square. The most-honored guest is seated facing the door. In China, the host will sit opposite him with his back to the door. In ancient times, this symbolically indicated the host knew of no planned attack, and was not afraid to have his back to the entrance. The guest, on the other hand, could see an attack coming. The second most important guest will sit to the left of the most important guest, the next most important guest, to the primary guest's right, and so on, so that the host is seated humbly between the two least important guests. The Japanese arrangement is the same, with the host in the least desirable location. At a long banquet table, the host would sit in the middle or the side, with the honored guest to his right, the next important to his left, etc. Women do not figure into the arrangement because at important dinners, the women often eat separately.

*Seating Arrangements—Middle East Importance of Position:* In the Middle East, seating is usually circular, but not necessarily around a table. Guests may sit on the floor. Communal bowls are usually placed at the center, equidistant from the diners. In this culture, someone's right-hand side is the preferred side, since the left hand is considered unclean. Therefore, it is easy to remember to seat the most important guest to the right of the host. Women usually eat separately.

## The Importance of Skill

There are three aspects of skill:

1. eating with cutlery
2. eating with chopsticks
3. eating with the hands

Eating with cutlery implies cutting, which is the distinguishing mark of this method. Continental style is the most dominant form of this type of eating. The entire Western world uses this method with the one exception, the United States, where we eat "zigzag." Your refined American table manners that your mother took great pains to teach you will make you look like a backwoodsman in any country that uses the continental style.

Eating with chopsticks precludes the need to cut food. All cutting is done in the kitchen, and only bite-sized pieces are served.

Whichever method you use, commit to it. Don't switch between American and continental style during a meal. To develop any skill, you must practice. Before traveling overseas, practice the method you will be using so you will appear polished and confident.

*American Style Cutlery Skill:* To cut, the fork is held in the left hand, tines down. The knife is held in the right hand and only used to cut. Both index fingers point down the utensils. After a piece is cut, the knife is rested across the side of the plate with the blade toward the center of the plate. The fork is switched to the right hand to eat the piece of food, tines up.

The fork remains in the right hand unless it is necessary to cut a piece of food.

The resting position is with knife along the edge of the plate and the fork in the center of the plate.

To signal that you are finished, place both knife and fork together, pointing toward the left side of the plate.

Napkins are kept in the lap.

When only the fork is being used, the left hand should be placed in the lap.

## CONTINENTAL STYLE OF DINING

*Continental Service:* There are four continental methods of serving the meal:

1. Service *a la francaise* requires you to serve yourself from a platter held to your left by a servant. Use the serving fork and spoon together and replace them on the tray next to each other when finished. This is the highest form of service and the least economical.
2. Service *a l'anglaise* allows a servant to serve you from a platter on your left.
3. Service *a la russe* presents the main course in one piece on a platter, usually on a cart beside the table. The meat is carved in front of the guests and a waiter places a plate in front of each guest. Often the cooking is completed at the table in this way, perhaps with a flaming sauce.
4. *American* service provides a complete serving on individual plates straight from the restaurant kitchen to the guest.

*Continental Style Cutlery:* The fork is held in the left hand with the tines facing down and the knife is held in the right hand. The knife is used to push the food onto the back to the fork.. The forefinger of each hand points down the utensil. The tines of the fork always face down. One does not cut and then put the knife down. Hold the food with the fork, and cut and push with the knife.

More than one food may be placed on the fork at one time, e.g., potatoes with a bite of meat.

Eat the food off the back of the fork. Don't twist the fork in your hands so that the tines face up as it enters your mouth.

The utensils for the fish course, which precedes the meat course, are handled a bit differently. The fish knife, which is broad and flat, is held like a pencil, not with the index finger in a position to push down for cutting. This is because the fish knife does more scooping than cutting if the fish is cooked properly. The fork is held in the left hand, tines down, with a gentler grip; the thumb and index finger extending to the same point, forming an O.

Salad is eaten with a knife and fork, using the knife to fold the lettuce onto the fork tines. Do not cut the lettuce.

The resting position is crossing the knife and fork with the tines of the fork pointing down on top of the knife. They form an angle of 90 degrees at the bottom of your plate. Don't leave your utensils like this at the end of the meal, because it signals the waiter that you are not done.

While in the rest position, keep your hands visible by resting your wrists on the edge of the table. Never rest your hands in your lap.

Do not use your personal butter knife for serving butter to your bread plate. Use the knife on the butter dish. Use your butter knife to butter one bite-sized piece of bread at a time. Your bread plate is to your left.

For a meal consisting of several courses, your place setting will have more than one fork, spoon, and knife. They are usually arranged with the utensils for the first course at the outer edges. Work your way in toward the plate.

Soup is eaten by spooning the soup away from you toward the center of the bowl. Eat the soup by sipping it from the side of the spoon. Do not place your other hand in your lap. Rest your wrists on the edge of the table.

Note that in Europe, the salad is served after the main course, and so the salad fork and knife will be placed closest to the plate.

The dessert fork and spoon are placed at the top of your place setting. In very formal service, the dessert spoon and fork will arrive on a plate with a doily and a small bowl of water: your finger bowl. Remove the fork to the left and the spoon to the right. Place the doily and the bowl to your upper left.

When dessert is served, use only the fork, if it is cake or pie, and only the spoon for ice cream or pudding. For anything else, use the spoon in your right hand and the fork in your left hand. The spoon is used to cut and raise food to your mouth. The fork is used to push the food onto your spoon.

When your dessert dish is removed, place the finger bowl and doily in front of you. Dip the fingertips of one hand at a time, drying one hand before dipping the other, patting the fingertips on your napkin. (Note: in Europe, the term for napkin is *serviette.* A napkin is a diaper.)

Wait until everyone is finished and the host and hostess make the suggestion to leave the table—only when you are finished. If you need to leave the table during a meal, the napkin is placed on the arm or seat of the chair.

Knife and fork are placed parallel to each other on the plate, pointing left, fork tines up.

Place your napkin to the left side of your plate before leaving the table.

## Dining Chinese Style (Chopsticks):

Tables are round or square, and guests sit equidistant from the serving dishes, which are placed on a revolving tray in the middle of the table.

Communal dishes of meat, fish, and vegetables are placed in the center. These are considered merely condiments. The real dinner is the rice.

Each person is given a small bowl of rice. The rice bowl is always accepted with two hands, not just one. Never eat the other foods before the rice is served, or you will be thought greedy.

When the host gives a signal, the guests may take food from the central serving dishes. There may be special serving chopsticks in some countries. Often, you just use your own chopsticks to take food. Use the larger end for dipping into serving dishes. Place the food in your rice bowl or directly into your mouth.

Chopsticks are never used to pierce the food. If cutting is necessary, one should prod the food until its natural fissures are exposed and it falls apart.

Chopsticks are held between the first three fingers. The bottom stick is held still while the top stick is maneuvered against it.

Never leave the chopsticks sticking into your rice. When resting, place them against the chopstick rest or across the top of the bowl. Never lick or bite the chopsticks to remove food stuck to them. Do not search through the serving dish with your chopsticks. Eat the piece in front of you. Do not grip single pieces of rice between chopsticks. The rice is sticky, and is lifted by the sticks to your mouth.

Hold the rice bowl in your left hand throughout the meal. When every last grain of rice is consumed, this indicates that you are done. Leaving rice in the bowl shows a lack of appreciation for the effort that people have made in producing the rice.

Don't pour sauces into your rice bowl. Use sauces for dipping.

All the common dishes should be shared equally. It is bad manners to look as though you favor one food over another. Try everything.

At the end of the meal, place your chopsticks side by side on the rest or the side of the bowl, not on the table.

At a Chinese banquet, the distinction between the lavish banquet and a normal meal is made by minimizing the importance of the rice. Meat, fish, and vegetables are now the important foods. Rice may not be served at all until the end of the meal. If you ask for rice, it means that you are through eating. Banquets could consist of twelve to twenty courses. Don't eat very much at the beginning.

The host should be praised excessively during the banquet.

*Japanese Variations:* Before the meal, hot towels are passed to the guests to wipe their hands. Some men also wipe their faces. Women do not. Napkins are not used during the meal.

Each person receives a tray with a rice bowl on the left, a soup bowl on the right (both of these bowls are covered), and an entree dish at the top. Remove the bowl covers to the left and right of the tray. Dishes remain on the tray, unless you pick one up to eat.

Start with the soup, lifting it to your mouth to drink a portion, then picking out a morsel from the broth with your chopsticks. Soup spoons are not provided.

Next, pick up the rice bowl and eat a small amount. The rice bowl will remain in your hand throughout the meal, only setting it down to pick up the soup bowl. The rice and the soup should last through the meal. All food should be paced to finish at the same time.

Leave a little rice in your bowl to receive more. You should eat at least two bowls of rice during a meal.

When eating noodles, it is good to slurp them in while sucking air.

If the host passes you a tray, put your rice bowl onto it to be refilled.

Save the pickles for the end of the meal.

Replace the covers on your rice bowl and soup bowl when you are done.

*Korean Variations:* When eating, don't raise the rice bowl or any other bowl to your mouth.

Soup spoons are provided. Place the soup spoon in your soup bowl or over your rice bowl, not on the table.

Don't completely clean your plate. This implies that your host did not provide enough food.

If you want seconds, refuse twice and accept the third time. If you are hosting, always offer food three times.

*Middle Eastern Variations:* Traditional Middle Eastern seating is on the floor with communal dishes at the center. Individual dishes are not always provided. Be sure the soles of your shoes do not face anyone.

Before the meal, a servant may bring a pitcher and a bowl. This is for washing your hands in full view of everyone, so everyone knows your hands are clean.

Eat with your right hand, keeping your left hand behind you.

Sauces are often provided for dipping bread.

The quantity of food will be huge. This is to show the guest that the host is not skimpy. Sometimes the tablecloth is removed after each course. To get an idea of how much food to expect, count the tablecloths.

Take food from the edge of the plate, rather than the center, or you might burn your hand.

Someone may put a choice piece of food on your plate (if there are plates). If you don't want it, you don't have to eat it.

Never reach beyond your space of the communal dish.

If you are not given a spoon to eat couscous, take a small handful and form it into a ball, then pop it into your mouth without touching your lips. Your hand will be returning to the communal dish!

Wipe your fingers on a piece of bread between bites. Lick your fingers only at the end of a meal to indicate you are done.

Don't clean your plate or you will insult your host. Leave a small amount.

Refuse second helpings several times before accepting.

## The Importance of Honor

The social function of dining is not only for the purpose of honoring a guest. Sharing a meal requires sharing the honors. Giving does not flow in one direction. The host gives food and honor to his guest; in return, the host receives praise and obligation from his guest. The host of a family/clan or group culture will entertain lavishly, providing more food than anyone needs, to show he is not stingy and that the guest is important. In so doing, he elevates himself and the guest. He expects to receive the same degree of hospitality in return. If he does not, this is a serious offense. The guest who does not reciprocate is greedy, selfish, and thoughtless of others. This is cause for excommunication from the tribe or group as it goes against the very basic values of the culture.

The individualistic cultures outwardly maintain the equality of the individual host and guest. They are equally important. The host and hostess sit in the most prominent locations, able to control the event from their "thrones." They surround themselves with the most interesting and honored guests. The hostess is served first, and all wait until she begins. The host and hostess do not humble themselves to their guests. It is quite the opposite. They maintain their position of honor and invite their guests to join them in that honor. Praise is not necessary. In fact, to some, praise would be an insult, implying that they are surprised to be served such a good meal. A simple thank-you is required, but praise is not. A diner should finish all his food as a compliment to the chef.

In family/clan and group cultures, there is an elaborate and symbolic dance of humility. The host offers the food. The guest declines. The host offers again. The guest refuses again. The host insists. The guest accepts. Never for a minute did anyone doubt that the guest would accept in the end, but to accept right away would appear greedy and self-centered. This "dance" applies to who walks through the dining room door first, who sits in the seat of honor, who takes the first serving from the common bowl, who takes the last serving from the bowl. The guest of honor does. When he eventually gives way and accepts these honors, he must praise the host effusively for his hospitality and insist upon his unworthiness. It is not enough to behave correctly and thank the host. The guest must convince everyone that he is truly impressed.

## More Dining Tips

Here are a few more dining tips that will prevent you from offending any family/clan or group host and being branded as an unappreciative guest:

- Accept the food as presented. Do not add salt or other seasoning, except for sauces. (In some pluralist cultures, salt is acceptable since individual tastes are valid.)
- Try everything. Never decline what is offered to you, unless it is so unusual that it might make you ill. In that case, make up a medical reason for declining.
- The locals in many cultures may not believe that eating quietly is good manners. Slurping, smacking, and belching all may be compliments to the host, indicating that the meal is being enjoyed. You, however, should not join in too exuberantly.
- Finishing everything on your plate implies that you have room for more, and that your host did not feed you enough.
- Business discussions have no place during a display of hospitality. Your host may bring up business after dessert, but you should never initiate a business discussion over a meal.

## Managing the Food

There are two categories of foods that should be avoided when hosting and should be anticipated for when visiting:

1. foods that are hard to eat
2. foods that are hard to swallow.

There is a difference. Foods that are hard to eat include artichokes, clams, corn –on –the cob, and spaghetti. Foods that are hard to swallow include monkey's brains, sheep's eyeballs, and stir-fried bees. One American traveler was entertained in Vietnam at a restaurant where the menu was kept in cages outside. The choices included cats, turtles, snakes, dogs, and other small creatures. The blood sauce was not euphemistically referred to as *au jus.*

The first rule of the game is not to judge another culture as being better or worse than your own. This applies to food as well. The best strategy is not to ask what it is, swallow it quickly, cut it into small pieces, and pretend it's chicken. Otherwise, pretend to eat by pushing the food around on your plate. In Asian cultures, you could try declining certain foods on the grounds that you are not worthy to eat whatever it is.

Also, consider that other cultures find some of our foods repulsive. The list includes corn (which others feed to animals only), grits, marshmallows, peanut butter, pecan or pumpkin pie, and commercially processed white bread. When hosting, consider the guest's normal diet. Avoid serving foods that are so traditionally American that they border on disgusting or boring.

Also, when hosting or ordering in a restaurant, avoid hard-to-manage foods. If you are served difficult foods, here is a selected short list of what to do.

- Artichokes: Whole artichokes are eaten with the fingers. Each leaf is pulled off one at a time; the soft part dipped in sauce then scraped off with the teeth. Place the remainder of the leaf on the side of the plate. Do not eat the leaf. When the leaves have been pulled off, the center thistle is removed by fork and knife. The heart, at the very bottom, is cut and eaten with a fork.

- Celery and radishes: Take them from the serving dish with your hands and eat them with your fingers.
- Caviar: Spread it on toast along with crumbled egg and other condiments if you like. Eat the caviar on toast held in your hand.
- Oysters, mussels, and clams: When served on the half shell, they are held by the shell in one hand and removed from the shell with a small oyster fork. Dip into sauce and eat in one bite.
- Soft-boiled eggs: Served in an egg cup, they are eaten out of the shell. Slice the top off with a knife.
- Fruit with seeds or pits: These can be eaten with the hands, removing the pits from your mouth by placing your hand over your mouth, dropping the pits into your cupped hand, and placing them on the side of your plate. In continental dining, most fruit is eaten with fork and knife. Follow the lead of your host or hostess.
- Pate de foie gras: Place on a piece of toast or bread with your knife and eat with your hands.
- Spaghetti: Use a fork to pull out a few strands at a time. Twirl them around your fork against the edge of the plate or bowl.
- Baked potatoes: Eat them from the skin with a fork. Do not mash them first. Place butter on the potato by taking butter from your own bread plate with your dinner knife. Do not use your dinner knife to take butter from the butter serving dish.
- Shrimp cocktail with the tails on: Hold by the tail with your fingers, dip into sauce, bite off the shrimp and discard the tail on your plate.
- Snails: If tongs are provided, hold the shell with the tongs. Otherwise, use your hand. Pull the snail out with the oyster fork. Eat it in one bite. The extra garlic butter sauce may be soaked up by a piece of bread.

## When Alcohol Is Served

Dining hosts may serve various wines and or other alcohol beverages. There will be toasts and certainly there is a protocol which one needs to be aware so as not to offend your host. One does not have to sip the wine or taste the alcohol beverages but neither should a visitor use this platform to preach the evils of alcohol. Let's look at the various protocol issues of the service of wine.

1. If the wine glasses are on the table, allow the first glass of wine to be poured. There will be a toast by the host, so the proper thing to do is raise your glass for the toast. One does not have to taste the wine or even pretend to taste it. Simply raise your glass in response to the toast. If the toast was in your honor, you do not have to raise the glass. All others at the table do. When a toast is given in a person's honor, the receiver has to reciprocate. When glasses are refilled, all that is necessary for the guest to do if he does not want his glass to be refilled is to simply place the forefinger of the rim of the glass.
2. People never pour their own drinks. Watch your neighbor's glass and refill it when it is dry. If there is some beverage left, do not refill the glass. Always lift your glass when someone pours for you.
3. A white wine goblet and champagne goblet are held by the stem. A red wine goblet is held by the bowl of the glass.
4. In Japan, sake, a potent rice wine, is served hot before the meal. It is poured into tiny ceramic cups and held with the right hand, supported by the left hand. It is polite to fill one another's cups.
5. If the host or a guest asks why you're not drinking, simply say you don't drink because of religious convictions or medical reasons. When you know in advance that drinking is part of the culture and you will be expected to partake, tell your hosts before you arrive and your reason for that decision.

## Dining Key Points

Dining is a game of position, skill, and honor.

Most cultures have some seating hierarchy that places the most important guest in a seat of honor relative to the host.

There are three types of skills: eating with cutlery, eating with chopsticks, and eating with the hands.

The game of honor is played between the host and the guest, with the interplay of giving and receiving. Some cultures raise this to a ritual.

Avoid serving or ordering foods that are difficult to eat and foods that are difficult to stomach.

# 9. Hosting the Foreign Internationalist on Home Turf

To some people of the world, such as the Chinese and the Russians, a business trip to the United States is a prestigious event. To others, it is an ordeal. Travelers around the world vary in their acceptance of novelty. If the traveler is not very adventurous and does not speak English, a trip to the United States can be very tiring. Working in another culture causes stress and distractions. If you hope your visitor will be productive while in the United States, it is to your benefit to see that he is well taken care of and that difficulties are minimized.

## Little Things May Cause a Glitch

Do you think that it is an advantage for you to interact with foreigners on familiar territory? It may not be. Often, when we are taken out of our comfort zone, our antennae go up. The very fact the surroundings are unusual and another language is being spoken prompts us to pay attention to small details that we might never notice at home. How often do you walk into your church, club, or work and think about how you will greet others? When someone walks into your office, do you offer him or her a chair? You probably just expect him or her to sit down. How many people do you refer to by nickname? We don't pay much attention to the customs of our own culture until we are asked to look at it through the eyes of a foreigner.

It is wise to take a look at your home environment, your church environment, your place of work, and your everyday behavior in light of the foreigner's expectations and cultural needs. Each major culture type presents a list of basic needs. The Asian must never be criticized and must always save face. The Arab must feel safe and in control and be able to fulfill the requirements of his religion. The northern European must be able to accomplish his goals without distraction or interference. Even when traveling, we each take with us our minimum cultural requirements. Are your visitor's needs likely to be met in your daily environment? If not, he will feel his basic needs are at risk.

Before a guest who is unfamiliar with your protocol and etiquette arrives, take these steps:

1. Look through your protocol mirror with a different perspective.
2. Have an objective.
3. Have a strategy and plan.

## WHOSE PROTOCOL RULES DO YOU USE?

Whose rules do you want to use? Yours make the most sense—or do they? It's much less work to use that with which you are familiar. But are you likely to build the relationship if you insist your rules be used? Let's assume you have already been to your guest's country, you studied his culture and protocol, and you behaved according to his expectations to show respect and to bring down the barriers between your two cultures. You have established some kind of relationship. That relationship was based on his comfort level working with you in his culture. If he arrives on your turf and you change the rules, do you think he might reconsider whether to continue the relationship?

When the rules of behavior change, you may have to start things all over again and establish trust, respect, and communication. Keep in mind just because the protocol has changed does not mean you have.

## Plan of Action

In planning events for your guest, you should not only consider the activity's objective, but also the underlying message that the form of the activities suggests.

- Will the event be casual or formal?
- Will you invite your guest to dinner at your home or at an expensive restaurant?
- What message do you want to communicate?
- Will you meet in your office? Or should you meet in a formal conference room? Is the meeting room at your office sufficient, or should you arrange for an elegant meeting room at a hotel?
- Will your family be included in the planned events?
- Are you expecting other members of their family to travel with your guest/s?
- If this is in connection with your Christian ministry, will there be church services, meetings, social gatherings, or other events?
- Will your guest/s want to explore your city with you or alone?
- When you entertain in a restaurant, what kind of cuisine will or will not be appropriate?
- How are you going to handle expected and unexpected introductions?

## Informing the Home Team

You may have been on your own when first meeting your counterpart abroad, or you may have been accompanied by others. When you invite your foreign guest to your turf, there are more participants on your side, such as your family, church staff, and members of your congregation. Consider this cadre of people as novices. They were not with you when you ventured abroad. They did not prepare as you did. They do not know the protocols or the people.

These participants can help you achieve your goal or hinder or reverse your progress. The respect they show you will not be lost on the visitor. And remember, your guest will be evaluating that respect relative to the norms in his own culture. For example, if your guest is Asian and your secretary is constantly interrupting you with requests, or calls you by your first name or a nickname, or makes a joke about your choice of tie, your guest will not be impressed by the degree of respect your secretary shows you.

Similarly, if you show your counterpart respect but not those below you in status, the message he receives will be mixed. Every person with whom he is likely to come in contact should be alerted as to the proper behavior to accomplish your team goals. Do not merely inform these people how to act, but explain why you would like them to behave in this way.

Consider whether you will need an interpreter and, if so, what you expect from this person. When people come to the United States, we often assume they will speak English. This is a burden to many visitors, especially people who did not learn English in school.

## Appoint a Liaison

A member of your team should be designated as the liaison person who will see to all arrangements for the visitor before he arrives and who will escort and support the guest while he is in the United States. If your guest does not speak English, it would be wise to hire your interpreter to perform this crucial role. If language is not a problem, then assign a person from your church, ministry, or office. It would be wise to choose a male for this role if your visitor is Asian, Latin American, or Arab. This will save both people from the obvious potential for miscommunication of intent. It will also make the foreign visitor's conduct toward this person less confusing, since American businesswomen will not (and should not) behave the same way in which a woman in his culture would behave toward him. Your liaison should work with the visitor's support staff in making arrangements prior to travel. Ask your counterpart to designate one liaison person on his side that your person can contact with all questions.

## Governing Principles for Hosting Visitors

*He will be coming to your turf.* Your visitor may bring his own cultural attitudes, or may leave them behind. Judgments he is likely to bring along include:

1. the definition of correct table manners
2. the definition of hospitality
3. his status-conscious protocol
4. his expectations of Americans

Be aware and prepared that tribal players, when away from the family/clan, may feel that they are not constrained by expected behavior and may do things they would never do at home.

## Approach as a Friend

Your guest may no longer be a stranger, but is he a friend? If you are still in the early stages of the relationship, you will probably not yet qualify as a friend by his standards. Be aware that in the United States, we tend to treat everyone as a friend. It is important to maintain the level of formality with which you interacted in his country. Let him continue to set the terms of the relationship.

You can show him that he is accepted in your hometown by surrounding him with friendly faces. Mutual friends or acquaintances, especially from his home country, could be invited to non-business functions, if appropriate. Notify his local consulate of his visit, if possible. The consulate may extend a special welcome. Provide an interpreter with whom he can speak easily and a liaison person upon whom he can depend.

## Humble Yourself

The guest always does the host an honor by his visit. The host humbles himself by providing hospitality for the guest. Refer to the previous chapters to be sure you use his definition of hospitality. To an Arab, this may mean that if you do not offer him three different meat entrees, you are stingy. Reciprocate the hospitality that you would receive in his country.

## Elevate Your Guest's Self-Worth.

Make your guest feel important in these ways:

- Make hotel reservations in advance. Pre-register him if possible. (Make it clear before the trip who will be paying.)
- Meet with the hotel staff and alert them to your visitor's special needs. If possible, stay at the hotel before your guest arrives so that you can anticipate any problems that might arise.
- Have flowers (appropriate number and color), a fruit basket, or candy in the room before his arrival.
- Have the liaison person meet him at the airport and handle baggage and transportation. Do not leave this to a limousine driver.
- Have the hotel provide him with his local newspaper, or one in his language, each morning if possible.
- Fly the flag of his country at your church or office.

- Always use china coffee cups and saucers, never plastic. Don't use tea bags. Find his usual beverage. (Wouldn't you have appreciated a cup of American coffee at his office?)
- Have a photographer take commemorative photos of the visit after checking in advance with his liaison to be sure this is appropriate.
- During meetings and when entertaining, be sure to pay attention to the seating arrangement. Most cultures have a prescribed seat for the guest of honor. Plan ahead your seating arrangements for meetings and restaurants and entertaining in your home.
- The greatest honor you can give a person in most family/clan or group cultures is to invite him to your home. Most foreigners would love to see how Americans live. It also shows the desire for friendship, an indication of trust, and further lowering of barriers. (One tip: household pets should not be invited to meet the guest, unless your visitor has expressed interest in your pet.) Brief your family on appropriate cross-cultural expectations as you did your staff at the church or office.

## Make Your Purpose His Welfare

- Consider his dietary restrictions and normal diet. Don't serve heavy sauces if his diet is simple. Don't serve pork if he is an Arab or Orthodox Jew, or beef if he is Hindu.
- Check with his liaison for any allergies or medical needs.
- If he smokes, consider how you will handle this if you work in a smoke-free environment.
- Give him access to your office communications so he can stay in touch with his office.
- Minimize his sense of insecurity in your culture. Take care of him personally. Don't assume he wants to be on his own to explore; ask.
- Ask what he would like to do while in the United States. Accommodate him whenever possible.

## SUPPLEMENTAL DATA

Here are notes for three specific cultures, each representing a major culture type.

*Germany*

- Be punctual at all times. Provide an agenda and start and end your meetings at the stated time.
- Advise your secretary, receptionist, and others that they will need to stand for the guest when introduced to him, and to greet him with a firm handshake each day when arriving and when leaving.
- Gift giving is not necessary.
- Allow the German guest sufficient time to explore on his own.
- In a home, the guest should be seated to the right of the hostess.

*Saudi Arabia*

- Make sure no food or sauces are prepared with pork.
- Provide a place where a Muslim may pray five times a day. Be observant of his prayer schedule when planning meetings. Check with his liaison.
- Do not rush meetings, and do not be upset if he is late. Notify drivers not to expect him to be on time.
- If he greatly admires a possession of yours in his culture you are expected to give it to him. It will not likely come up, but be aware of the custom and plan a response. He will be obligated to reciprocate.
- Provide bottled water, fruit, and olives in his hotel room.
- Tell stories, legends, or fables that are germane to your region.
- Instruct your staff, especially your female staff, about what to expect when being introduced to an Arab. Advise your team that he may stand close to them when speaking, and that they should not back away. Women should not be physically close. They will have to extend their hand first to shake hands when introduced.

- Provide him a place to smoke.
- When dinner is over, end the evening soon thereafter.
- If dining at home, be sure to offer food three times or your guest may starve. He will refuse twice before accepting.
- Do not offer alcohol or prepare any sauces with alcohol.
- Do not give him an expensive gift that could be considered a bribe.

*Japan*

- Do not serve cream sauces. Japanese have a low tolerance for lactose.
- Suggest that your visitor send you in advance menus and recipes he would like your chef to prepare.
- Serve good quality beef and melon when entertaining. These are very expensive in Japan.
- Take him to the best restaurant or club in your town, not one with "character."
- Be specific about the appropriate dress code. "Casual" has different meanings around the world.
- Have a photo taken of the entire delegation in front of your church or company with the church name or company logo and yourself visible. Give it as a memento.
- If you entertain the visitor in your home, he will want to meet your family and have photos taken with you and your family.

## A Warning Regarding Colors

Many Americans underestimate the psychological power of color. Many of the more symbolic cultures have clear meanings associated with colors. One American company lost a deal with an Asian company by decorating a ballroom in black and white. Here are a few pointers:

- Black and white represents death in Asian countries.
- Purple symbolizes death in Mexico and Brazil.

- Blue, representing heaven, is the color associated with death in Syria.

When hiring an event planner or hotel designer to decorate for a function, ask that person to research color and other symbolism regarding your visitor's culture. It could be a very important decision.

## HOSTING SUMMARY

- If you have already met with your visitor in his country, do not change the rules when he arrives on your turf. It will be too confusing.
- Plan an agenda to accomplish your goals.
- Determine who will be on the home team.
- Notify *all* employees whenever a foreign visitor is arriving. Do not merely inform them how to act, but explain *why.*
- Some person should be designated as a liaison who will see to all arrangements for the visitor before he travels and will escort and support him while he is in the United States. Make sure that you or the liaison takes care of all arrangements and every detail at the airport, hotel, and office.

# Appendix: Alphabetical Country-by-Country Summary

## Quick Country Reference Guide

The following pages serve as a quick reference guide to many individual nations. Determine which major culture type the country falls under and follow the methodology presented in previous chapters.

The listings are arranged alphabetically. For each listing, there will be important information regarding culture, local factors that may modify the culture as categorized with emphases on primary motivations, plan of action, and protocol and etiquette guidelines. This brief information will give you a cultural orientation so you will have the essential knowledge you need to be effective in your travels, service, or business. Refer to the background information for the culture group listed before arriving at your destination.

## ARGENTINA SUMMARY

**Cultural Data**

*Culture Type:* Family/Clan

*Region:* Latin America

*Local Influences:* Eighty-five percent of the population is of European descent, including Italian, Spanish, German, English, French, and Russian. Be cognizant of the person's background, even if he speaks Spanish as his first language. There is likely to be a cross-cultural influence. Buenos Aires is a very cosmopolitan city with European sophistication.

*Primary Motivations:* The family's status, power, and welfare come first.

*Plan of Action:*

- Always address the Argentine formally, using his title and family name (next to last name).
- Expect to spend time establishing a relationship. Don't press a business discussion until your counterpart offers an opening.
- Maintain formality in dress, posture, and speech until he relaxes the interaction.
- Your image is important in communicating your own status.
- Don't back away if your counterpart chooses to stand close during conversation.
- Establish contact through a well-regarded local agent.
- The first meeting should be on his turf.
- Send the most senior person from your company, along with one or two subordinates.
- Plan on using an interpreter. Translate materials into Latin American Spanish.
- Minimize risks in any proposal.
- Do not assume you hold the most power because you are from the United States.
- Entertain at the best restaurants. Dine continental style.
- Once a relationship has been established, your church or organiza-

tion should not change the U.S. contact person, or the process will have to begin again.

*Local Protocol & Etiquette:*

- Use a firm grip when shaking hands. Maintain good eye contact.
- Argentines might make personal observations about you. This just means that the person is comfortable with you.
- Opera and soccer (futbol) are good topics of conversation.

## AUSTRALIA SUMMARY

**Cultural Data**

*Culture Type:* Individualistic

*Region:* Australia

*Local Influences:* The country was born of the disenfranchised. English class structure was not transported to Australia. The society fosters a strong masculine stereotype. Identity is not derived from the family, but through the individual.

*Primary Motivations:* No man is a servant and no man is a master. Personal welfare is primary.

*Plan of Action:*

- Keep equality in mind at all times, from the structure of your business proposal to opportunities for socializing.
- Return the Australian's informality, but don't initiate it.
- Bargaining is considered to be a waste of time.
- Be sure to communicate the importance of your mutual objectives. Do not defer to him, yet do not project superiority.
- Be straightforward.

*Local Protocol & Etiquette:*

- Greet an Australian with a firm handshake and "hello." They tire of hearing non-Australians say "G'day." Begin with last names, but if he uses your first name, respond in kind.

- Give your business card at the introduction. Your counterpart may not give you one; cards are not very important in Australia.
- Titles and degrees are not impressive. The Australian will make his own judgment as to the quality of the person with whom he is speaking.
- Appropriate attire is conservative and not overly elegant. Leave the gold chain and other ostentatious jewelry at home. It is not only too showy, it is not "masculine" for a man to wear this.
- Be friendly, relaxed, modest, and unpretentious. Don't try to impress your host.
- Gifts are not given unless you are invited to someone's home.
- Don't fill your presentation with hype or glitz. A simple, direct presentation is more effective. Get to the point.
- Sports are an excellent topic of conversation. Become familiar with Australian rules of football and rugby. When discussing sports, do not use the term "root" as in "root for the home team." It means something obscene.
- There is a difference between "afternoon tea" and "tea." "Tea" is actually the meal served between 6 and 8 P.M.
- Women are legally equal but socially an underclass, although men may not admit it.

## BELARUS SUMMARY

### Cultural Data

*Culture Type:* Progressive Family/Clan

*Region:* Central and Eastern Europe

*Local Influences:* Belarus has been dominated by Poland, Lithuania, and Russia throughout much of its history. The country is seeking an identity.

*Primary Motivations:* Individualistic affiliation is especially important in Belarus because of its weak national identity. Individualistic welfare is the primary focus.

*Plan of Action:*

- Confirm and be modest. Do not flaunt affluence.
- Do not entertain lavishly.
- Sharing is important. Gift giving is common and should be reciprocated.
- Presentations should stress minimizing risks.
- Respect age. However, be aware that the younger generation is more entrepreneurial since the demise of the communist system.

*Local Protocol & Etiquette:*

- Shake hands with a firm grip while stating your last name. Men and women shake hands with each other.
- Small gifts are appreciated.
- Dress conservatively.
- Use manners outlined in the Russia summary.
- Accept hospitality, whether invited to a restaurant or to a home.

## BELGIUM SUMMARY

### Cultural Data

*Culture Type:* Individualistic, Family/Clan

*Region:* Western Europe

*Local Influences:* Belgium is a transition country between the strong individualism of the Netherlands and the more individualism French to the south. Ethnic identity is an issue, and can become contentious. Brussels is predominantly French in its culture. Most likely, you will be interacting with people in this section of Belgium and therefore should study the French profile as well.

*Primary Motivations:* Self-interest and individualism welfare is of utmost importance.

*Plan of Action:*

- Know the comfort level of the primary person with whom you will be meeting. Does he speak French or Dutch? Prepare to use an interpreter.

- Project a sophisticated but not supercilious image. Use good, formal manners, and be knowledgeable about world affairs.
- Do not try to find common cultural ground, but show knowledge of the Belgian culture.
- Presentations should be logical and linear. Appeal to the Belgian's self-interest; solve his problems.

*Local Protocol & Etiquette:*

- Shake hands on meeting and leaving. Shake quickly with a light pressure. When being introduced, repeat your name.
- Be sure to shake hands with secretaries when arriving and leaving.
- At a large party, allow your host to introduce you. You don't have to shake hands with everyone.
- Belgians value tact and diplomacy over bluntness.
- Don't discuss the country's language differences. However, if you translate your materials, provide both French and Dutch.
- The first meeting is usually for getting acquainted. Belgians lean to the individualism side on this point. In the Flemish north, this will not always be the case.
- Schedule business entertaining over lunch. Belgians like to spend the evening with their families.
- If a businesswoman wants to entertain a Belgian businessman, arrange payment in advance. He won't allow her to pay otherwise.

## BOLIVIA SUMMARY

**Cultural Data**

*Culture Type:* Family/Clan

*Region:* Latin America

*Local Influences:* The population is 50 percent Indian, 30 percent mestizo, and 15 percent European.

*Primary Motivations:* Family status, power, and welfare come first.

*Plan of Action:*

- Plan on using an interpreter. Translate materials into Latin American Spanish.

- Always address the Bolivian formally, using his title and family name (next to last name).
- Expect to spend time establishing a relationship. Don't press toward a business discussion until your counterpart offers an opening.
- Maintain formality in dress, posture, and speech until he relaxes the interaction.
- Your image is important in communicating your own status.
- Don't back away if your counterpart chooses to stand close during conversation.
- Minimize risks in any proposal.
- Do not assume you hold the most power because you are from the United States.
- Entertain at the best restaurants.
- Dine continental style.
- Once a relationship has been established, don't change the U.S. contact person, or the process will have to begin again.

*Local Protocol & Etiquette*

- Machismo is very strong.
- It is permissible to talk business over lunch, but not over dinner.
- Our hand gesture that means "so-so"—palm down, rocking the hand back and forth—means no in Bolivia.

## BRAZIL SUMMARY

### Cultural Data

*Culture Type:* Family/Clan

*Region:* Latin America

*Local Influences:* Brazil is the only Portuguese country in South America. The population contains a larger number of people of African descent than the neighboring Hispanic countries. The African-Brazilians are descendants of the slaves imported by the Portuguese. They have been assimilated into the population, predominantly in the north. In the south, there is a substantial Japanese community. Germans are also represented in São Paolo, the largest city.

*Primary Motivations:* Family status and welfare and the enjoyment of life are strong motivators.

*Plan of Action:*

- Plan on using an interpreter. Translate materials into Portuguese.
- Always address the Brazilian formally, using his title and family name (next to last name).
- Expect to spend time establishing a relationship. Don't press toward a business discussion until your counterpart offers an opening.
- Maintain formality in dress, posture, and speech until he relaxes the interaction.
- Your image is important in communicating your own status.
- Don't back away if your counterpart chooses to stand close during conversation.
- Minimize risks in any proposal.
- Do not assume you hold the most power because you are from the United States.
- Entertain at the best restaurants.
- Dine continental style.
- Latinos trust people, not companies.

*Local Protocol & Etiquette:*

- The Brazilians are better than most Latinos at abstract thinking, but still make decisions based on feelings and personal interests.
- Look for German and Japanese influence in São Paulo. This city operates more like northern cities. Expect a faster pace.
- The Brazilians seem very different from their Hispanic neighbors. Their attitude is very light and optimistic. They have good expectations for the future. One does not get this optimism in the other countries of Latin America.
- When thinking, don't absentmindedly rub your fingers under your chin, as some men with beards do. It means you don't know the answer to a question.

## BULGARIA SUMMARY

**Cultural Data**

*Culture Type:* Progressive Family/Clan

*Region:* Central and Eastern Europe

*Local Influences:* The Ottoman Turks dominated Bulgaria until World War I. The country was part of the Axis during World War II and then came under Soviet influence. Communist domination ended in 1990.

*Primary Motivations:* The welfare of their family group and the security of their nation is their motivating factor.

*Plan of Action:*

- Trust must be established before you will be accepted.
- Conform and be modest. Do not flaunt affluence.
- Do not entertain lavishly.
- Sharing is important. Gift giving is common and should be reciprocated.
- Presentations should stress minimizing risks.
- Respect age. However, be aware that the younger generation is more entrepreneurial since the demise of the communist system.

*Local Protocol & Etiquette:*

- Bulgarians admire the entrepreneurial spirit of the United States and Western Europe, and apply it in an individualism sense.
- The family is taken into consideration during any decision-making.
- Bulgarians have a strong work ethic. However, management skills are lacking.
- Bulgarians respect openness, strength, competence, honesty, and loyalty.
- European manners are used. Respectful behavior toward others is important.
- The head-nodding gesture Americans use for "yes" and "no" are reversed in Bulgaria.

## CANADA SUMMARY

**Cultural Data**

*Culture Type:* Family/Clan, Individualistic

*Region:* Canada

*Local Influences:* Canada can be divided into French-speaking Quebec, English-speaking Ontario, and the western provinces. The major difference between the United States and Canada is that the United States tends to assimilate diverse cultures into one system. Canada holds ethnic groups separate.

*Primary Motivations:* Self-interest of the ethnic group in the east and individual progress in the west is the Canadian's primary motivation.

*Plan of Action:*

- Do not project superiority because you live in the United States, and do not assume Canadians wish they did.
- In Quebec, cater to the French culture. Try to speak French. This will greatly enhance your image. If you are meeting with someone in Vancouver, remember there is a large community from Hong Kong in that city.

*Local Protocol & Etiquette, Quebec:*

- Physical space is closer. They may touch you while conversing.
- Use a reasonably firm handshake, and shake upon first meeting, greetings, and departures.
- Use last names until your host switches to first. He may go back and forth.
- Eat continental style.

*Local Protocol, English-Speaking Canada:*

- Handshakes are firm. Shake upon greeting and introduction, but not upon leaving.
- Use last names when introduced. First names will be used very soon thereafter. Wait for your host to initiate this.
- English-Canadians are not comfortable touching or speaking at close range.
- Privacy is important.

- Business meals are common. At dinner, wait for your host to bring up business.
- In business situations, maintain good posture. One can be more relaxed in social settings.
- Business gifts should be modest. Gifts are opened immediately. An invitation to a restaurant is considered a gift.
- Eat continental style.

## CHILE SUMMARY

**Cultural Data**

*Culture Type:* Family/Clan

*Region:* Latin America

*Local Influences:* Chile's population is 95 percent European, primarily Spanish, German, and Italian. Use global protocol.

*Primary Motivations:* Family status, power, and welfare are motivating factors.

*Plan of Action:*

- Plan on using an interpreter. Translate materials into Latin American Spanish.
- Always address the Latino formally, using his title and family name (next to last name).
- Expect to spend time establishing a relationship. Don't press toward a business discussion until your counterpart offers an opening.
- Maintain formality in dress, posture, and speech until he relaxes the interaction.
- Your image is important in communicating your own status.
- Don't back away if your counterpart chooses to stand close during conversation.
- Minimize risks in any proposal.
- Do not assume you hold the most power because you are from the United States.

- Entertain at the best restaurants.
- Dine continental style.
- Latinos trust people, not companies.

*Local Protocol & Etiquette:*

- There are more professional women here than in any other Latin American country. This is the best place for a businesswoman to work, but it is still very difficult.
- The Northern European influence results in a strong desire for progress and advancement through education. There is a significant middle class.
- Avoid aggressive behavior.
- Don't raise your right fist to head level. This is a communist gesture.
- Try to overcome the Chilean's sense of physical isolation by making frequent trips and keeping in contact.
- Gifts are not customary. If someone gives you a gift, open it immediately.

## CHINA SUMMARY

**Cultural Data**

*Culture Type:* Group

*Region:* Asia/Pacific

*Local Influences:* Chinese culture dominates the Far East. It is based on Confucian philosophy.

*Primary Motivations:* The welfare of the group is paramount. People work to benefit the group and to uphold its honor.

*Plan of Action:*

- Personal relationships must be established before business is done. Do not assume this means you are a personal friend.
- Negotiations will be time-consuming. Expect to make many trips. Be patient.
- One who is powerful and successful shows his humility.

- Harmony must be maintained. Do not confront or question anyone in a negative way. Never say no. Expect the Chinese to always say yes, which might mean no.
- Allow the Chinese to win something in negotiations.
- Recognize and respect the social position of all you encounter.
- Never compliment a person directly. Never praise someone in front of his superiors. Praise the group.
- Negotiations may appear cyclical rather than linear. Be prepared to discuss any subject out of sequence at any time.

*Local Protocol & Etiquette:*

- Everything shuts down between noon and 2 P.M.
- Avoid colors in your presentation. Colors have symbolic meaning.
- Bring at least twenty copies of your proposal. You will meet with many groups.
- Relationships are important before a deal is closed.
- At the end of a meeting, leave before the Chinese.
- Reciprocate banquets, but never outdo your host in lavishness. Spouses may be invited. Guests arrive on time for banquets.
- Refuse hospitality two times and on the third invitation accept it. This way you don't look greedy.
- Wait for the host to eat or drink.
- If you are greeted by applause, applaud back.
- Never put your hands in your mouth.
- Gift giving is technically illegal. Don't give anything expensive in front of others. A gift from your church or organization to the Chinese organization is acceptable. When giving or receiving a gift, use both hands. The gift is not opened in the presence of the giver. Chinese will decline a gift three times to not appear greedy. Keep insisting. Never give a clock; it is associated with death. Do not give gifts until all business is concluded.
- Everyone belongs to a work unit, which becomes their group. The work unit takes care of housing, medical needs, and vacation plans as well as employment. The smallest unit of survival is the group.

## COLOMBIA SUMMARY

**Cultural Data**

*Culture Type:* Family/Clan

*Region:* Latin America

*Local Influences:* The population is 58 percent mestizo and 20 percent European. The business elite is primarily European.

*Primary Motivations:* The welfare, status, and power of the family group are most important.

*Plan of Action:*

- Plan on using an interpreter. Translate materials into Latin American Spanish.
- Always address the Latino formally, using his title and family name (next to last name).
- Expect to spend time establishing a relationship. Don't press toward a business discussion until your counterpart offers an opening.
- Maintain formality in dress, posture, and speech until he relaxes the interaction.
- Your image is important in communicating your own status.
- Don't back away if your counterpart chooses to stand close during conversation.
- Minimize risks in any proposal.
- Do not assume you hold the most power because you are from the United States.
- Entertain at the best restaurants.
- Dine continental style.
- Once a relationship has been established, do not change the U.S. contact person, or the process will have to begin again. Latinos trust people, not companies.

*Local Protocol & Etiquette:*

- The only professional title that is used is *doctor.*
- Be sure when meeting someone that you drag out the greeting. Don't be in a rush. Chat for a minute.

- Gifts are not opened in front of the giver.
- Women are restricted in some aspects of business.
- Leave small amounts of food on your plate to indicate that you are done and don't want more.

## COSTA RICA SUMMARY

**Cultural Data**

*Culture Type:* Family/Clan

*Region:* Latin America

*Local Influences:* The population is 95 percent European, which is unusual for a Central American country. Costa Rica has maintained a fairly stable government and a dynamic capitalism.

*Primary Motivations:* This is an individualism culture with strong tendencies toward equality. People work for the benefit of their individualism, but also value personal achievement. There is a strong work ethic, but they are not completely goal-oriented.

*Plan of Action:*

- Plan on using an interpreter. Translate materials into Latin American Spanish.
- Always address the Latino formally, using his title and family name (next to last name).
- Expect to spend time establishing a relationship. Don't press toward a business discussion until your counterpart offers an opening.
- Maintain formality in dress, posture, and speech until he relaxes the interaction.
- Your image is important in communicating your own status.
- Don't back away if your counterpart chooses to stand close during conversation.
- Minimize risks in any proposal.
- Do not assume you hold the most power because you are from the United States.

- Entertain at the best restaurants.
- Dine continental style.

*Local Protocol & Etiquette:*

- Be punctual. This is the most punctual of all Latin American countries.
- Use a slightly limp handshake.
- Women tend to be accepted in business, more than in other individualism countries.
- Both machismo and the class system are maintained, but these are tempered by a sense of equality and respect for the individual.

## CROATIA SUMMARY

**Cultural Data**

*Culture Type:* Progressive Family/Clan

*Region:* Central and Eastern Europe

*Local Influences:* Croatia was ruled by the Hapsburg dynasty for centuries. After the fall of the Austro-Hungarian Empire following World War I, Croatia, Slovenia, Bosnia, and Serbia were held together in a federation known as Yugoslavia. After the fall of the Soviet Union, nationalism and ethnicity separated these countries. Strong individualism identity now operates.

*Primary Motivations:* The welfare of the family/clan/group and the security of the larger ethnic group are the motivating factors.

*Plan of Action:*

- Trust must be established before you will be accepted.
- Participate in the Croats' conformity and modesty. Do not flaunt affluence.
- Do not entertain lavishly.
- Negotiate a win-win outcome.
- Sharing is important. Gift giving is common and should be reciprocated.
- Presentations should stress minimizing risks.

- Respect age. However, be aware that the younger generation is more entrepreneurial since the demise of the communist system.

*Local Protocol & Etiquette:*

- Croatians are primarily Roman Catholic. Expect a stronger power hierarchy and centralized decision-making.
- Croats value kinship bonds, education, and a good career.
- European manners are used.
- It is acceptable to express emotion and opinions.

## CZECH REPUBLIC SUMMARY

**Cultural Data**

*Culture Type:* Progressive Family/Clan

*Region:* Central and Eastern Europe

*Local Influences:* Forty percent of Czechs are Roman Catholic, and the majority of the rest are unaffiliated Christians. They believe in a personal relationship with a "universal being."

*Primary Motivations:* The welfare of the individualism group and the security of the ethnic group determine Czechs' motivation.

*Plan of Action:*

- Trust must be established before you will be accepted.
- Participate in their brand of conformity and modesty. Do not flaunt affluence.
- Do not entertain lavishly.
- Sharing is important. Gift giving is common and should be reciprocated.
- Presentations should stress minimizing risks.
- Respect age. However, be aware that the younger generation is more entrepreneurial since the demise of the communist system.

*Local Protocol & Etiquette:*

- Cooperation and contribution are valued over individual accomplishments. The family unit is considered in all decision-making.
- Hierarchies tend to be formed. Leadership is valued.

- Most important values: education, social standing, modesty, and cleverness.
- European manners are followed.
- Translation of material into Czech will impress them, but English is acceptable.
- Czechs are detail-oriented, and will study all aspects of an agreement. Expect negotiations to move slowly.
- Present information clearly, highlighting major points and using visual aids when possible.
- Don't get down to business too abruptly. Relationships are important and slow to form.
- Dinner entertainment is more common than lunches. Do not discuss business during a meal.
- Greet someone with a firm but brief handshake. Use the last name, which is the family name. Use professional titles when they are known. Wait to be introduced if there are more than two people present.
- Avoid using your index finger, waving, or beckoning.
- Keep your feet on the floor.
- Business gifts should be inexpensive, but of good quality.
- Dress conservatively.

## DENMARK SUMMARY

### Cultural Data

*Culture Type:* Individualistic

*Region:* Western Europe

*Local Influences:* Denmark once ruled Scandinavia, but now is an equal neighbor. Still, ancient animosities remain among its former colonies. Danes recognize that theirs is a small country, and accept the value of international trade.

*Primary Motivations:* An ordered life, cooperation among people, and individual destiny are guiding forces.

*Plan of Action:*

- Be sure to treat them as equals. Do not compare Danish and U.S. standards of living. They do not care. Danes accept their place in the world, and do not strive anxiously to get ahead. They are not impressed by your wealth, possessions, or status.
- Do not refer to a Dane as a Scandinavian.
- Your proposal should emphasize efficiency, simplicity, and cost savings.
- Danes are not rigidly formal, but polite formality should be maintained. Don't be stiff or present a severe or overly elegant image.
- Management is not elitist. Socializing among ranks is accepted.
- During conversation, avoid personal questions. Privacy is important.

*Local Protocol & Etiquette:*

- A handshake is as good as a contract. If you agree on something and shake hands, you had better perform.
- Shake hands on meeting and leaving. Use a firm grip.
- Don't comment on someone's clothes, even with a compliment. It is too personal and considered odd.
- Feel free to introduce yourself in a group.
- American businesswomen will have no trouble in Denmark.
- Appropriate gifts are products from your area and coffee table books. Gifts are not expected in business.
- Dine continental style.
- When invited to someone's house, never go empty-handed. Bring flowers or candy.

## ECUADOR SUMMARY

**Cultural Data**

*Culture Type:* Family/Clan

*Region:* Latin America

*Local Influences:* The population is 65 percent mestizo and 25 percent Indian. There are few pure Europeans, but they are the power elite.

*Primary Motivations:* The family status, power, and welfare are paramount.

*Plan of Action:*

- Plan on using an interpreter. Translate materials into Latin American Spanish.
- Always address the Latino formally, using his title and family name (next to last name).
- Expect to spend time establishing a relationship. Don't press toward a business discussion until your counterpart offers an opening.
- Maintain formality in dress, posture, and speech until he relaxes the interaction.
- Your image is important in communicating your own status.
- Don't back away if your counterpart chooses to stand close during conversation.
- Be prepared to make concessions, but only after appropriate resistance. Do not appear to negotiate these concessions.
- Minimize risks in any proposal.
- Do not assume you hold the most power because you are from the United States.
- Entertain at the best restaurants.
- Dine continental style.
- Latinos trust people, not companies.

*Local Protocol & Etiquette:*

- Ecuadorians have a more self-centered form of individualism. They show more personal interest.
- There is a strong work ethic, but they are not goal-oriented.
- Don't use head motions to indicate yes or no; use words.

## EGYPT SUMMARY

**Cultural Data**

*Culture Type:* Family/Clan

*Region:* Arab

*Local Influences:* Egyptians are proud of their ancient civilization, but Islam is so dominant to the present culture that ancient influences do not prevail.

*Primary Motivations:* The welfare of the individual, along with maintaining and increasing its power and status while upholding the laws of Islam and the security of the nation, guide all action.

*Plan of Action:*

- Be cognizant of the nature of Islamic law and morality. It dictates behavior.
- You must be present to be of consequence. Meetings should be at your potential partners' offices.
- Relationships and trust come before business.
- Business associates must stay in constant communication for the relationship to continue.
- Expect delays in appointments. Time is not linear. Be patient and expect to take a long time completing a transaction.
- Humility is highly regarded, especially in a powerful person.
- An Egyptian loves to bargain, but do not inflate your price too much. Your first offer must be good enough to attract his attention.
- Minimize risks and uncertainty in your proposals. Praise and appreciation for your counterpart must be verbalized often.
- Maintain formality in behavior, appearance, and address.
- Project a successful image.
- Never refuse hospitality. Always reciprocate.
- Never reprimand or criticize directly. Failure is not directly acknowledged. Honor is very important. Deal with negatives euphemistically.

- Never say that you are a "self-made man." Lineage is important to Arabs. You are a reflection of your entire family.
- Proposals, plans, and negotiations should focus on the "people" issues, which are most important to Egyptians.

*Local Protocol & Etiquette:*

- Do not use first names immediately. Wait for your host to offer.
- Don't take any criticism of the U.S. government personally.
- Do not discuss bad news on a social occasion.
- The U.S. gesture for waving good-bye means "come here."
- Women should avoid direct eye contact with men and avoid crowds, where men may try to touch.
- Finishing everything on your plate is considered rude. Leaving food indicates the abundance of the host.
- Law requires that a company doing business in Egypt must have an Egyptian agent. Get separate agents for Cairo and Alexandria.
- Political contacts do not have the same influence in Egypt as they do in other Arab countries.
- In the cities, women will not have difficulty doing business. Entertain at European-style hotel restaurants.

## ENGLAND SUMMARY

**Cultural Data**

*Culture Type:* Family/Clan, Individualistic

*Region:* Western Europe

*Local Influences:* Great Britain includes England, Scotland, and Wales. The United Kingdom further includes Northern Ireland. While England is Individualistic, Scotland and Wales are Individualist.

*Primary Motivations:* Maintenance of both status and the status quo are important factors.

*Plan of Action:*

- Form first, deference second, competence last.
- English derive their identity from the family and its place in society.

- A prestigious third-party introduction will open doors and speed the process.
- England is a nation of managers. Form a "coalition" with your counterpart, as well as with subordinates.
- Formal manners, attending to every detail, are necessary.
- Be punctual.
- Image is everything, but don't play a game of one-upmanship.
- Avoid comments about one's stature, power, or financial status. This would be rude. Personal comments should be avoided in general.
- Privacy is important. Do not repeat conversations or distribute information unless your English counterpart is informed in advance.
- In presentations, appeal to the Englishman's rational side and his desire to maintain tradition.

*Local Protocol & Etiquette:*

- Shake hands only when meeting. Always wait for a woman to extend her hand first. Say "How do you do?" rather than "Hello," and expect the same reply. No answer is expected.
- If you say something is "quite good," you have not given a compliment. In general, remember that British English and American English are not the same. There are many words that have different meanings.
- To get a waiter's attention, use eye contact. Don't wave.
- Businesswomen might find men condescending, depending on their age and the type of business.
- If you and your English counterpart agree on action items for each side, don't make changes to the plans unless you get together again. He will feel that you are usurping his power if you do anything not agreed on.
- Wait for a British businessperson to offer the first invitation to lunch. You should reciprocate when possible.
- Don't offer business gifts.
- Dine continental style.

## ESTONIA SUMMARY

**Cultural Data**

*Culture Type:* Individualistic

*Region:* Central and Eastern Europe

*Local Influences:* Although Estonia has been in the Russian sphere of influence, historically its existence was closely tied with the Scandinavian countries, especially Sweden. This produced a strong individual orientation, which is unusual for Central and Eastern Europe.

*Primary Motivation:* Personal achievement and progress.

*Plan of Action:*

- Third-party introductions are not necessary, but always useful.
- Greet someone with a firm handshake.
- Wait until you are invited to use someone's first name.
- Remain formal in your manners and posture, even though you are using first names.
- Contracts can be verbal. If you assent to an agreement verbally, expect to be held to your word.
- Keep your presentation precise, logical, and straightforward.
- Dine continental style.

## FINLAND SUMMARY

**Cultural Data**

*Culture Type:* Individualistic

*Region:* Western Europe

*Local Influences:* Finland is a Scandinavian country that has been ruled at times by Russia and Sweden. Many customs are shared.

*Primary Motivation:* Logic and self-interest are important to success. Finns also wish to preserve their unique national identity.

*Plan of Action:*

- Third-party introductions are not necessary, but always useful.
- Most Finns with whom you will be meeting speak English. However, do not take this for granted. Check to see if you should have information translated and use an interpreter.

- Greet someone with a firm handshake.
- Finns commonly use first names, but wait until you are invited to use someone's first name.
- Remain formal in your manners and posture, even though you are using first names.
- Contracts can be verbal. If you assent to an agreement verbally, expect to be held to your word.
- Be warned that Finns are very straightforward with their opinions, and will aggressively assert their position.
- Keep your presentation precise, logical, and straightforward.

*Local Protocol & Etiquette:*

- Shake hands when introduced and when leaving.
- Don't stand with your arms folded. It is a sign of arrogance.
- At a meal, the host and hostess toast their guests. They never receive toasts from their guests.
- Don't leave food on your plate.
- An invitation to a sauna is the equivalent of an invitation to an American golf course. An invitation is unlikely if you are a woman dealing with men.
- Foreign businesswomen are accepted.
- An agreement is usually celebrated by a long lunch.

## FRANCE SUMMARY

**Cultural Data**

*Culture Type:* Individualistic, Family/Clan

*Region:* Western Europe

*Local Influences:* France is caught between two cultures and so has blended both: family/clan in the south and individualists in the north.

*Primary Motivation:* Personal freedom, not personal achievement, is important to the French.

*Plan of Action:*

- The French are status-conscious.
- Translate everything into French. Use an interpreter. It is helpful if you speak French.
- A handshake may not be offered. If it is, use a moderate grip.
- Show some sophistication. Be knowledgeable about French culture and history.
- Do not attempt to find common ground in a social sense. The French do not want to relate to you personally.
- Your appearance should be impeccable and elegant, a bit on the formal side.
- Your proposal must be compelling. The French do not like to deal with foreigners.
- Do not trust words. Get it in writing. Get a contract signed.
- Appeal to their self-interest.
- Time is not money. It is power and is used as a manipulative device.
- Use formal etiquette, last names, and titles.
- Do not try a hard sell. The French disdain selling.
- Use the continental dining style or you will be thought of as a barbarian.

*Local Protocol & Etiquette:*

- Shake hands when meeting and leaving with a quick light grip. No pumping.
- When entering a room, greet everyone in it.
- Be careful not to speak or laugh loudly. The French speak more quietly than Americans.
- Place your bread on the table next to your plate. There are no bread plates.
- Finish everything on your plate.
- Businesswomen will be more accepted in the north than in the south. Businessmen may treat a woman flirtatiously, but not condescendingly. Businesswomen should give special attention to their dress. They must be fashionable and elegant.
- Contracts are written in precise detail, but they tend to be adviso-

ry. The French may not honor all contract points. Stress often the points that are most important to you.

- Business lunches are more popular than dinners. Don't expect to talk business. Lunch could last two hours.
- If you are hosting a meal at a restaurant, be sure you get a menu that has prices. Some restaurants give the prices only to the host. If you are a guest with a menu without prices, let your host order or ask what he recommends.
- The best gifts are those with some intellectual or aesthetic appeal instead of logo gifts. Don't give a gift until you have met someone several times.

## GERMANY SUMMARY

**Cultural Data**

*Culture Type:* Individualistic

*Region:* Western Europe

*Local Influences:* Germany varies from strong pluralism in the north to individualism tendencies in the Catholic south. Reunification with East Germany has revealed a strong communist cultural influence on a generation of people. It may take another generation to reawaken their pluralist nature. When dealing with former East Germans, a study of the chapter on Central and Eastern Europe would be wise.

*Primary Motivation:* Personal achievement and power are the driving forces.

*Plan of Action:*

- Do not assume that meetings will be conducted in English. Translate all material and use an interpreter.
- All documents should look polished and professional.
- Maintain formality at all times. Self-control is very important.
- Dress very conservatively and formally.
- Be prepared to back up all of your figures. Allow some room for negotiation.

- Germans value intelligence. They are impressed by thoughtful questions.
- Don't compliment Germans. They offer compliments only if something is outstanding.
- Your presentation should highlight how the Germans' performance will be enhanced. You must prove all your claims.
- Privacy is important. Don't ask personal questions.
- Dine continental style.

*Local Protocol & Etiquette:*

- When introduced, use a firm handshake with one distinct shake, and state your last name.
- Shake hands when meeting and leaving. Be sure to include the secretary.
- Relationship-building comes after business for the Germans. At the end of business discussions a German may ask you to stay and share a brandy with him. Please be aware so you can make a proper decision.
- At a party or business meeting, wait to be introduced by a third person.
- Never say anything negative about soccer or the local team. Germans take the sport very seriously.
- It is not customary for a woman to thank a man when receiving a compliment.
- Men should allow people of higher status (and, in social situations, women) to walk through a door first. But when entering a restaurant, a man should walk in front of a woman.
- Never eat with your fingers, not even a sandwich.
- Never use your knife to cut potatoes, pancakes, or dumplings. It implies the food isn't cooked right.
- Finish everything on your plate, even in restaurants, or make an excuse.
- The guest makes the first move to go. If you are visiting someone and your host does not refill your glass, it is an indication that you should go.

- Don't ask for coffee with a meal. It is served afterward.
- A businesswoman will be perceived as not having authority to make decisions. Make your corporate authority clear with a letter of introduction from the head of your church or organization.
- Any gift should be small and simple. Large, expensive gifts are considered tasteless. If you are sending flowers to a hostess, never send red roses. They mean love. Avoid chrysanthemums, also. Send an odd number, but not thirteen.

## GREECE SUMMARY

**Cultural Data**

*Culture Type:* Progressive Family/Clan

*Region:* Greece

*Local Influences:* The present-day Greek's attachment to his ancient Greek ancestors separates him from a Western Europe historically ruled by Rome. The Greek looks eastward, but is strongly democratic and capitalistic.

*Primary Motivation:* Individualistic welfare and advancement motivates the Greeks.

*Plan of Action:*

- Relationship-building is important, and friendship comes with obligation.
- Be punctual, even though your Greek counterpart will not be.
- Shake hands with a firm grip, and don't break away too quickly.
- Use last names and titles when introduced, showing special respect for older people.
- Business cards should be printed in both Greek and English. Hand the card Greek side up, being sure that the writing is right side up.
- Dress conservatively.
- Presentations should include a variety of presentation techniques, many visual.
- Treat the senior member in a group with respect. Authority usually

rests with him, although there is a need for consensus in decision-making groups.

- Expect to bargain and make quick decisions.
- Patience is important in negotiations, but be prepared to move quickly on a moment's notice.
- Language is often exaggerated and emotional.

*Local Protocol & Etiquette:*

- Business is often done over a cup of coffee. Informal meetings may be held in a coffeehouse.
- Lunch is the main meal of the day. Dinner is small and is served late.
- The communal approach is followed in some restaurants where diners share several dishes.
- The head-nodding gestures indicating "yes" and "no" can be confusing because they are traditionally reversed in Greece.
- A smile can mean anger as well as pleasure.
- Don't give business gifts at the first meeting. Don't give token gifts merely to display your company logo.

## HONG KONG SUMMARY

**Cultural Data**

*Culture Type:* Group

*Region:* Asia/Pacific

*Local Influences:* Hong Kong was a British crown colony until 1997, when it reverted to Chinese rule. It will be allowed to keep its capitalist system until 2047.

*Primary Motivation:* Self-determination and group prosperity motivate the Hong Kong.

*Plan of Action:*

- Personal relationships must be established first. Do not assume this means you are a personal friend.

- Negotiations will be time-consuming. Expect to make many trips. Be patient.
- One who is powerful and successful shows his humility.
- Harmony must be maintained. Do not confront or question anyone in a negative way. Never say no. Expect the Hong Konger to always say yes, which might mean no.
- Recognize and respect the social position of all you encounter.
- Never compliment a person directly. Never praise someone in front of his superiors. Praise the group.
- Negotiations may appear cyclical rather than linear. Be prepared to discuss any subject out of sequence at any time.

*Local Protocol & Etiquette:*

- Greet everyone when you arrive, beginning with the most senior person. Use a light handshake. Address people with their surname and title.
- Be punctual.
- Never refuse an invitation to lunch or dinner. If you must, offer an alternative date.
- Accept tea if it is offered. Wait for your host to drink first.
- A banquet is appropriate at the end of negotiations. Always reciprocate if you are given one.
- Refuse hospitality three times before accepting, so you don't look greedy.
- Decorum is important to both the Chinese and British cultures in Hong Kong.
- Men should not cross their legs, but keep them on the floor.
- Do not wear blue or white. These colors are reserved for mourning.
- Do not open a gift in the presence of the giver.

## HUNGARY SUMMARY

### Cultural Data

*Culture Type:* Progressive Family/Clan

*Region:* Central and Western Europe

*Local Influences:* Hungary came under the influence of the Hapsburg dynasty in the sixteenth century; in 1867 a dual monarchy with Austria was declared, beginning the Austro-Hungarian Empire. This was a union of Germanic and Slavic people that lasted until the end of World War I. In 1949, Hungary became a communist socialist state. It is now a democracy, and is one of the most prosperous Eastern European nations.

*Primary Motivation:* Individualistic welfare and national identity motivates the Hungarians.

*Plan of Action:*

- Trust must be established before you will be accepted.
- Participate in their brand of conformity and modesty. Do not flaunt affluence.
- Do not entertain lavishly.
- Negotiate a win-win outcome.
- Sharing is important. Gift giving is common and should be reciprocated.
- Presentations should stress minimizing risks.
- Respect age. However, be aware that the younger generation is more entrepreneurial since the demise of the communist system.

*Local Protocol & Etiquette:*

- The country is two-thirds Roman Catholic and one-quarter Protestant. Religion is not a big part of their lives.
- Vertical hierarchy is preferred, but consensus decision-making may prevail until greater confidence in business is achieved.
- Hungarians value family, education, job security, private property, and travel.
- They admire professionals and intellectuals over the merely wealthy.
- Intentions, feelings, and opinions may be directly expressed. Deviousness is not respected.

- Your host probably will entertain you. Hospitality is important to the Hungarians. At the end of negotiations, you should host a cocktail party or dinner at a good hotel.
- A firm handshake is used when meeting and leaving. Use family names until invited to use first names. In Hungary, the family name precedes the given name.
- When visiting a company, bring many small gifts for everyone you meet.
- Hungarians love horses. You may be invited to go riding. If you ride, this is a good topic of conversation.

## INDIA SUMMARY

**Cultural Data**

*Culture Type:* Family/Clan, Group

*Region:* India

*Local Influences:* India must be understood in context with its religious beliefs. Hinduism, followed by more than 80 percent of the population, is central to their lives.

*Primary Motivations:* The welfare of the family/group is important.

*Plan of Action:*

- A medium firm handshake is the proper greeting for business. You may see people greeting each other with the *namaste,* which one does by placing the hands together as if in prayer, fingers pointing up, and bowing the head slightly.
- Use his last name along with Mr. It is not appropriate for a foreigner to use the term *sahib.*
- Don't shake a woman's hand unless she offers it. Men generally do not touch women in public. It is polite to refer to women as "ladies."
- A business card printed in English should be provided. Your card should have your title, academic degrees, and professional affiliations. This will help the Indian position you in his universe.

- Be punctual. Your host may not be.
- Relationship is important, but the Indian will get down to business fairly quickly.
- Accept any hospitality offered.
- Social distance may be close, but touching is not common in conversation.
- British manners prevail. Be subdued. Self-control is favored over impulsiveness. A quietly self-confident aura breeds trust and respect. However, one should be friendly and communicative.
- Be cautious in giving criticism. Indians take offense easily.
- Use the right hand when passing papers and objects and when eating.
- Keep shoes and feet on the floor.
- Whistling is considered rude.
- Your first meeting should include the head of the company, who will probably make the final decision on your proposal. Always try to match the status of meeting participants. If you send your chief technical person, make your appointment with a technical person. Speak to the secretary of your targeted person to be sure you are contacting the right person at the appropriate level.
- A business lunch is appropriate after an interest in your business has been established. It is acceptable to talk business over the meal.
- Dinner invitations should be offered only after some sort of relationship is established.

*Local Protocol & Etiquette*

- Entertaining is usually done in private clubs or in restaurants.
- The guest of honor should be seated to the right of the host. There are no other seating formalities.
- There is no toasting ritual. Your host may offer a toast in the British manner if he has spent time in England.
- Continental style of eating is used in most Westernized restaurants. The traditional manner of eating is by using the right hand and no utensils.
- Hindi do not eat beef.

- Gifts are a sign of friendship. They should be modest and reserved for later meetings.
- There is a significant Muslim population, especially in the northern section of the country. Study the Arab chapter. Be considerate of Muslims, who will be fasting during the month of Ramadan from sunrise to sundown, and remember that they don't eat pork or drink alcohol.

## INDONESIA SUMMARY

**Cultural Data**

*Culture Type:* Group, Family/Clan

*Region:* Pacific Rim

*Local Influences:* Indonesia has the largest Muslim population in the world. See the Arab profile; much of that protocol is appropriate here. However, Indonesia is naturally a group culture base with Islamic culture overlaid. Hierarchies tend to be more authoritarian. A majority of Indonesian businesspeople are ethnic Chinese, so it is important to know the Asia/Pacific profile as well.

*Primary Motivation:* The welfare, status, and security of the family individualism and group motivate the Indonesians.

*Plan of Action:*

- Personal relationships must be established before business is done. Do not assume this means you are a personal friend.
- Top management should be present at the first meeting. Your church or organization should be represented by a group of specialists at this first meeting. Do not include a lawyer.
- Negotiations will be time-consuming. Expect to make many trips. Be patient.
- One who is powerful and successful shows his humility.
- Harmony must be maintained. Do not confront or question anyone in a negative way. Never say no. Expect them to always say yes, which might mean no.

- Recognize and respect the social position of all you encounter.
- Never compliment a person directly. Never praise someone in front of his superiors. Praise the group.
- Negotiations may appear cyclical rather than linear. Be prepared to discuss any subject out of sequence at any time.

*Local Protocol & Etiquette:*

- In the Bahasa Indonesia language, it is difficult to converse with a person until you know his status relative to yours. Pronouns depend on relative status.
- At social gatherings, those of lesser status should arrive first. An invitation may tell you when to arrive. If you are asked to arrive early, you can be sure you are not the most important guest.
- Indonesians follow the Arab concept of time. Chinese expect punctuality.
- The response, "yes, but..." means no.
- Facts are "degrees of probability." Compromise and accommodation are always in order.
- Decisions require consensus.
- Indonesians are accustomed to physical touching within the same sex. This is often part of a close relationship, unlike in other parts of Asia.
- Shake hands only upon initial introduction and before and after a long separation. Use a weak handclasp. Do not rush the greeting.
- Naming conventions are not standardized. Some people have one name, some have several. Ask how to address the person. If he is Chinese, use the first name.
- Gifts are given often. Any small occasion is appropriate, even when someone comes to tour the factory. They need not be expensive. Do not open gifts in the presence of the giver. Refuse the gift three times before accepting.
- A dinner guest should wait to begin eating or drinking until asked to do so. If you are the guest of honor, refuse the honor several times before accepting.

- Do not invite a Muslim to lunch during the month of Ramadan. He will be fasting.

## IRAQ SUMMARY

**Cultural Data**

*Culture Type:* Family/Clan

*Region:* Arab World

*Local Influences:* There are so many changes in Iraq that where once all business had to go through the Iraq government, this isn't true today. One must wait to see how the country will be shaped for future business.

*Primary Motivation:* Individualistic power, status, and prosperity, as well as national security and the rule of religious law, are the prime motivators.

*Plan of Action:*

- Be cognizant of the nature of Islamic law and morality. It dictates behavior.
- Make your first approach through a well-connected local representative.
- You must be present to be of consequence. Meetings should be at the Iraqis' offices.
- Relationships and trust come before business.
- Business associates must stay in constant communication for the relationship to continue.
- Expect delays in appointments. Time is not linear. Be patient and expect to take a long time completing a transaction.
- Humility is highly regarded, especially in a powerful person.
- An Iraqi loves to bargain, but do not inflate your price too much. Your first offer must be good enough to attract his attention.
- Minimize risks and uncertainty in your proposals. Praise and appreciation for your counterpart must be verbalized often.
- Maintain formality in behavior, appearance, and address.
- Project a successful image.

- Never refuse an Iraqi's hospitality. Always reciprocate.
- Never reprimand or criticize directly. Failure is not directly acknowledged. Honor is very important. Deal with negatives euphemistically.
- Never admit that you are a "self-made man." Lineage is important; you are a reflection of your entire family.
- Proposals, plans, and negotiations should focus on the "people" issues.

*Local Protocol & Etiquette:*

- Use first names as soon as you are introduced.
- When offered food or drink, refuse the first time, then accept.
- Iraq is much less formal than other Arab countries.
- Iraqis don't like the excessive praise and flowery language of other Arab nations.
- Women have had equal rights for twenty years.
- Never try to bribe anyone.
- The best business gift is a book.

## IRELAND

### Cultural Data

*Culture Type:* Family/Clan

*Region:* Western Europe

*Local Influences:* Ireland is not a part of the United Kingdom, but it shares heavily in the cultural history that formed the British Isles. The Roman Catholic Church has maintained its dominant position in Ireland since the fifth century. Remember that Northern Ireland is predominantly Catholic and is part of the United Kingdom, not Ireland.

*Primary Motivation:* Family or clan welfare and enjoyment of life.

*Plan of Action:*

- The attitude toward business is more relaxed than in other Northern European nations.

- Use more formal manners in Ireland than you would in the United States.
- Relationship-building is important. Don't hurry into business discussions.
- Dress conservatively, but do not be overly formal.
- Shake hands upon greeting and leaving. Use last names until invited to use first names.
- The Irish are very tolerant of foreigners. They will not take offense easily.
- Business cards are not commonly used in Ireland. Bring them with you to leave with a secretary if the person you want to see is out.

*Local Protocol & Etiquette:*

- Keep gestures to a minimum.
- Wear tailored clothing, even for casual wear. Dress warmly.
- Gift giving in business is not done. If you go to someone's home, don't go empty-handed. Flowers (not roses, not red or white, not an even number, not thirteen, and not wrapped), candy, and cheeses all make good hostess gifts. If someone gives you a gift, open it immediately.
- When shaking hands, wait for a woman to extend her hand first.
- At a large party, introduce yourself. In a small group, wait to be introduced.
- When the Irish describe someone as plain, it's a compliment.
- When offered a drink, raise the glass before you drink and say "Cheers."
- At dinner, the small plate next to your dinner plate is not for bread. It is for the peelings you remove from boiled potatoes. Bread is rarely served at dinner.
- There are few businesswomen, but American businesswomen will be taken seriously.

## ISRAEL SUMMARY

### Cultural Data

*Culture Type:* Family/Clan, Individualistic

*Region:* Israel

*Local Influences:* Only 60 percent of the population is native to Israel. Business practices may be North American, Russian, European, or Mediterranean.

*Primary Motivations:* Family and personal gain and security, and the security of Israel are important. Protocol and etiquette support the needs of the family over the needs of the individual.

*Plan of Action:*

- Jews are divided into two ethnic heritages. Sephardic Jews come from the Mediterranean area, Northern Africa, and the Middle East. Ashkenazic Jews come from Europe. The Ashkenazic Jews are dominant in politics and religion, and the Sephardic Jews are more present in government and business.
- Ashkenazic Jews tend to show strong individualists tendencies, while the Sephardic Jews are family/clan oriented. The Jewish religion promotes, or rather, reflects, a family/clan perception. Even though some Ashkenazic Jews come from strong pluralist countries such as Germany and the Netherlands, their culture has always maintained the family/clan hierarchy.
- About 50 percent of the Jews in Israel are Orthodox Jews. They share many customs with Muslims.
- The approach to Israel is to study general individualism culture, the Arab profile, the Russian/Central Europe profile, and the European/individualists profile.
- The plan of action for a Sephardic contact is similar to that of the Arab plan of action. The plan of action for Ashkenazic contacts is more European in style.

*Local Protocol & Etiquette:*

- Israel is a democratic and egalitarian culture that values competition.

- The Israeli negotiating style is much more confrontational. They love to argue and debate.
- Women are legally equal in status and even serve in the military. Men still dominate, as in all family/clan societies.
- The security of the state is taken into consideration when making major decisions.
- The holy days are Friday and Saturday each week. Judaism and Islam both use lunar calendars. Israelis are used to thinking in twenty-eight-day months.
- Use engraved business cards. Print them in both English and Hebrew (Arabic, if you are visiting an Israeli Arab).
- Businesswomen should not extend their hand to greet an Orthodox Jewish male. His religion has laws against touching women. She should also never hand something directly to him, but put it next to him so he can pick it up. Orthodox Jews can usually be identified by their yarmulkes, or skullcaps. Half of Israel's Jews are considered secular and do not observe these rituals.
- The common greeting is to shake hands and address the person using Mr., etc., plus the surname. *Shalom,* which means peace, is said when greeting and leaving.
- Conservative business suits are appropriate, and in general, modest dress is required.
- The continental style of eating is most widely used.

## ITALY SUMMARY

### Cultural Data

*Culture Type:* Family/Clan, Individualistic

*Region:* Western Europe

*Local Influences:* There are two Italys: the north, dominated by Milan, and the south, dominated by Rome. Most business is done in the north. Government is attended to in Rome.

*Primary Motivation:* In the individualistic north, personal achievement is the important factor; in the family/clan south, the welfare of the family is the driving force.

*Plan of Action:*

- Use formal manners, but do not be overly stiff.
- Use last names unless asked to do otherwise.
- Do not gesture with your hands in the north. They value self-control.
- Dress should be conservative, yet fashionable.
- Sincerity is important.
- Shake hands when meeting and leaving.
- An introduction from a mutual business associate is very useful.
- First meeting should take place at his offices.
- Business will take precedence over relationship-building.

*Local Protocol & Etiquette:*

- In the south you may encounter more physical touching during greetings, like a hand on the shoulder.
- When eating spaghetti, don't cut it or twirl it against a spoon. Twirl it against the side of the dish.
- Even if you have invited people to a restaurant, there will be fighting over the check. You must insist on paying. A businesswoman has almost no chance of picking up the bill unless payment is arranged ahead and she explains that her church or organization has paid.
- A woman will be taken seriously in business, but if she is traveling with a man, she will be taken for his secretary. A woman must dress very formally and expensively to give the signal that she is a person of some authority. Always place academic degrees and titles on your business card.
- Don't discuss business or hand out business cards in a social setting.
- When you invite an Italian businessperson to a meal, ask which of his colleagues should be included in the invitation.

## JAPAN SUMMARY

**Cultural Data**

*Culture Type:* Group

*Region:* Asia/Pacific

*Local Influences:* Although Japan is related to other Asian countries through its inheritance of Chinese Confucian philosophy, for much of its history the country was isolated from other cultures, developing a unique culture and homogeneous society.

*Primary Motivations:* The welfare and honor of the group are important.

*Plan of Action:*

- One who is powerful and successful shows his humility.
- Harmony must be maintained. Do not confront or question anyone in a negative way. Never say no. Expect them to always say yes, which might mean no.
- Approach a potential partner through a local representative.
- Personal relationships must be established before business is done. Do not assume this means you are a personal friend.
- Top management should be present at the first meeting. Your company should be represented by a group of specialists at this first meeting. Do not include a lawyer.
- Negotiations will be time-consuming. Expect to make many trips. Be patient.
- Recognize and respect the social position of all you encounter.
- Never compliment a person directly. Never praise someone in front of his superiors. Praise the group.
- Negotiations may appear cyclical rather than linear. Be prepared to discuss any subject out of sequence at any time.

*Local Protocol & Etiquette:*

- The Japanese language is very subtle. There is much left unspoken, but to a Japanese all is understood.
- Use of an interpreter is recommended, even if the Japanese say they speak English. Provide your own interpreter. The two languages

require completely different thought processes, and they will probably understand only half of what you are saying. When they respond to your remarks with a big smile, they have not understood.

- Numbers should always be written on a piece of paper for clarity.
- Letters will not be answered if the sender is not known.
- Foreign companies do not have to go through trading companies to do business in Japan. However, it is important to have an intermediary or agent to make introductions and set appointments, especially if your organization is small.
- Use an intermediary to discuss bad news.
- Be punctual for meetings. For social engagements, be somewhat late.
- Greet someone with a weak handshake and a nod of the head. If someone bows to you, bow to him exactly as low as he bowed to you. Cast your eyes down and put your hands against your sides.
- Present business cards after shaking hands.
- Address the person by his last name. Use Mr. and the last name. Foreigners should not use the honor term *san* after the name.
- The smallest gesture may have great meaning. Keep your hands and face quiet.
- Don't blow your nose in public, and never use a cloth handkerchief. Use a disposable one.
- Gestures indicating a negative response can be fanning the right hand in front of the face and sucking air.
- Maintain greater separation between people when conversing than is normal in the United States.
- Gift giving is very important to the Japanese. The ceremony is equally as important as the present itself. Business gifts must be given January 1 and July 15 (year-end and midyear). Gifts are often exchanged on first meeting. Wait for your host to offer a gift first. Reciprocate with a gift of equal quality. Remember, image is everything. Logo gifts from well-known Western stores are appre-

ciated. Never give an even number of anything, especially avoiding the number four. Avoid giving anything predominantly white, which signifies death. Have gifts wrapped in Japan by a service or hotel service. They have their own notions of what is attractive. The wrapping is part of the symbolism. Bows are not used.

- Wear slip-on shoes because you will be removing them frequently. Slippers are provided for guests when entering a home and some restaurants.
- If you wear a kimono, or kimono-style wrap clothing, always wrap left over right. Only corpses are wrapped right over left.
- The term "manager" does not mean *the* manager, but is more likely one of many managers in a group. Be careful of Japanese corporate hierarchy and use their title that best describes your status. Do some company research.
- Unless the visitor is selling, your host will make the first invitation for evening entertainment. Entertainment is lavish and should be reciprocated. Keep parity of status in mind when initiating an invitation.
- Group seating arrangements at a restaurant are important. See this book's Dining section.
- During meetings, sit opposite the person who matches your rank.
- Refuse hospitality three times before accepting, so you don't look greedy.

## JORDAN SUMMARY

### Cultural Data

*Culture Type:* Family/Clan

*Region:* Arab World

*Local Influences:* Jordan has allowed Western influence in some aspects of its culture while remaining an Islamic nation.

*Primary Motivations:* The welfare of the individualism family group, and adherence to Islam.

*Plan of Action:*

- Be cognizant of the nature of Islamic law and morality. It dictates behavior.
- Humility is highly regarded, especially in a powerful person.
- A Jordanian loves to bargain, but do not inflate your price too much. Your first offer must be good enough to attract his attention.
- Make your first approach through a well-connected local representative.
- You must be present to be of consequence. Meetings should be at your potential partner's offices.
- Relationships and trust come before business.
- Business associates must stay in constant communication for the relationship to continue.
- Expect delays in appointments. Time is not linear. Be patient and expect to take a long time completing a transaction.
- Minimize risks and uncertainty in your proposals. Praise and appreciation for your counterpart must be verbalized often.
- Maintain formality in behavior, appearance, and address.
- Project a successful image.
- Never refuse hospitality. Always reciprocate.
- Never reprimand or criticize directly. Failure is not directly acknowledged. Honor is very important. Deal with negatives euphemistically.
- Never admit that you are a "self-made man." Lineage is important. You are a reflection of your entire family.
- Proposals, plans, and negotiations should focus on the "people" issues.

*Local Protocol & Etiquette:*

- English is Jordan's second language.
- Address people you don't know well by the English titles, Mr., Mrs., and Miss.
- Jordan is much less conservative than other Arab nations. Women may dine out with men.

- Private businessmen are much more straightforward in Jordan than in other Arabic countries.
- If a woman must do business in Jordan, she is given honorary male status.

## KUWAIT SUMMARY

**Cultural Data**

*Culture Type:* Family/Clan

*Region:* Arab World

*Local Influences:* Kuwait is a very small, very wealthy, independent state.

*Primary Motivations:* The status, power, and wealth of the family/clan group are important.

*Plan of Action:*

- Be cognizant of the nature of Islamic law and morality. It dictates behavior.
- Humility is highly regarded, especially in a powerful person.
- A Kuwaiti loves to bargain, but do not inflate your price too much. Your first offer must be good enough to attract his attention.
- Make your first approach through a well-connected local representative.
- You must be present to be of consequence. Meetings should be at your potential partner's offices.
- Relationships and trust come before business.
- Business associates must stay in constant communication for the relationship to continue.
- Expect delays in appointments. Time is not linear. Be patient and expect to take a long time completing a transaction. Minimize risks and uncertainty in your proposals. Praise and appreciation for your counterpart must be verbalized often.
- Maintain formality in behavior, appearance, and address.
- Project a successful image.

- Never refuse hospitality. Always reciprocate.
- Never reprimand or criticize directly. Failure is not directly acknowledged. Honor is very important. Deal with negatives euphemistically.
- Never admit that you are a "self-made man." Lineage is important. You are a reflection of your entire family.
- Proposals, plans, and negotiations should focus on the "people" issues.

*Local Protocol & Etiquette:*

- When you see someone bowing and kissing someone's hand, do not feel that you must do likewise.
- After any meal, leave after you finish coffee.
- Suggest that instead of meeting at the man's office that you meet at your hotel lobby. There won't be so many interruptions—or so much coffee. Remember that you are now the host and must be generous in your hospitality.
- When meeting with a group from a Kuwaiti company, the person who sits, listens, and says nothing is usually the decision-maker.
- Kuwaitis are very punctual. Don't be even ten minutes late.
- Don't send a woman to do business.
- Never whistle in public.

## LATVIA SUMMARY

### Cultural Data

*Culture Type:* Individualistic

*Region:* Central and Eastern Europe

*Local Influences:* Along with Estonia, Latvia has historically been associated with the Scandinavian countries, especially Sweden. In the post-Soviet Union world, Latvia is returning to its individualistic ways.

*Primary Motivations:* Personal achievement and progress are the motivating factors.

*Plan of Action:*

- Third-party introductions are not necessary, but are always useful.

- Many people you will be doing business with speak English. However, do not take this for granted. Check to see if you should have information translated and use an interpreter.
- Contracts can be verbal. If you assent to an agreement verbally, expect to be held to your word.
- Keep your presentation precise, logical, and straightforward.

*Local Protocol & Etiquette:*

- Greet someone with a firm handshake.
- Wait until you are invited to use someone's first name.
- Remain formal in your manners and posture, even though you are using first names.
- Dine continental style.

## LITHUANIA SUMMARY

**Cultural Data**

*Culture Type:* Progressive Family/Clan

*Region:* Central and Eastern Europe

*Local Influences:* Lithuania and Poland have had close ties for centuries, including their Roman Catholic faith. For most of the twentieth century, Lithuania was under Russian or Soviet rule, but it became independent in 1990.

*Primary Motivation:* The welfare and security of the family/clan and ethnic group are important.

*Plan of Action:*

- Approach with a personal reference or through a local agent.
- The first meeting should be at your potential partner's offices.
- Trust must be established before you will be accepted.
- Conform and be modest. Do not flaunt affluence.
- Do not entertain lavishly.
- Negotiate a win-win outcome.
- Sharing is important. Gift giving is common and should be reciprocated.

- Presentations should stress minimizing risks.
- Respect age. However, be aware that the younger generation is more entrepreneurial since the demise of the communist system.

*Local Protocol & Etiquette:*

- Customs and protocol are similar to Poland.

## MALAYSIA SUMMARY

**Cultural Data**

*Culture Type:* Group

*Region:* Asia/Pacific

*Local Influences:* According to the constitution, a Malay is someone who speaks the Malay language, professes Islam, and practices Malay customs. Eighty percent of the inhabitants speak Bahasa Malaysia, and many speak English. Arab traders brought Islam to the region. Read the section in Chapter Five regarding the Arab world and Islamic customs.

*Primary Motivation:* The welfare of the individualism group is the driving force.

*Plan of Action:*

- One who is powerful and successful shows his humility.
- Harmony must be maintained. Do not confront or question anyone in a negative way. Never say no. Expect them to always say yes, which might mean no.
- Approach through a local representative.
- Personal relationships must be established before business is done. Do not assume this means you are a personal friend.
- Top management should be present at the first meeting. Your church or organization should be represented by a group of specialists at this first meeting. Do not include a lawyer.
- Negotiations will be time-consuming. Expect to make many trips. Be patient.
- Recognize and respect the social position of all you encounter. Do not expect them to require equality.

- Never compliment a person directly. Never praise someone in front of his superiors. Praise the group.
- Negotiations may appear cyclical rather than linear. Be prepared to discuss any subject out of sequence at any time.

*Local Protocol & Etiquette:*

- Remember that the holy days of rest are Thursday and Friday (this varies in different parts of Malaysia). The overlay of Islam and Arab culture onto a previously group culture shows in the necessity for praise and self-esteem. Credit is lavished on the smallest successes. Status and power are not just organizing principles, they must be demonstrated.
- Do not invite a Muslim to lunch during the month of Ramadan. He will be fasting.
- Greeting with Westerners is done by a very light handclasp, which may be held for ten seconds. Don't rush the greeting. Ethnic Malays used to have no family name. Use the first name. This is also used for ethnic Chinese. It is all right to ask the proper form of address. When you explain how they should address you, match their level of formality.
- There is a significant Indian population in Malaysia. Reciprocity and public recognition facilitate decision-making. Cash is not commonly used to speed up decisions.
- Economic control lies with the Chinese minority.
- Representation in Malaysia is essential. Large trading companies usually control the importing of goods. Personal contacts are important.
- A simple, moderate handshake is an appropriate greeting. The family name comes first in sequence. Use titles and first name. The term "manager" does not denote someone very senior in the organization.
- Gifts should not be given on the first meeting. Never give trivial or token gifts such as corporate mementos.
- The visitor should never shout, show emotion, or curse.

- Never challenge the status, power, or prestige of Malaysians.
- Early presentations should include a history of your company, leading executives, special awards, and important customers.
- Malay executives value problem avoidance, and will not easily agree to anything new.
- Status is important, and is indicated on the business card by titles and degrees.
- Dress for hot weather, but white long sleeved shirts are a mark of prestige. A "lounge suit" is a dark business suit.
- Do not blow your nose in public. Spitting is forbidden.
- Do not host a social event until you have been invited as a guest. Let your host make the first invitation.
- Avoid giving any gift that might be construed as a bribe.
- Although the weather is hot, dress formally until you determine the degree of informality that is accepted by the people you are meeting.
- Refuse hospitality three times before accepting, so you don't look greedy.

## MEXICO SUMMARY

**Cultural Data**

*Culture Type:* Family/Clan

*Region:* Latin America

*Local Influences:* Mexico's proximity to the United States does not necessarily translate into a blend of cultures at the borders. Mexico remains strongly individualism.

*Primary Motivation:* The status, power, and welfare of the family are the motivating factor.

*Plan of Action:*

- Always address the Mexican formally, using his title and family name (next to last name).
- Expect to spend time establishing a relationship. Don't press

toward a business discussion until your counterpart offers an opening.

- Maintain formality in dress, posture, and speech until he relaxes the interaction.
- Your image is important in communicating your own status.
- Don't back away if your counterpart chooses to stand close during conversation.
- Establish contact through a well-regarded local agent.
- The first meeting should be on his turf.
- Send the most senior person from your company, along with one or two subordinates.
- Plan on using an interpreter. Translate materials into Latin American Spanish.
- Be prepared to make concessions, but only after appropriate resistance. Do not appear to negotiate these concessions.
- Minimize risks in any proposal.
- Do not assume you hold the most power because you are from the United States.
- Entertain at the best restaurants.
- Dine continental style.
- Once a relationship has been established, your company should not change the U.S. contact person, or the process will have to begin again. Mexicans trust people, not companies.

*Local Protocol & Etiquette:*

- The population is 60 percent mestizo, 30 percent Indian, and 9 percent European.
- Be careful not to make comparisons with the United Sates.
- In price negotiations, don't start with a very high price, expecting to bargain. This is insulting. Leave a little room for movement, but don't expect ignorance of the marketplace.

## MOROCCO SUMMARY

### Cultural Data

*Culture Type:* Family/Clan

*Region:* Arab World

*Local Influences:* French occupation shaped some of the customs and tendencies of this nation. Islam still remains the organizing force.

*Primary Motivation:* The welfare and security of the family group are the driving force.

*Plan of Action:*

- Be cognizant of the nature of Islamic law and morality. It dictates behavior.
- Make your first approach through a well-connected local representative.
- You must be present to be of consequence. Meetings should be at the Moroccan's offices.
- Relationships and trust come before business.
- Business associates must stay in constant communication for the relationship to continue.
- Expect delays in appointments. Time is not linear. Be patient and expect to take a long time completing a transaction.
- Humility is highly regarded, especially in a powerful person.
- A Moroccan loves to bargain, but do not inflate your price too much. Your first offer must be good enough to attract his attention.
- Minimize risks and uncertainty in your proposals. Praise and appreciation for your counterpart must be verbalized often.
- Maintain formality in behavior, appearance, and address.
- Project a successful image.
- Never refuse hospitality. Always reciprocate.
- Never reprimand or criticize directly. Failure is not directly acknowledged. Honor is very important. Deal with negatives euphemistically.
- Never admit that you are a "self-made man." Lineage is important. You are a reflection of your entire family.

- Proposals, plans, and negotiations should focus on the "people" issues.

*Local Protocol & Etiquette:*

- Women should never make eye contact with men who are strangers. They will interpret it as an invitation.
- Moroccan bureaucracy was patterned after the French. Business is conducted formally
- Print business cards in both Arabic and English.
- French is spoken by much of the business class. Use an interpreter.
- Business is never done without serving tea first.
- You will probably be invited to a home dinner. Men and women eat separately. The women get the leftovers.

## NETHERLANDS SUMMARY

**Cultural Data**

*Culture Type:* Individualistic

*Region:* Western Europe

*Local Influences:* The Dutch have always looked beyond their small country to the world beyond. They have an international focus.

*Primary Motivation:* Personal achievement and productivity are important.

*Plan of Action:*

- The Dutch have an aversion to chaos and an affinity for self-organizing systems.
- Realism and structure are important concepts. Be well-organized and realistic.
- Punctuality and precise scheduling are important.
- Greet with a firm handshake. Begin by using last names. Your potential partner may invite you to use first names fairly early on.
- Introduce yourself to others in a large group. Self-control is a virtue. Control of the body indicates a disciplined mind.
- Privacy is important. Don't ask very personal questions.

- Dress in a traditional, understated business suit.
- Your presentation material should be in English. A translator will probably not be necessary.
- Negotiate a win-win outcome.

*Local Protocol & Etiquette:*

- Shake hands when meeting and leaving. As you are introduced, repeat your last name. Always stand when being introduced.
- If you don't introduce yourself before speaking, the Dutch may be offended by your casual behavior.
- Be prepared to discuss world politics with the Dutch.
- Don't offer compliments until you know someone well.
- Don't get up during a meal, even to go to the bathroom. It is considered rude.
- When entertaining at a restaurant, the host usually chooses and orders for the whole party.
- Women are treated as equals in business.
- Business dinners are more popular than business lunches.
- Invitations should not be spontaneous.

## NEW ZEALAND SUMMARY

### Cultural Data

*Culture Type:* Individualistic, Family/Clan

*Region:* Australia

*Local Influences:* Australians originally colonized New Zealand. Later, more cultivated settlers arrived from England. New Zealand tends to be more English than Australia, but is still closer to the individualists profile than to the family/clan profile of the British.

*Primary Motivations:* Personal welfare is important.

*Plan of Action:*

- Return New Zealanders' informality, but don't initiate it.
- Decrease their sense of isolation by holding the first meeting at their offices.

- A local agent is not necessary, but a third-party introduction always makes contact easier.
- Keep a local representative on staff to keep up on local developments and give you a local presence.
- Keep equality in mind at all times, from the structure of your business proposal to opportunities for socializing.
- Be sure to communicate to your potential partner the importance to you of your mutual business objectives. Do not defer to him, yet do not project superiority.
- Be straightforward.

*Local Protocol & Etiquette:*

- Greet with a firm handshake and "hello." Begin with last names, but first name usage will follow almost immediately.
- Give your business card at the introduction, but know that your counterpart may not give you one.
- Titles and degrees are not impressive. A New Zealander will make his own judgment as to the quality of the person with whom he is speaking.
- Business dress is conservative, and not overly elegant.
- Be friendly, relaxed, modest, and unpretentious. Don't try to impress your host.
- Gifts are not given, unless you are invited to someone's home.
- Don't fill your presentation with hype or glitz. A simple, direct presentation is more effective. Get to the point.
- Decision-making can occur at lower levels, but things still take longer than in the United States.
- You may be invited out for a drink after work. Don't bring up business unless your host does. New Zealanders make a clear distinction between work and play.

## NORWAY SUMMARY

**Cultural Data**

*Culture Type:* Individualistic

*Region:* Western Europe

*Local Influences:* Norway stresses its own independence, having been ruled by Denmark and then Sweden for much of its history. Norwegians are adamant about projecting a national identity.

*Primary Motivation:* Self-interest and national self-determination are important factors.

*Plan of Action:*

- Be sure to treat them as equals. Do not compare Norwegian and U.S. standards of living. They do not care. They are fiercely defensive of Norwegian culture.
- Do not refer to a Norwegian as a Scandinavian.
- Norwegians are not rigidly formal, but polite formality should be maintained. Don't be stiff, or present a severe or overly elegant image.
- Third-party introductions are not necessary, but they are always helpful.
- Use English in all business dealings.
- Management is not elitist.
- Power is valued over wealth, since the tax system equalizes everyone's wages.
- During conversation, avoid personal questions. Privacy is important.

*Local Protocol & Etiquette:*

- Shake hands when meeting and leaving.
- Never speak in a loud voice.
- Women will not have difficulty being taken seriously in Norway.

## PAKISTAN SUMMARY

**Cultural Data**

*Culture Type:* Family/Clan

*Region:* Arab World

*Local Influences:* Pakistan was established as a separate Muslim state during the British partitioning of India in 1947. The government is a democracy. The country is not Arab, but conforms to Islamic law. Arab customs, which proceed from Islamic law and family/clan culture, largely apply to Pakistan.

*Primary Motivation:* The welfare of the family/clan is the driving force.

*Plan of Action:*

- Be cognizant of the nature of Islamic law and morality. It dictates behavior.
- Business associates must stay in constant communication for the relationship to continue.
- Expect delays in appointments. Time is not linear. Be patient and expect to take a long time completing a transaction.
- Humility is highly regarded, especially in a powerful person.
- Make your first approach through a well-connected local representative.
- You must be present to be of consequence. Meetings should be at your potential partner's offices.
- Relationships and trust come before business.
- A Pakistani loves to bargain, but do not inflate your price too much. Your first offer must be good enough to attract his attention.
- Minimize risks and uncertainty in your proposals. Praise and appreciation for your counterpart must be verbalized often.
- Maintain formality in behavior, appearance, and address.
- Project a successful image.
- Never refuse hospitality. Always reciprocate.
- Never reprimand or criticize directly. Failure is not directly

acknowledged. Honor is very important. Deal with negatives euphemistically.

- Never admit that you are a "self-made man." Lineage is important. You are a reflection of your entire family.
- Proposals, plans, and negotiations should focus on the "people" issues. People are most important to family/clan cultures.

*Local Protocol & Etiquette:*

- Urdu and English are the official languages. Note that the Urdu words for yesterday and tomorrow are the same.
- Forms of address are very complicated, since there are many variations on Pakistani names. Ask how they should be addressed.
- Men should never wear a suit and tie from November through March. The jacket need never be worn except when seeing government officials.
- Never gesture with a closed fist.
- Women are generally not well received in business.

## PARAGUAY SUMMARY

**Cultural Data**

*Culture Type:* Family/Clan

*Region:* Latin America

*Local Influences:* The population is 95 percent mestizo, which seems to indicate a more egalitarian social structure. The European minority still holds economic power.

*Primary Motivation:* Family status and power determine a person's prosperity.

*Plan of Action:*

- Maintain formality in dress, posture, and speech until your potential partner relaxes the interaction.
- Your image is important in communicating your own status.
- Don't back away if your counterpart chooses to stand close during conversation.

- Establish contact through a well-regarded local agent.
- The first meeting should be on the Paraguayan's turf.
- Send the most senior person from your company, along with one or two subordinates.
- Plan on using an interpreter. Translate materials into Latin American Spanish.
- Always address the Paraguayan formally, using his title and family name (next to last name).
- Expect to spend time establishing a relationship. Don't press toward a business discussion until your counterpart offers an opening.
- Be prepared to make concessions, but only after appropriate resistance. Do not appear to negotiate these concessions.
- Minimize risks in any proposal.
- Do not assume you hold the most power because you are from the United States.
- Entertain at the best restaurants.
- Dine continental style.
- Once a relationship has been established, your church or organization should not change the U.S. contact person, or the process will have to begin again. Paraguayans trust people, not companies.

*Local Protocol & Etiquette*

- Formal titles are used, but someone with a university degree is referred to as *licenciado* instead of doctor, which is reserved for PhDs and medical doctors.
- Don't wink. It has sexual connotations.

## PERU SUMMARY

### Cultural Data

*Culture Type:* Family/Clan

*Region:* Latin America

*Local Influences:* Peru was the seat of the Incan civilization. The population is 45 percent Indian, 37 percent mestizo (European and Indian mix), and 15 percent European. The business class is mostly the European minority. There are also a significant number of Japanese and Chinese businesspeople in Peru.

*Primary Motivation:* The family status and welfare come first.

*Plan of Action:*

- Always address the Peruvian formally, using his title and family name (next to last name).
- Establish contact through a well-regarded local agent.
- The first meeting should be on the Peruvian's turf.
- Send the most senior person from your company, along with one or two subordinates.
- Plan on using an interpreter. Translate materials into Latin American Spanish.
- Expect to spend time establishing a relationship. Don't press toward a business discussion until your counterpart offers an opening.
- Maintain formality in dress, posture, and speech until your counterpart relaxes the interaction.
- Your image is important in communicating your own status.
- Don't back away if your counterpart chooses to stand close during conversation.
- Be prepared to make concessions, but only after appropriate resistance. Do not appear to negotiate these concessions. Latinos like zero-sum games.
- Minimize risks in any proposal.
- Do not assume you hold the most power because you are from the United States.
- Entertain at the best restaurants.
- Dine continental style.
- Once a relationship has been established, your church or organization should not change the U.S. contact person, or the process will have to begin again. Peruvians trust people, not companies.

*Local Protocol & Etiquette:*

- Unlike other South American countries, men should not cross their legs one knee over the other. One ankle on the other knee is all right.

- Peruvians use lots of hand gestures when they speak. Be careful of your own.
- It is best not to discuss ancestry or politics in Peru. There is an extremely strong caste system in Peru based on ancestry.
- If you are invited to a home, bring the hostess flowers. They must be roses or they will think you are cheap. Avoid red, which means love.

## PHILIPPINES SUMMARY

**Cultural Data**

*Culture Type:* Group

*Region:* Asia/Pacific

*Local Influences:* The Philippines is a predominantly Catholic country. The Christian culture overlays an inherent group base. The result is an emphasis on power. The public sector is important to all private business transactions. The country operates under a system of guided free enterprise. Power is ultimately held in the government.

*Primary Motivation:* The status, power, and wealth of the family guides behavior.

*Plan of Action:*

- Approach through a local representative.
- Personal relationships must be established before business is done. Do not assume this means you are a personal friend.
- Top management should be present at the first meeting. Your church or organization should be represented by a group of specialists at this first meeting. Do not include a lawyer.
- Negotiations will be time-consuming. Expect to make many trips. Be patient.
- One who is powerful and successful shows his humility.
- Harmony must be maintained. Do not confront or question

anyone in a negative way. Never say no. Expect them to always say yes, which might mean no.

- Recognize and respect the social position of all you encounter. Do not expect them to require equality.
- Never compliment a person directly. Never praise someone in front of his superiors. Praise the group.
- Negotiations may appear cyclical rather than linear. Be prepared to discuss any subject out of sequence at any time.

*Local Protocol & Etiquette:*

- Greet the Filipino with a firm handshake, but not with much pumping. Titles should be used along with the surname. Many names are Spanish, as the Philippines was colonized by Spain. Therefore, the proper surname would be the next to the last name, the name of the father's family.
- The culture exhibits its family/clan behavior by encouraging praise and building self-esteem through compliments, unlike most of Asia. This is a country that learned machismo from its Spanish ancestors.
- Business is not discussed at the first meeting. If the host casually says that he would like to hear your proposal sometime, that is a signal to leave and schedule another appointment with the secretary. The second meeting should include a luncheon invitation from you.
- A confrontational style is not appropriate in negotiations. Harmony should prevail. The presenter should plan a multimedia presentation. Local representatives should be present at all negotiations.
- Upper management does not respond to detail. Rather, they prefer to see the big picture. Control on all issues rests with the CEO.
- Filipinos are not punctual. They do expect you to be on time. Waiting is often a status game.
- If decisions are delayed, negotiators may require a commission, rebate, or bonus. This is a complex issue for Americans, who can-

not, by law, provide kickbacks. This is all the more reason to have a local agent to counsel you on tactics.

- Dinner invitations are the sign of a good relationship. Entertainment will be lavish. Dinners are social affairs and may include wives. Reciprocate invitations.
- The visitor should project an air of importance and subtle power. Wealth and social status are important.
- Filipinos are more relaxed about business cards. You should offer yours first. They may or may not give you theirs.
- At the end of a business deal, invite your counterpart and associates to dinner. You may have to ask several times whenever issuing an invitation, since an invitation may casually be offered as a polite gesture.
- Dress conservatively until you know how casually the people you are meeting with will be dressed.

## POLAND SUMMARY

### Cultural Data

*Culture Type:* Progressive Family/Clan

*Region:* Central and Eastern Europe

*Local Influences:* Poland has been a Roman Catholic country for over one thousand years. Even under Communism and in the decades during which Poland did not officially exist, the Polish identity was maintained through the Roman Catholic Church. The country is now democratic, with a free-market economy.

*Primary Motivation:* The welfare of the family group and the security of the ethnic group are the motivation factors.

*Plan of Action*

- Conform and be modest. Do not flaunt affluence.
- Do not entertain lavishly.
- Sharing is important. Gift giving is common and should be reciprocated.

- Presentations should stress minimizing risks.
- Respect age. However, be aware that the younger generation is more entrepreneurial since the demise of the communist system.
- Approach with a personal reference or through a local agent.
- First meeting should be at your potential partner's offices.
- Trust must be established before you will be accepted.

*Local Protocol & Etiquette:*

- Poles value punctuality, skill and intelligence, privacy, family, and loyalty to the Polish nation.
- They have a strong work ethic.
- They are critical of themselves and their institutions.
- Direct communication is preferred.
- Facts are more important than emotions in decision-making, but relationships are more important than laws.
- Poland has strong power hierarchies and is a male-dominated society.
- Translate materials into Polish.
- A local representative will make business and social arrangements much easier.
- Business lunches and dinners are popular. Expect to stay out late, or you may insult your potential partners.
- Shake hands to meet, greet, and say good-bye. Use last names.
- Avoid loud behavior in public.
- Polish men have more traditional views of women. A woman should not talk to a strange man, or it will be considered flirting.
- A gift is appropriate at the first meeting.
- Dress conservatively.

## PORTUGAL SUMMARY

**Cultural Data**

*Culture Type:* Family/Clan

*Region:* Western Europe

*Local Influences:* Portugal has a strong national identity separate from Spain in spite of their proximity and relative size. The Portuguese have traditional ties with England, and feel comfortable emulating their behavior. The Portuguese are certainly Individualistic, without the modifying influence of England's strong Celtic character. Business procedures would be more like the Spanish in terms of the need for security and relationship building, but more formal and reserved in style.

*Primary Motivation:* The welfare and security of the family group are important factors.

*Plan of Action:*

- Plan on using an interpreter. Translate materials into Portuguese.
- Always address a Portuguese formally, using his title and family name (next to last name).
- Expect to spend time establishing a relationship. Don't press toward a business discussion until your counterpart offers an opening.
- Maintain formality in dress, posture, and speech until he relaxes the interaction.
- Your image is important in communicating your own status.
- Don't back away if your counterpart chooses to stand close during conversation.
- Establish contact through a well-regarded local agent.
- The first meeting should be on your potential partner's turf.
- Send the most senior person from your church or organization, along with one or two subordinates.
- Be prepared to make concessions, but only after appropriate resistance. Do not appear to negotiate these concessions.
- Minimize risks in any proposal.
- Entertain at the best restaurants.

- Dine continental style.
- Once a relationship has been established, your church or organization should not change the U.S. contact person, or the process will have to begin again.

*Local Protocol & Etiquette:*

- Shake hands when meeting and leaving. Shake hands with everyone present.
- Business cards need not be translated, but plan on bringing an interpreter to meetings. Exchange business cards at the beginning of a meeting.
- The Portuguese respect professional women. Dress elegantly, but conservatively.
- Portuguese tend to be somewhat unreliable in meeting deadlines.
- Give gifts after you have begun business dealings. Ask your contact if he would like anything from the United States. He may appreciate access to technical products, like computer programs, books, or CDs.
- Dinner is always social. Do business at lunch only.
- Finish everything on your plate. Never eat with your hands. Keep your napkin on the table or you will be offered one continually.

## ROMANIA SUMMARY

### Cultural Data

*Culture Type:* Progressive Family/Clan

*Region:* Central and Eastern Europe

*Local Influences:* The early history of Romania was dominated by the Roman Empire, of which Romania was a province. Its language is based on Latin. However, its proximity to the subsequent Byzantine Empire along with its progressive Individualistic nature resulted in a predominantly Orthodox Christian state. After World War II, Romania came under the influence of Soviet Union. Today, Romania is a democratic republic, and one of the poorest countries in Europe.

*Primary Motivation:* The welfare of the family group is the motivating factor.

*Plan of Action:*

- Participate in their brand of conformity and modesty. Do not flaunt affluence.
- Do not entertain lavishly.
- Sharing is important. Gift giving is common and should be reciprocated.
- Presentations should stress minimizing risks.
- Respect age. However, be aware that the younger generation is more entrepreneurial since the demise of the communist system.
- Approach through a personal reference or through a local agent.
- First meeting should be at your potential partner's offices.
- Trust must be established before you will be accepted.

*Local Protocol & Etiquette:*

- Romanians distrust authority, and are reverting to insular Individualistic structure.
- They have very weak business management skills.
- The more educated the Romanian, the more objective he is in decision-making. Subjective emotions do play a part.
- The current priority for all Romanians is to feed and house their families.
- Opinions and emotions are freely expressed.
- Send letters in English. A letter that must be translated is more respected.
- Distrust makes it difficult to make contacts. Use local representatives. Once you are accepted, the relationship will be a strong bond.
- Romanians are status-conscious. Stay in the best hotel. Have your title and degrees printed on business cards.
- Small gifts are appreciated at the first meeting.
- Shake hands often when coming and going, each time you see someone in a day, and when being introduced. Use a firm grip. Use last names and professional titles.

- Romanians gesture a lot with their hands. You should not, since many U.S. gestures can be seriously misunderstood.
- Eat continental style.
- Use European manners.

## RUSSIA SUMMARY

**Cultural Data**

*Culture Type:* Progressive Family/Clan

*Region:* Central and Eastern Europe

*Local Influences:* Russians have an affinity for Americans. This may be because both are used to life on a broad canvas. Their nations' territories are extensive, and their political powers have been broad. Although they stood at opposite ideological poles, there is much the two peoples have in common.

*Primary Motivation:* The welfare and security of the family group are the driving forces.

*Plan of Action:*

- Approach with a personal reference or through a local agent.
- First meeting should be at their offices.
- Trust must be established before you will be accepted.
- Conform and be modest. Do not flaunt affluence.
- Do not entertain lavishly.
- Negotiate a win-win outcome.
- Sharing is important. Gift giving is common and should be reciprocated.
- Presentations should stress minimizing risks.
- Respect age. However, be aware that the younger generation is more entrepreneurial since the demise of the communist system.

*Local Protocol & Etiquette:*

- Don't hire an expatriate Russian to represent you in Russia.
- Russians see themselves as rational and conscious realists. They are also romantic and sentimental.

- Private business is done on trust. This makes relationships very important to doing business. Initial contacts should be made through a trusted third-party.
- European manners are used. Keep your hands out of your pockets, use good posture, don't cross your ankle over the other knee, and remember that whistling indoors brings bad financial luck.
- Be punctual. They may not be.
- Shake hands coming and going and when introduced. Use a firm handshake.
- Address your host by last name. Do not use the term "comrade." When you become friendly, he may suggest any variety of nicknames.
- Observe age and rank, and adjust your protocol to honor these.
- You will probably need an interpreter. But the presence of an interpreter doesn't mean the Russians with whom you are dealing do not understand English. Translate written materials into Russian, especially sample contracts, to save time in translation.
- Bring many business cards, printed in English and Russian. There are few telephone books, so people collect cards. They may not have a good supply themselves. Write down a list of meeting participants and their phone numbers.
- Token gifts are often exchanged at the first meeting. Go to Russia prepared to give a lot of gifts, and bring an extra bag for the ones they will give to you.
- Business will begin soon after a bit of conversation. The Russians may ask you to sign an agreement of cooperation, which is not a contract to work together, but to express mutual interest. It is all right to sign it.
- Be clear of your intentions for this first meeting. If it is merely exploratory, say so. The Russians may have expectations of you as their savior.
- The Russian negotiating team will usually have specialists with different interests. The head of the team will do the most talking and you should direct most of your remarks to him.

- If you want to make a big impression on them, invite them to come visit you in the United States. You will be responsible for their expenses during the visit, but they will pay the airfare.
- Negotiations may take time. Time is not money. Time is wisdom.
- Management skills are often lacking. Don't leave anything unsaid. Don't assume they will fill in the blanks properly.
- Presentations should be concrete, visual, and factual with detailed specifications.
- Decisions are often made subjectively, based on emotion. Logic is considered second.
- Russians are not afraid to express emotion, and use it as a tool. Sometimes they will storm out of a meeting, only to return later. Don't lose your temper, but it is wise to meet emotion with emotion. It is often necessary to play hardball.
- End all meetings with a summary of the meeting and action items for the next meeting.
- Very few people stop for lunch. Lunch is taken more often in Moscow than elsewhere. There are only a few decent restaurants, anyway. At the end of talks, host a dinner at a hotel restaurant. Wives are generally not included.
- The continental style of eating is used.
- If you are invited to someone's home, which is rare, bring an odd number of flowers. Even numbers are for funerals.
- Businesswomen are respected in Russia. There will be no risk of harassment.

## SAUDI ARABIA SUMMARY

### Cultural Data

*Culture Type:* Family/Clan

*Region:* Arab World

*Local Influences:* Saudi Arabia maintains the strictest Islamic code of behavior with no tolerance of transgressions, even by foreigners.

*Primary Motivation:* The welfare and security of the family/clan and upholding Islamic law are the driving forces in this culture.

*Plan of Action:*

- Be cognizant of the nature of Islamic law and morality. It dictates behavior.
- Expect delays in appointments. Time is not linear. Be patient and expect to take a long time completing a transaction.
- Humility is highly regarded, especially in a powerful person.
- Make your first approach through a well-connected local representative.
- You must be present to be of consequence. Meetings should be at the Saudis' offices.
- Relationships and trust come before business.
- Business associates must stay in constant communication for the relationship to continue.
- A Saudi loves to bargain, but do not inflate your price too much. Your first offer must be good enough to attract his attention.
- Minimize risks and uncertainty in your proposals. Praise and appreciation for your counterpart must be verbalized often.
- Maintain formality in behavior, appearance, and address.
- Project a successful image.
- Never refuse hospitality. Always reciprocate.
- Never reprimand or criticize directly. Failure is not directly acknowledged. Honor is very important. Deal with negatives euphemistically.
- Never admit that you are a "self-made man." Lineage is important. You are a reflection of your entire family.
- Proposals, plans, and negotiations should focus on the "people" issues.

*Local Protocol & Etiquette:*

- Whenever someone enters the room, always rise and shake hands.
- Never enter the country with Western magazines. The wife of a foreign businessman was deported for carrying a copy of *Cosmopolitan.*

- Arabs usually wait to be asked more than once before accepting second helpings of food.
- Whenever something is offered, refuse first, then accept.
- Never send a woman to do business, even as a member of a team. There are strict legal restrictions on women's activities.
- Print business cards in both Arabic and English.
- Present a modest gift after meeting someone two or three times.

## SINGAPORE SUMMARY

**Cultural Data**

*Culture Type:* Group

*Region:* Asia/Pacific

*Local Influences:* Capitalism reigns in Singapore, and the Chinese are in control, representing 76 percent of the population. Singapore is the closest thing to a meritocracy in the Far East. Few people get ahead without long hours and hard work.

*Primary Motivation:* The welfare of the family and ethnic group are the motivating factors.

*Plan of Action:*

- One who is powerful and successful shows his humility.
- Harmony must be maintained. Do not confront or question anyone in a negative way. Never say no. Expect them to always say yes, which might mean no.
- Approach through a local representative.
- Personal relationships must be established before business is done. Do not assume this means you are a personal friend.
- Top management should be present at the first meeting. Your church or organization should be represented by a group of specialists at this first meeting. Do not include a lawyer.
- Negotiations will be time-consuming. Expect to make many trips. Be patient.
- Recognize and respect the social position of all you encounter.

- Never compliment a person directly. Never praise someone in front of his superiors. Praise the group.
- Negotiations may appear cyclical rather than linear. Be prepared to discuss any subject out of sequence at any time.

*Local Protocol & Etiquette:*

- Even though Singaporeans appear Western in their work ethic and meritocracy, all other protocol is generally along the Chinese model. Communication and feedback is not direct, saving face is important, and relationships are a must.
- Sending low-level representatives is a waste of time.
- Be punctual.
- Singaporeans laugh as a sign of anxiety or embarrassment, not levity.
- Use a limp handclasp as a greeting. Use the person's title and first name, which is usually the family name, or the appropriate given name, if the person is a Muslim Malay.
- Singapore prides itself on being the least corrupt state in Asia. Gifts are given only to friends. Decline a gift three times and do not open it in the presence of the giver.
- Business moves fairly quickly by Asian standards. Communication channels are usually clear.
- After an initial meeting of about forty-five minutes, the visitor should initiate leaving.
- An invitation to one of Singapore's private clubs confers prestige.
- Refusing hospitality shows bad manners.

## SLOVAKIA SUMMARY

### Cultural Data

*Culture Type:* Progressive Family/Clan

*Region:* Central and Eastern Europe

*Local Influences:* Until World War I, Slovakia was under Hungarian rule for about a thousand years. After World War II, it was united with the Czech Republic as Czechoslovakia. In 1948, the country came under communist domination. In 1989, Czechoslovakia became an independent democracy, but nationalism surfaced. In 1992, the Czech Republic and Slovakia became separate nations.

*Primary Motivations:* The welfare of the family/clan and that of the national ethnic identity are the motivating factors.

*Plan of Action:*

- Participate in the Slovaks' brand of conformity and modesty. Do not flaunt affluence.
- Do not entertain lavishly.
- Approach with a personal reference or through a local agent.
- First meeting should be at the Slovak's offices.
- Trust must be established before you will be accepted.
- Sharing is important. Gift giving is common and should be reciprocated.
- Presentations should stress minimizing risks.
- Respect age. However, be aware that the younger generation is more entrepreneurial since the demise of the communist system.

*Local Protocol & Etiquette*

- Slovaks are proud of their peasant roots and peasant values, which include hard work, generosity, honesty, and modesty.
- They view entrepreneurs as greedy.
- They do not value aggressiveness and individualistic self-confidence.
- Education is valued above wealth.
- Use titles when greeting someone.
- Print your titles and degrees on your business card.
- Many hand gestures are used. Avoid using American gestures as some of them are offensive.
- European manners are appropriate.

## SOUTH KOREA SUMMARY

**Cultural Data**

*Culture Type:* Group

*Region:* Asia/Pacific

*Local Influences:* In comparing South Koreans to the Japanese, one Westerner observed that they are less ethnocentric, less anti-foreign, and less chauvinistic. They are strongly capitalistic and are familiar with Western business.

*Primary Motivations:* Group power, wealth, and security are the driving forces in this culture.

*Plan of Action:*

- One who is powerful and successful shows his humility.
- Harmony must be maintained. Do not confront or question anyone in a negative way. Never say no. Expect them to always say yes, which might mean no.
- Approach through a local representative.
- Personal relationships must be established before business is done. Do not assume this means you are a personal friend.
- Top management should be present at the first meeting. Your church or organization should be represented by a group of specialists at this first meeting. Do not include a lawyer.
- Negotiations will be time-consuming. Expect to make many trips. Be patient.
- Recognize and respect the social position of all you encounter.
- Never compliment a person directly. Never praise someone in front of his superiors. Praise the group.
- Negotiations may appear cyclical rather than linear. Be prepared to discuss any subject out of sequence at any time.

*Local Protocol & Etiquette:*

- Be punctual for all appointments.
- Shake hands with a moderate grip, and add a slight bow. To indicate added respect, support your right forearm with your left hand.
- The junior person should initiate the greeting and be the first to

bow. The senior person will extend his hand first. Women do not commonly shake hands. A businesswoman will have to initiate a handshake with a Korean man.

- Do not introduce yourself in a group. Wait to be introduced.
- Address the person by his family name, which comes first, along with his title or Mr. When writing, use the greeting "To my respected..." with the title and full name.
- Relationships and hospitality are important, but Koreans are most familiar with Western practices.
- Although harmony is very important, Koreans are the most likely of all Asian societies to express emotion and to be direct and even somewhat aggressive during negotiations. You, however, should remain calm.
- Try to match the rank of individuals who are meeting. Age is an important determining factor in establishing rank.
- Koreans often hold one-on-one meetings. This does not contradict their group nature. The person you meet with is acting as an intermediary who must present your proposal to the entire company. It is important to establish a good relationship with this person.
- Do not use triangle shapes in your presentation. They have a negative connotation.
- Silence can be a clue that you were not understood. Do allow some silence for thought, but follow up by rephrasing your last point.
- Koreans are more likely than other Asians to say no, but will still avoid it when possible.
- If during the meeting the Koreans return to social small talk, it is an indication that they are through discussing business for the day.
- Meetings begin and end with a bow. If the ending bow is deeper and longer than the opening bow, it is an indication that the meeting went well.
- Do not bring gifts from Japan or mention contacts or travel there. Koreans hold great animosity toward the Japanese.
- Offer your business card with your right hand. Treat it with digni-

ty. Don't put a person's card in your wallet, and then put the wallet in your back pocket.

- Do not write a person's name in red ink. It means the person is deceased.
- Do not talk business over a meal unless your host does. When eating, do not finish everything on your plate. This indicates that the host did not provide enough food and you are still hungry. Always refuse food twice before accepting.
- Never blow your nose in public.
- Eye contact shows sincerity and attentiveness to the speaker.
- When giving or receiving gifts, use both hands. Do not open the gift in the presence of the giver. Expect the gift to be refused at first. This is good manners. Reciprocate gifts and hospitality.

## SPAIN SUMMARY

**Cultural Data**

*Culture Type:* Family/Clan

*Region:* Western Europe

*Local Influences:* Spain's history is dominated by Roman, Islamic, and Catholic rule at various times. Each influence was resident for centuries. These three cultural powers were all family/clan in nature, with strong authoritarian power structures.

*Primary Motivation:* The power and welfare of the family group are the driving forces.

*Plan of Action:*

- Plan on using an interpreter. Translate materials into Spanish.
- Always address the Spaniard formally, using his title and family name (next to last name).
- Expect to spend time establishing a relationship. Don't press toward a business discussion until your counterpart offers an opening.
- Maintain formality in dress, posture, and speech until he relaxes the interaction.

- Your image is important in communicating your own status.
- Don't back away if your counterpart chooses to stand close during conversation.
- Establish contact through a well-regarded local agent.
- The first meeting should be on the Spaniard's turf.
- Send the most senior person from your church or organization, along with one or two subordinates.
- Be prepared to make concessions, but only after appropriate resistance. Do not appear to negotiate these concessions. The Spanish like zero-sum games.
- Minimize risks in any proposal.
- Entertain at the best restaurants.
- Dine continental style.
- Once a relationship has been established, your church or organization should not change the U.S. contact person, or the process will have to begin again.

*Local Protocol & Etiquette:*

- Shake hands when meeting and leaving.
- Older people and people of high rank may address you by your first name. Don't take this as a signal to use theirs. Use their surname until invited to do otherwise. If a person of high rank asks you to use his first name, precede it by "Don" as a sign of respect.
- Beware of casual U.S. gestures. Some of them are offensive. Use the whole hand, not the fingers, to gesture.
- Dressing well at all times gives the impression of accomplishment.
- Businesswomen must project a professional air. Dress elegantly, but conservatively. Don't be flirtatious in any way. Men may make comments to women as they walk by. Be sure not to react or acknowledge them in any way. If you return the gaze of a man, he will think you are interested in him.
- Correspond with a Spanish company in formal English. Do not have letters translated into Spanish. The translation will probably not be sufficiently formal, flowery, and poetic, and might offend.

- Be careful in gift giving. Wait until you have formed a relationship. Products or artwork representative of your home state are appropriate gifts.

## SWEDEN SUMMARY

**Cultural Data**

*Culture Type:* Individualist

*Region:* Western Europe

*Local Influences:* Similar to Denmark and Norway, Sweden has turned its natural sense of independence and equality into a legislated equality by economic conformity. They are strongly capitalistic, though, and not as protectionist as Norway. Unlike the Norwegians, Swedes have a history of strong and adventurous monarchs. Their power hierarchy is stronger than Norway, but not as strong as Germany.

*Primary Motivations:* Equality and self-determination are the motivating factors.

*Plan of Action:*

- Be sure to treat them as equals. Do not compare Swedish and U.S. standards of living. They are not impressed by your wealth, possessions, or status.
- Do not refer to a Swede as a Scandinavian.
- Third-party introductions are not necessary, but they are always helpful.
- Use English in most business dealings.
- Your proposal should emphasize efficiency, simplicity, and cost savings. It should be rational and linear in its presentation.
- Swedes are not rigidly formal, but polite formality should be maintained. Don't be stiff, or present a severe or overly elegant image.
- During conversation, avoid personal questions. Privacy is important.
- Swedes highly value intelligence and education.

*Local Protocol & Etiquette:*

- Shake hands when meeting and leaving.

- Upper-class Swedes address each other in the third person, as in "How is Mr. Nordstrom today?" instead of "How are you?"
- Businesswomen will be taken seriously, and can invite men to business lunches without feeling awkward.

## SWITZERLAND SUMMARY

**Cultural Data**

*Culture Type:* Individualist

*Region:* Western Europe

*Local Influences:* The Swiss are strong Individualistic and have formed strong power structures. They are made up of people from France, Germany, and Italy, combining the independent nature in each of these cultures into a contiguous set of provinces called cantons. They are insistent on their own identities and self-determination. The Swiss believe in national unity, but not uniformity.

*Primary Motivations:* Personal accomplishment and self-determination.

*Plan of Action:*

- Maintain formality at all times. Self-control is very important.
- Dress very conservatively and formally.
- Be prepared to back up all of your figures. Allow some room for negotiation.
- The Swiss value intelligence. They are impressed by thoughtful questions.
- Your presentation should highlight how their business will be enhanced. You must prove all your claims.
- The Swiss prefer the power position of meeting on their own turf.
- A third-party introduction is imperative. Bankers and lawyers make appropriate references.
- Assume that meetings will be conducted in English. Translate all material and use an interpreter only if you know the language of the person you will be meeting.

- All documents should look polished and professional.
- Privacy is important. Don't ask personal questions.
- Dine continental style.

*Local Protocol & Etiquette*

- When you write to a Swiss company, address the letter to an individual, but address the envelope to the company.
- Business cards should include titles in English.
- Hand your card to the receptionist when you arrive.
- Business lunches are more common than dinners. Dinner is purely a social occasion.
- Appropriate gifts include whiskey or brandy, food products from your home state, and coffee table books.

## SYRIA SUMMARY

**Cultural Data**

*Culture Type:* Individualistic

*Region:* Arab World

*Local Influences:* Although Syria is an Arab country and nearly all its citizens profess Islam, it is officially a secular country.

*Primary Motivations:* The welfare and status of the family group.

*Plan of Action:*

- Be cognizant of the nature of Islamic law and morality.
- Expect delays in appointments. Time is not linear. Be patient and expect to take a long time completing a transaction.
- Humility is highly regarded, especially in a powerful person.
- Make your first approach through a well-connected local representative.
- You must be present to be of consequence. Meetings should be at the Syrians' offices.
- Relationships and trust come before business.
- Business associates must stay in constant communication for the relationship to continue.

- A Syrian loves to bargain, but do not inflate your price too much. Your first offer must be good enough to attract his attention.
- Minimize risks and uncertainty in your proposals. Praise and appreciation for your counterpart must be verbalized often.
- Maintain formality in behavior, appearance, and address.
- Project a successful image.
- Never refuse hospitality. Always reciprocate.
- Never reprimand or criticize directly. Failure is not directly acknowledged. Honor is very important. Deal with negatives euphemistically.
- Never admit that you are a "self-made man." Lineage is important. You are a reflection of your entire family.
- Proposals, plans, and negotiations should focus on the "people" issues.

*Local Protocol & Etiquette:*

- Educated Syrians are cosmopolitan, but conservative.

## TAIWAN SUMMARY

**Cultural Data**

*Culture Type:* Group

*Region:* Asia/Pacific

*Local Influences:* Taiwan largely consists of Chinese who fled communist rule in mainland China. There is deep animosity between the two nations.

*Primary Motivation:* The welfare and progress of the family and group are the motivating factors.

*Plan of Action:*

- One who is powerful and successful shows his humility.
- Harmony must be maintained. Do not confront or question anyone in a negative way. Never say no. Expect them to always say yes, which might mean no.
- Approach through a local representative.

- Personal relationships must be established before business is done. Do not assume this means you are a personal friend.
- Top management should be present at the first meeting. Your church or organization should be represented by a group of specialists at this first meeting. Do not include a lawyer.
- Negotiations will be time-consuming. Expect to make many trips. Be patient.
- Recognize and respect the social position of all you encounter.
- Never compliment a person directly. Never praise someone in front of his superiors. Praise the group.
- Negotiations may appear cyclical rather than linear. Be prepared to discuss any subject out of sequence at any time.

*Local Protocol & Etiquette:*

- Have written materials translated by a Taiwanese expert. Chinese characters are different in Taiwan and China.
- In a group, sit according to rank, with the most important member at the center, the next important to his right, third important to his left, etc.
- Greet someone with a slight bow and light handshake. If someone asks you, "Have you eaten?" the correct response is yes, even if you have not.
- Use the person's title or Mr. or Madam, with the family name, which comes first.
- Do not point with the index finger, use your whole hand. Chinese indicate themselves by pointing to their nose, instead of their chest as Americans do.
- Gifts may be given on the first trip. If offered a gift, always decline three times before accepting. Avoid giving clocks, or anything that cuts like a letter opener. Avoid the colors white, black, or blue.
- Evening business entertainment is very important. Dinner may be followed by entertainment at bars or clubs.
- The guest samples the food first. Eat lightly, leaving a small amount of food in the bowl. There may be as many as twenty

courses. If your bowl is empty it will be refilled. Refuse food three times before accepting, so you don't look greedy.

## THAILAND SUMMARY

**Cultural Data**

*Culture Type:* Group

*Region:* Asia/Pacific

*Local Influences:* Thais are very proud that their country never came under foreign rule, as did much of Southeast Asia. Thai means "free." The ethnic Chinese make up most of the business community. Ethnic Thais are more likely to be found in government positions. A cooperative, yet competitive, triumvirate of bureaucracy, military, and commercial elite rules Thailand.

*Primary Motivation:* The welfare and security of the group.

*Plan of Action:*

- One who is powerful and successful shows his humility.
- Harmony must be maintained. Do not confront or question anyone in a negative way. Never say no. Expect them to always say yes, which might mean no.
- Approach through a local representative.
- Personal relationships must be established before business is done. Do not assume this means you are a personal friend.
- Top management should be present at the first meeting. Your church or organization should be represented by a group of specialists at this first meeting. Do not include a lawyer.
- Negotiations will be time-consuming. Expect to make many trips. Be patient.
- Recognize and respect the social position of all you encounter.
- Never compliment a person directly. Never praise someone in front of his superiors. Praise the group.
- Negotiations may appear cyclical rather than linear. Be prepared to discuss any subject out of sequence at any time.

*Local Protocol & Etiquette:*

- The greeting in Thailand is the *wai.* It is done by pressing your hands together as if in prayer and pointing the fingers outward. Elbows are close to the body. You lower your head toward your hands. The higher the hands are placed, the greater the respect. Westerners may shake hands, but Thais appreciate the effort.
- Titles are very important. Use titles plus the person's first name.
- Be punctual.
- Entertaining is done in the evening. If you are hosting, you may invite your counterpart's wife to a dinner. Some evening entertainment is for men only. Don't bring your spouse unless specifically invited.
- Thais eat continental style except they use a fork and spoon instead of a fork and knife. Cut with the spoon. It is an honor to be offered the last bit of food on a serving dish. Refuse several times before accepting.
- Dress well as a sign of status, but avoid wearing a black suit, which is reserved for funerals.
- A smile could mean yes, hello, thank you, never mind, or excuse me.
- The first meeting is to get acquainted, but you should eventually restate your business so the Thais can determine who should be at the next meeting, if there is a next meeting.
- Eye contact is desirable.
- Thais hesitate to ask questions. It implies that someone is a poor presenter. Public criticism is a form of violence.

## TUNISIA SUMMARY

### Cultural Data

*Culture Type:* Family/Clan

*Region:* Arab World

*Local Influences:* Tunisia is the most Western of Arab nations because of its long dominance by France.

*Primary Motivations:* The status and prosperity of the family/clan is important.

*Plan of Action:*

- Be cognizant of the nature of Islamic law and morality. It dictates behavior.
- Expect delays in appointments. Time is not linear. Be patient and expect to take a long time completing a transaction.
- Humility is highly regarded, especially in a powerful person.
- A Tunisian loves to bargain, but do not inflate your price too much. Your first offer must be good enough to attract his attention.
- Make your first approach through a well-connected local representative.
- You must be present to be of consequence. Meetings should be at your potential partner's offices.
- Relationships and trust come before business.
- Business associates must stay in constant communication for the relationship to continue.
- Minimize risks and uncertainty in your proposals. Praise and appreciation for your counterpart must be verbalized often.
- Maintain formality in behavior, appearance, and address.
- Project a successful image.
- Never refuse hospitality. Always reciprocate.
- Never reprimand or criticize directly. Failure is not directly acknowledged. Honor is very important. Deal with negatives euphemistically.
- Never admit that you are a "self-made man." Lineage is important. You are a reflection of your entire family.

- Proposals, plans, and negotiations should focus on the "people" issues.

*Local Protocol & Etiquette:*

- When greeting someone in business circles for the first time use the French title *Monsieur.*
- At a home meal, it is important to wash your hands in front of everyone. The servant will bring a bowl and pitcher.
- Hire a French interpreter.
- Give your business card to the senior man first and then others.

## TURKEY SUMMARY

**Cultural Data**

*Culture Type:* Family/Clan

*Region:* Arab World

*Local Influences:* Turkey is the bridge between Europe and Asia. It is the home of the former Ottoman Empire, which came to an end after the First World War. It is a democratic, secular state. Turkey is not an Arab nation, but 90 percent of the population is Muslim. Eighty-five percent are ethnic Turks. Turkey shares many customs with Arab nations.

*Primary Motivation:* The welfare and security of the family/clan are important factors.

*Plan of Action:*

- Be cognizant of the nature of Islamic law and morality. It dictates behavior.
- Expect delays in appointments. Time is not linear. Be patient and expect to take a long time completing a transaction.
- Humility is highly regarded, especially in a powerful person.
- Make your first approach through a well-connected local representative.
- You must be present to be of consequence. Meetings should be at your potential partner's offices.
- Relationships and trust come before business.

- Business associates must stay in constant communication for the relationship to continue.
- A Turk loves to bargain, but do not inflate your price too much. Your first offer must be good enough to attract his attention.
- Minimize risks and uncertainty in your proposals. Praise and appreciation for your counterpart must be verbalized often.
- Maintain formality in behavior, appearance, and address.
- Project a successful image.
- Never refuse hospitality. Always reciprocate.
- Never reprimand or criticize directly. Failure is not directly acknowledged. Honor is very important. Deal with negatives euphemistically.
- Never admit that you are a "self-made man." Lineage is important. You are a reflection of your entire family.
- Proposals, plans, and negotiations should focus on the "people" issues. People are most important to family/clan cultures.

*Local Protocol & Etiquette:*

- Turks do not shake hands when leave-taking.
- The form of address upon introduction is the surname preceded by *Bay* for men and *Bayam* for women.
- Most entertaining is done in restaurants.

## UKRAINE SUMMARY

### Cultural Data

*Culture Type:* Progressive Family/Clan

*Region:* Central and Eastern Europe

*Local Influences:* Ukraine was controlled by Russia for centuries. The Russians feel it is truly part of Russia. The Ukrainians do not.

*Primary Motivation:* The welfare of the family group and national self-determination are the motivating factors.

*Plan of Action:*

- Approach with a personal reference or through a local agent.

- First meeting should be at the Ukrainian's offices.
- Trust must be established before you will be accepted.
- Participate in their brand of conformity and modesty. Do not flaunt affluence.
- Do not entertain lavishly.
- Negotiate a win-win outcome.
- Sharing is important. Gift giving is common and should be reciprocated.
- Presentations should stress minimizing risks.
- Respect age. However, be aware that the younger generation is more entrepreneurial since the demise of the communist system.

*Local Protocol & Etiquette:*

- Ukrainians are independent thinkers, capable of both objective analysis and subjective decision-making.
- Beware of both "yes" and "no" during decision-making. Both are used tactically, either to stall talks until more information has arrived, or to keep you talking when you seem to be losing interest. Nothing is certain until the contract is signed.
- Negotiations may become emotional. Play hardball.
- Avoid compromises. They make you appear weak. Ukrainians are schooled in business the same as the Russians. See the previous notes on Russia.
- European manners are used.
- Ukrainians are generally more easygoing than are Russians. Otherwise, many business and social customs are similar.

## URUGUAY SUMMARY

**Cultural Data**

*Culture Type:* Family/Clan

*Region:* Latin America

*Local Influences:* Uruguay is the most secular of the Latin American countries. The population is 88 percent European, mostly Spanish and Italian.

*Primary Motivations:* The status, power, and prosperity of the family group are primary factors.

*Plan of Action:*

- Establish contact through a well-regarded local agent.
- The first meeting should be on the Uruguayan's turf.
- Send the most senior person from your church or organization, along with one or two subordinates.
- Plan on using an interpreter. Translate materials into Latin American Spanish.
- Always address the Latino formally, using his title and family name (next to last name).
- Expect to spend time establishing a relationship. Don't press toward a business discussion until your counterpart offers an opening.
- Maintain formality in dress, posture, and speech until he relaxes the interaction.
- Your image is important in communicating your own status.
- Don't back away if your counterpart chooses to stand close during conversation.
- Be prepared to make concessions, but only after appropriate resistance. Do not appear to negotiate these concessions.
- Minimize risks in any proposal.
- Do not assume you hold the most power because you are from the United States.
- Entertain at the best restaurants.
- Dine continental style.
- Once a relationship has been established, your church or organization should not change the U.S. contact person, or the process will have to begin again.

*Local Protocol & Etiquette:*

- Uruguayans have a reputation for being pessimistic and opinionated.
- There are more professional women than men in Uruguay, yet still men are dominant and women's rights are restricted.

- It is common to be invited back to someone's home for coffee after dinner in a restaurant. Don't stay very long.

## VENEZUELA SUMMARY

**Cultural Data**

*Culture Type:* Family/Clan

*Region:* Latin America

*Local Influences:* The population is 70 percent mestizo, with Spanish, Italian, Portuguese, Arab, German, African, and Indian making up the balance.

*Primary Motivation:* The power, status, and prosperity of the family group are the motivating factors.

*Plan of Action:*

- Establish contact through a well-regarded local agent.
- The first meeting should be on the Venezuelan's turf.
- Send the most senior person from your church or organization, along with one or two subordinates.
- Plan on using an interpreter. Translate materials into Latin American Spanish.
- Always address the Venezuelan formally, using his title and family name (next to last name).
- Expect to spend time establishing a relationship. Don't press toward a business discussion until your counterpart offers an opening.
- Maintain formality in dress, posture, and speech until he relaxes the interaction.
- Your image is important in communicating your own status.
- Don't back away if your counterpart chooses to stand close during conversation.
- Be prepared to make concessions, but only after appropriate resistance. Do not appear to negotiate these concessions.
- Minimize risks in any proposal.

- Do not assume you hold the most power because you are from the United States.
- Entertain at the best restaurants.
- Dine continental style.
- Once a relationship has been established, your church or organization should not change the U.S. contact person, or the process will have to begin again.

*Local Protocol & Etiquette:*

- A businesswoman going out at night with a businessman will be misconstrued.
- Announce your full name when shaking hands.
- Businesswomen should not give gifts to their male counterparts.

## VIETNAM SUMMARY

**Cultural Data**

*Culture Type:* Group

*Region:* Asia/Pacific

*Local Influences:* One misconception about the Vietnamese is that they hate Americans. This is not so. They are eager to become players in the international marketplace.

*Primary Motivation:* The prosperity and security of the group are important factors.

*Plan of Action:*

- One who is powerful and successful shows his humility.
- Harmony must be maintained. Do not confront or question anyone in a negative way. Never say no. Expect them to always say yes, which might mean no.
- Approach through a local representative.
- Personal relationships must be established before business is done. Do not assume this means you are a personal friend.
- Top management should be present at the first meeting. Your church or organization should be represented by a group of specialists at this first meeting. Do not include a lawyer.

- Negotiations will be time-consuming. Expect to make many trips. Be patient.
- Allow them to win something in negotiations.
- Recognize and respect the social position of all you encounter. Do not expect them to require equality.
- Never compliment a person directly. Never praise someone in front of his superiors. Praise the group.
- Negotiations may appear cyclical rather than linear. Be prepared to discuss any subject out of sequence at any time.

*Local Protocol & Etiquette:*

- The typical group pattern is followed: group meetings, greeting every person at the meeting, accepting hospitality, discussing business only when the host is ready, and establishing trust and friendship before business is done.
- The Vietnamese should be addressed using his given name, which comes last.
- Refuse hospitality three times before accepting, so you don't look greedy.

# Research References

AMG International *(Advancing the Ministries of the Gospel).* Chattanooga, TN: AMG International 2004.

Johnstone, Patrick and Mandryk, Jason. *Operation World: When we Pray God Works.* Waynesboro, GA: Gabriel Resources, 2001.Leaptrott, Nan. *Rules of the Game: Global Business Protocol.* Cincinnati, OH: Thomson Executive Press, 1996.

Lingenfelter, Sherwood G., and Mayers, Marvin Keene. *Ministering Cross-Culturally: An Incarnational Model for Personal Relationships.* Grand Rapids, MI; Baker Publishing Group, 2002.

Morrison, Terri, Conaway, Wayne, and Borden, George A. *Kiss, Bow, or Shake Hands: How to Do Business in Sixty Countries.* Holbrook, MA: B. Adams, 1995.

Geolux Communications, Brigham University *Culturgrams,* Lindon, Utah, 2004

Internet Resources

http://www.mnnonline.org/
http://www.au.org/
http://www.omf.org/
http://www.bible.acu.edu/missions/page.asp?ID=574
http://www.au.omf.org/content.asp?Id=13106
http://www.evangelicalalliance.org.au/broc/ministries.php/
http://www.adventures.org/

# Index

## A



## B

## C



## D

## E



## F



## G

## H



## I

## J



## K



## L



## M

## N



## O



## P



## Q



## R

## S

## T



## U



## V



## W